Davis B. Casseday

The Hortons

Davis B. Casseday

The Hortons

ISBN/EAN: 9783337054724

Printed in Europe, USA, Canada, Australia, Japan

Cover: Foto ©ninafisch / pixelio.de

More available books at **www.hansebooks.com**

THE HORTONS:

OR

American Life at Home.

BY

DAVIS B. CASSEDAY.

FOR SALE BY
JAMES S. CLAXTON, PHILADELPHIA:
D. APPLETON & Co., NEW YORK: LEE & SHEPPARD, BOSTON:
R. W. CARROLL & Co., CINCINNATI: S. C. GRIGGS & Co., CHICAGO:
TRÜBNER & Co., LONDON.
1866.

TO

ARTHUR W. MITCHELL,

OF

MARYLAND,

THIS BOOK IS AFFECTIONATELY INSCRIBED.

Contents.

	PAGE
CHAPTER I.	
Bad News by the Telegraph—Father and Daughter..................	5
CHAPTER II.	
The Breakfast-room at Belair—The Merchant in his Counting-house—An Old Clerk...	11
CHAPTER III.	
A Commercial "Panic"—Bartimeus Scroggs, and other creditors.....	21
CHAPTER IV.	
Flower-fancies...	29
CHAPTER V.	
Autumn days, and the Family at Belair—A Cavalier encountered at Farmer Gregg's...	33
CHAPTER VI.	
Women in town and country contrasted—Caroline Mellen..............	43
CHAPTER VII.	
A Birthday Party at Belair, and what was said and done thereat....	47
CHAPTER VIII.	
Some account of the Crosbys, and of a poor neighbor of theirs......	60
CHAPTER IX.	
A Storm at Sea, and a Calm Ashore—Bradley Horton....................	67
CHAPTER X.	
The Spirits in Clement Horton's Counting-house........................	73

CHAPTER XI.
Bradley Horton at The Cedars—Lydia Bardleigh—The Sick-chamber.. 88

CHAPTER XII.
Bloker and Ball—The Captain's Widow.. 100

CHAPTER XIII.
A small Dinner-party at Belair, including two representatives of Commerce.. 107

CHAPTER XIV.
How the Anniversary of the Battle of Hickory Hollow was celebrated at Slumptown... 115

CHAPTER XV.
A Moonlight Excursion on the water—Doctor Pledget tells the Story of a Nervous Patient, and becomes acquainted with an Astronomer... 126

CHAPTER XVI.
Warned to Move.. 145

CHAPTER XVII.
At The Cedars—Rail-shooting.. 149

CHAPTER XVIII.
A Farm-house at evening—Two Lovers talk reasonably in the moonlight... 157

CHAPTER XIX.
Clinkers and Charity.. 163

CHAPTER XX.
A Woman's Letter—Christmas at Belair without Grog, and what the guests thought of it... 174

CHAPTER XXI.
Too much Whiskey-punch, together with a queer Experience of Mr. Broon's.. 185

CHAPTER XXII.
Winter in the Country, Sleighing and Courtship, and a Lover called to answer... 196

CHAPTER XXIII.
Judge Bardleigh talks Ghost in the twilight.................. 205

CHAPTER XXIV.
A Notable Couple—How Bartimeus Scroggs failed to go to Congress, and how Orator Puffin went.................. 210

CHAPTER XXV.
Father and Daughter again.................. 216

CHAPTER XXVI.
Brentlands—Scenery and Humor of the Country—Max Heyhurst—A Talk about Poetry, and Political Morals.................. 219

CHAPTER XXVII.
Brentlands—A day's duck-shooting.................. 229

CHAPTER XXVIII.
Brentlands—Bradley Horton as a Farmer—Field, Wood, and Garden—Tom Hance—Mr. Potteril of New Paradise, and his man, Simon Horseradish.................. 234

CHAPTER XXIX.
At The Cedars—The Lovers—Uncle Steve Trencher.................. 248

CHAPTER XXX.
Lydia Bardleigh at Aunt Dinah's death-bed.................. 259

CHAPTER XXXI.
Jane Warner—Sewing for Bread—Little Lame Frank—An Accident and an Old Acquaintance.................. 262

CHAPTER XXXII.
Jane Warner—Jacob Bloker—The Private Mad-House.................. 274

CHAPTER XXXIII.
Tare and Tret out at Grass—Little Frank—Henry Davenport seeks for information.................. 282

CHAPTER XXXIV.
Bloker's Benevolence.................. 292

CHAPTER XXXV.
How a Christian woman can die.................. 297

CHAPTER XXXVI.
At the Old Clerk's—A Discovery.. 304

CHAPTER XXXVII.
A party in a city mansion, at which there is conversation both grave and gay: together with some account of Doctor Peter Mellen, and how a dispute concerning Hydrophobia was settled... 308

CHAPTER XXXVIII.
A Conference concerning Jane Warner.. 321

CHAPTER XXXIX.
A Search for Jane Warner, and a Habeas Corpus.................................. 327

CHAPTER XL.
Some pleasant rides behind an old cab-horse—Friends part............ 333

CHAPTER XLI.
A Funeral at The Cedars—Bradley Horton at Brentlands—Hail—The old saddle sorrel... 337

CHAPTER XLII.
New York—Bradley Horton becomes an "Able Editor".................. 342

CHAPTER XLIII.
Washington Patriots, vulpine and vulturine—The Great Horse Fair at Hepzidam—Bloker reaps the Field of Blood............................. 345

CHAPTER XLIV.
Bartimeus Scroggs is loyal to the Administration, and makes a Name in History.. 349

CHAPTER XLV.
Paul Mervine... 353

CHAPTER XLVI.
A Death, and a Marriage... 358

CHAPTER XLVII.
A Few Last Words.. 361

THE HORTONS.

CHAPTER I.

*Believe me, sir, had I such venture forth,
The better part of my affections would
Be with my hopes abroad. * *
And every object that might make me fear
Misfortune to my ventures, out of doubt,
Would make me sad.*—MERCHANT OF VENICE.

THE slow, soft breeze of a July night, odorous with the exhalations of the landscape, sported capriciously along the elm-bordered terrace, and bore its benison through the open windows of the drawing-room at Belair. Clement Horton sat gazing at shadows of foliage, traced by the moonlight, that trembled on the pallid marble of an opposite pedestal. Without, between the droning trees, were vistas and uncertain reaches of amber-tinted prospect, where growing corn and oat-fields sentinelled with shocks merged in the indistinguishable meadows that margin the Tarnell.

The clank of a closing gate aroused the watcher. Rising, with alert step he passed to the terrace. A sound of hoofs upon a wooden bridge, which fell harsh and heavy upon his heart, then a duller thud approaching on the gravelled avenue, and a horseman emerged from a clump of shrubbery.

"Is it you, Walsh? The steamer's in, then?"

"Yes, sir; and here is the dispatch."

"You will find your room ready. Goodnight." And Mr. Horton reëntered the house and retired to his chamber.

Warm as was the night he shut the jalousie with scrupulous care, and drew the curtains close, as if he would stifle in the pent-up air from all the world the impressions of impending disaster which oppressed him. Eagerly, but with unsteady hands, he broke the envelope of the dispatch. For a moment its contents seemed blurred; then, at a glance, he comprehended all. His fears were more than realized. A heavy fall in the value of sugars in the British markets, in a measure indicated by previous advices, which involved the sacrifice of large shipments that he had made, and the failure of the old and extensive house of Price, Irving & Co., custodians of his affairs abroad, was announced. The magnitude of his misfortune was sharply defined in the mind of Clement Horton. Hope offered no illusion to break the force of the blow, which was bankruptcy.

Very curious are the alternations of feeling occasioned by calamity in men of rugged fibre. The countenance of the merchant to him who had surveyed it then would have betrayed little indication of care or struggle of passion. Nor was it the face of one stunned to insensibility. The tension of suspense was loosed, and for the moment the conflict of hope and apprehension was allayed. A conflict, ah! how agonizing to a man who beholds in his fears the belief of others in him, the result of laborious years and fidelity to honorable courses, passing into suspicion and censure. Allayed for the moment; fleeting and fallacious relief! Disquiet returned strengthened, like the evil spirit to its swept and garnished house. It is scarcely extravagance of language to declare that Clement Horton groaned in his anguish out of a body of death. As he contemplated the wreck of his fortune, too fragmented to float him over the gulf—the sudden shutting of the grooves of his career, his soul sank within him, and, casting himself upon the floor of his chamber, the stricken man wrestled and moaned away the sultry summer night.

Mr. Horton was a widower. Imbued with an abiding regard for the memory of his wife, although at the meridian of life and possessed of an ample fortune, in seven years he had not again married. While it was a sterling, Clement Horton's was not altogether an attractive character. With a disposition to confide, justly checked by knowledge of the world and habits of self-reliance, his manners were not prepossessing. His temper was somewhat rigorous. While he conscientiously cherished the larger virtues, and was aware, as one is when educated by books and travel, of the conventionalism of society, he bestowed an insufficient cultivation upon the smaller, those benevolences that are called the amenities of life. Truthful, punctual, inflexibly honest, unostentatiously generous as an almsgiver, scorning sneakingness in all its shapes, he was respected and trusted; unbending, taciturn, occasionally severe, he restrained in others germs of regard from ripening to ardent friendship.

Mr. Horton's surviving children were a son and daughter. The abounding life of nineteen flowed rejoicingly in the veins of Emily Horton. Far above the level of that womanhood where millinery ecstacies blend with platitudes of affected simplicity and lackadaisical complaints, the lineaments of her character displayed in well-harmonized proportions delicacy and strength; for, as it sexually should, delicacy predominated. A rare union of qualities, which in a better social organization will be more frequent, when determination and sentiment shall not, as now, expend themselves in distinct and often conflicting courses. Bodily exercise in full measure had made her robust, though not ungraceful. Dumb-bells alternated with French, and she tripped lightly and eagerly from the music-stool to the saddle. Carefully taught, at her father's requirement, the matronly duties of the household, the art, seldom possessed, of investing coarse, common-place labors with seemliness, dignified her industry. A healthy constitution of mind was made fruitful by culture. Tall and symmetrical in figure, her carriage was buoyant with athletic animation. Of fair complexion, her countenance, tranquilized by the play of eyes which were tender in repose, derived an air of archness from a nose slightly *retroussé*. Luxuriant tresses of light brown hair depended from a simple coiffure. Here was not the lithe loveliness of oriental beauty, fashioned in the fervor which purples the clusters of the lilac, and paints with Persian noons the voluptuous cheek of the peach—a faultless mould about a shrivelled core of soul, but the sound and spiritualized result of a lusty Christian civilization.

The moral character of a true woman, in which the virtues stand thick, may seem easy of analysis. Serenity, earnestness, self-sacrifice, endurance, and benevolence quicken and ennoble life. But unexpected developments of excellence constantly occur, and suggest in turn latent and indefinite possibilities. Besides, there is abatement for alloy. He who has felt the influence of such a character most, knows how hard it is to adequately express it; like light, it is a diffused beneficence—pure, pervading, and subtle. Enough, to remember the presence of a spiritual woman as that of one, like Spenser's Una, whose

> "——angel's face,
> As the great eye of heaven, shined bright,
> And made a sunshine in the shady place."

Yet there are wretched beings among men, Iagos and Stenos of society, whose souls are shut to this refreshing; who sneer with the incredulity of the pit at every portraiture of female purity, and value it by the attributed standard of the *coulisse*. So infernal frogs know only the ooze of Acheron. Even Satan, in the presence of Eve,

> "——abstracted stood,
> From his own evil."

But the virtues and graces are not necessarily associated. Often the most dangerous thing in bad women is their fascinating self-possession; while goodness is of plain case and uncourtly. Correggio, instinctively truthful, has depicted the Furies not old, withered, and deformed, the awful Memories of Æschylus in shapes of hideous sisterhood, but as women, comely with the rounded freshness of youth, a solitary serpent filletting each head, but faces—faces infernally implacable with perverted passions.

Emily Horton's nature was not ductile. Her virtues and defects tended to the positive. Hence she shunned shams, and was without prudery. Some caprices she showed, being a woman, but claimed no prerogative to cherish them; and in matters of moment, she was not uncertain. Least of all was there varying in the steadfastness of her love, which did not cling with the wantonness of whim, but clave with the directness and strength of passion. She strove to inspire her actions with a pure regard for wisdom and goodness; to live in the exercise of charity, which is the method of a comprehensive righteousness. Self-appreciation sometimes disported on the level of a spiritualized pride, which was not Pharisaism. Excess was apt to be the measure of her antipathies. The contemplation of wrong and meanness swelled her resentment to hatred, or sank it to contempt. Her nature, sensitive in its strength, capable alike of love and loathing, was rich in solace for sore occasions.

CHAPTER II.

Men are as so many emmets, busy, busy still, going to and fro, in and out, and crossing one another's projects, as the lines of several sea-cards cut each other in a globe or map. Now light and merry, but by-and-by sorrowful and heavy; now hoping, then distrusting; now patient, to-morrow crying out.—ANATOMY OF MELANCHOLY.

ORNING, attended by the warm South, was trailing her pall, glittering with dew, upon wood and field. From the bay-window of the breakfast-room a parterre of verbenas violet-hued and crimson, orange-suited jonquils, and roses of imperial aspect though garbed in saintly white, stretched picturesquely irregular until it was lost behind a copse of shrubbery. Gravelled avenues exhaling coolness in the shadow of overarching trees, alleys meandering through sunny spaces of turf, a jubilant choir of robins fresh from the morning feast of cherries, the sober and familiar wren, the oriole, a gleam of gold and jet, cleaving the tresses of the willow, the bugles of bees faintly blowing in the jessamine-scented air, contributed their several delights to the enchanting summer morning scene.

It was not until twice summoned that Mr. Horton, but little refreshed by daylight dozes, appeared. If this unusual breach of punctuality excited the attention of his daughter, his haggard look, despite an assumption of briskness as little like healthy animation as the restlessness of fever, aroused her solicitude. It was new to her, that look of one whose "heart taketh not rest in the night."

"Breakfast has been ready this half-hour, father; you are late, and seem ill."

"The hot night and wakefulness, Emily. I confess to being out of sorts, and I don't feel hungry now I'm here."

The repast proceeded in an uneasy silence.

"Really you should not call that a breakfast, *mon pere*—a bit of meat no bigger than a lozenge! Try this pigeon."

"No, child; nature is clogged. After all, I believe a cup of strong coffee is the best crutch for an ailing man."

"Don't the doctors forbid it?"

"Yes—and drink it. In India, I knew captains of the country ships who lived almost on curry and coffee. One shrivelled, sallow-skinned old fellow took a score of cups a day, was eighty when I met him, and perfectly clear-headed, but, it must be owned, much like a palsy in a bundle of parchment."

Reserved as was Mr. Horton in his intercourse with the world, with his daughter he was easy and unrestrained; still this bizarre sprightliness was unusual, and set awkwardly upon him. A servant announced the carriage, and Mr. Horton rose.

"Be quiet to-day, father, and keep from the sun. I think I shall be in the city for some dresses. If we go to Newport next month I must get ready. A note from Caroline Mellen tells me that she will be at my service, and you know ladies hate solitary shopping. Did you like the pearl-colored silk I showed you?"

"Yes, Emily, I thought it pretty, but—your taste is better taught than mine."

Newport! The word to the merchant was a pang. But the carriage wheels had not ceased to crunch the gravel of his grounds when weightier cares thronged his mind. Much of his paper was daily falling due, and large payments would be demanded within the week. He could still go on for some days, perhaps several weeks, at the price of further involvement. To this as an upright man he would not consent. Yet hardly was he resolved to stop at once, when a more sanguine mood controlled him. He could yet contrive to get through his difficulties without the humiliation of proclaimed failure; it only needed management and nerve, and both were his. He would accomplish all by a masterly adroitness; there should be no equivocal finesse. The unsullied credit and large concerns of his house, the fair growth of a quarter of a century, should not thus topple in an hour. Brief beguilement. Behind it, an enduring background, was necessity, stark and stringent, and importunate as an avenging shade.

Along the dusky highway; cityward. The plodding

teamster swerves with call and crack of lash his sinewy leader, and thinks the smart equipage which hurries by, the very shrine of happiness. A misanthropic butcher's boy, driving a herd of beeves, contorts his tallow-hued expanse of face to a scowl of envy, curses in shamble-seasoned adjectives his scurvy fortune, and poles the nearest ox. A pedler in the hedge, biting his frugal crust, catches a glimpse of cosy cushions and a portly gentleman in spruce attire, and thinks of the burden of the long, sweaty day. A brace of fast young gentlemen ogle languidly the carriage and its occupants, and bandy sententious comments. "Old Horton—rich as a Jew—'mazing pretty daughter, Bob: Old f'ler himself 'cidedly slow—s'prisin how them 'fernal slow men wear!" Across converging railroad tracks; by brick-yards, patches of truck, and grimy factories; by suburban taverns redolent of bitters, with their groups of morning idlers, and hostlers doing stable sleights with chunks of sponge and empty buckets; by limbo-looking spaces cumbered with refuse lumber, car-wheels, and grindstones, and superannuated coaches, warped, blistered, bare, and dismal, doing righteous penance for the hypocrisy of their running days when they were never full; by cemeteries, where falsehood suns itself in stone atop, while underneath reality takes refuge in dead night and the wormy corpse-stuffed mould; then on the street, among the currents of existence that set toward the greedy vortex of the town.

The counting-house of Clement Horton was entered from a narrow lane which skirted the river. You reached it along an entry dimly lighted by a single cobwebbed window, and a flight of well-worn steps. Over a stone archway, through which heavy drays laden with bales and tierces from the adjacent wharves rumbled all day long, scraping the damp granite sides, and rats scudded stealthily in the black mud, it garnered year by year its inky fruit in iron chests, between ponderous lids of tawny leather, and upon stems of wire that cropped along the walls. Its prospect was a lean slice of water scenery sandwiched in a brick perspective; ships at their moorings discharging cargo, or sweltering lazily in the caulker's reek of pitch, and passing steamboats that left legacies of smoke athwart the view. The region and its dwellers wore a dingy, not to say Stygian aspect. The huge warehouses rose sullenly above the life which surged beside them and took nothing of its impress; a sense of separateness like that of coffins from the funeral concourse striking the beholder, who as he passed the open doors and got glimpses of porters laboring far back in the cavernous gloom thought they seemed rummaging a sepulchre. From the coopers' shops came the knocking of busy adzes, and an odor of freshly whittled oak. Weighmasters and their men bustled among bales and bags, and stevedores shoved with slow labor grating casks. Massive anchors and coils of rust-eaten chain, stowed in sideway recesses, mocked humanity with their grim impassiveness. For the habitable buildings, they were groggeries and junk-shops, where thieves sold their plunder, sailor boarding-houses, and brothels of the baser sort—pustules into which run the peccant humors of urban civilization. The inhabitants were chiefly remarkable for an avoidance of cleanliness, a tendency to blear-eyes, and the consumption of clams. The musty air was toned with an exhaustless smell of onions. Such was the hallowed ground where Mammon owned his altars.

Seated in his private office, Mr. Horton engaged with accustomed regularity in the perusal of the day's correspondence. He was interrupted while making some memoranda concerning it by the entrance of his confidential clerk, who, having received the instruction which he sought, was retiring, when the merchant with an effort detained him.

"Mr. Davenport, please wait a moment: I have something to say."

The pause which followed, and the steady and serious gaze of the speaker disconcerted his subordinate.

"Henry, I am a broken man; (twitching of the mouth) I must stop."

"You are joking, sir," faltered Davenport,—"trying me?"

"Would to God I were!"

Then a new notion possessed the clerk—his employer's mind was unbalanced. If Henry Davenport had faith in anything, not properly the object of devotion, it was the stability of the house of Horton. Identified with it by a service of nearly twenty years, no waking thought or nightmare of mercantile disaster had ever disturbed him. As soon would he have confessed the rats could demolish the old granite archway.

Often had he counted Mr. Horton's estate; a quarter of a million at low valuation—not a dollar less. It was growing yearly, too, with improved vicinity and growth of revenue. He knew of losses, indeed, in excess of the customary business per centage; but compared with the capital which was pitted against them they might justly seem insignificant; as well question a ship's staunchness for the barnacles upon its bottom—and failed? Lunacy, clearly lunacy; dulness itself might see it. And so, his mind a tumult of incredulity, Davenport gazed upon his principal, who was refolding mechanically the morning's letters. Presently the merchant broke the silence.

"There is ruinous news from Europe, where I have large consignments. I operated silently, looking for a happy stroke of fortune, and mortgaged my property to make payments. My sagacity has been at fault, and I have lost. In the present tightness of money I see it is impossible for me to go on; and that only do I see plainly. I must consult my friends. My farms at Brentlands will be attached, of course, and I desire some special debts to have priority, and that may prevent an arrangement with all my creditors, which I hope for, but hardly expect. It is a shocking business, but I will hold nothing back; they shall impute to me no dishonesty. I have extended indulgence to others in distress; heaven knows whether I shall receive it!"

The old clerk blew his nose with energy, and replied in a husky voice:

"If it be so bad as you think, sir, still it cannot be desperate. The house of Clement Horton has a

2*

character which must command terms. No creditor however churlish, dare brave public opinion by re fusing them. After so many years, this is a rough turn of affairs for me, sir. But," he quickly added, with an attempt at cheerfulness which, despite the jaunty flourishing of his bandana, was sorry assurance, "it will all come right, and end a balance in our favor."

"God bless you for your sympathy, my friend! I hope I shall meet the worst firmly, as becomes an upright man," responded the merchant.

The law of the old clerk's life was method, stronger than the utmost spite of fortune, and he trod his round of duties with the same systematic steps, but his heart reeled beneath the burden of a noble sorrow. The young men over whom he presided observed that his characteristic equanimity, happily tempered with decision, had given place to a restless and querulous demeanor. Aroused from moodily brooding over his accounts, he would respond to the occasion with splenetic activity.

"By George, Wilson!" whispered Snively—seventeen, with a faint down on his upper lip—"old Dav's bagged at last. Now I know the meaning of the flashy vest he sported Sunday. Reg'lar loud pattern—saw one of the Vigee boys as Dav passed her house look as if he'd like to garote him for it—Twig?"

The interrogated, sucking the tip of his pen-holder the while, regarded his superior with an air of sentimental interest, lapsed into a despairing sigh, and, under cover of his desk-lid, whistled *sotto voce* a bar of "Unhappy Jeremiah."

Fancy not, O brother, who art travelling through "this vale," that our afflictions, thine and mine, will be read aright; or understood, educe tearful responses from Stokes, or Gibbs, or Thompson, fellow-creatures altogether lovely though they be, and parcel of the general caravan. The rue we cherish may not exhale their favorite odor, nor possess for them an inspiring tint. Leave them without upbraiding to the flora of their choice. Their orange blossoms, roses, poppies, will seem even to us, for all our present drapery of woe, a twelve-month hence less vapid. Let drollery then do on, and laugh, if it will, behind its hand, with dear, delightful Elia, at a funeral.

Mr. Horton confided his difficulties to two business and personal intimates. Relieved by the hearty offer of their services, and the relinquishment of part of his burden—its *shearing* in our meaning-full Saxon tongue—he was about to go home, when Davenport entered and handed him a package.

"There is something, sir, I will thank you to use for me."

"Use! What is it? Stop, Henry!"

"Well, if I must,—certificates of stock. I have invested about nine thousand dollars. Half of it is devoted to the support of my mother, should I die before her; with her frugal habits, and a small annuity of her own, it will be enough. For myself, I cannot live without employment. Besides, just in my prime—lustier than half the sickly spawn of twenty, now-a-days. Whatever happens, I shall tick on till I run down. Eh! don't smile, sir; a little bald, but it runs in the family—sign of a strong constitution, they say, and convenient for shower-baths."

"I thank you with all my heart, but I cannot—."

"Nor can I," exclaimed the ardent Davenport with brisk determination, as he disappeared.

"What *is* the matter with old Dav, Snively?" asked Wilson that night in a convivial lull at the weekly union of the "Musical Owls,"—Juddle, of the wholesale provision line, famous for his stunning solo of the "Blue-tailed Fly" to a jews-harp accompaniment, in the chair. "Hang me, sir, if I didn't see him this afternoon, when you'd all gone, before the glass ticing fancy knots in his cravat, and looking a perfect Romeo. Well, when he turned quick and caught me spotting him, and some astonished I was I rather think, he laughed, took his hat, gave me a parting punch in the ribs with a volume of McCullough, and sloped."

"Hit by the little archer, my boy! Wooman; lovely woo-man!" and the experienced youth thrust the suction-tube, with scientific precision, through the centre of a slice of lemon in his cobbler.

CHAPTER III.

How now, Shylock? what news among the merchants?
                                   MERCHANT OF VENICE.

"WHAT splendid sunsets we have, father," remarked Emily. They were lingering over their tea.

"Yes? I confess inattention. Perhaps I appreciate sunset more as a relief -this hot weather than a show."

"Look! I think of Italian skies, and Bradley. Are 'blue Friuli's mountains' laved by a more imperial flood? I fancy it is an efflux of paradise, where sainted shadows, untouched by gross influences, may lean and listen to our clamor, and find their happiness increased." Perhaps she was invoking good angels for the absent, and so came to think it, for she immediately added, "I wonder brother Bradley has not written in so long a time; it is more than a month."

There had been no such pressure in the money market as now prevailed, since the memorable crisis inaugurated by the "smash," as it was emphatically called, of the famous firm of Splinter & Splurge. That, it will be recollected, brought down half the banks of the country by the run. Splinter was thought to have made a rather good thing of the failure, being "smart." Certain it is that he lived in pious opulence ever after on the income of a bankrupt, was particular about his wines, sold his billiard table, built a private chapel, and entertained the bishop with holy hospitality. It is also consolatory to know, as showing that secular merit is, at least, rewarded in this calumniated world, that Splurge was subsequently elected secretary of the Epirus and Bungville Railroad, "realized" a snug sum by an over-issue of its bonds, and died, in an affluence of bequests, proprietor of a Cuban sugar estate and two hundred tattooed and musculous Bozales. The pressure was growing daily, too. Stout gentlemen, with double chins and claret-colored countenances, discussed with lean and bilious gentlemen at the insurance offices whether it would become a panic, delivering, as they swung their watch-seals, portentous periods in a big, infallible tone, to which the bilious men croaked confirmatory tremendous prophecies of woe. There was the same unflagging buzz of voices on 'Change, the droning worship of Plutus, till the janitor came and rang it out, when it stagnated on the steps, and eddied in the passages, and flowed into the convenient refectory to mix with the ring of glasses and the tinkle of pounded ice. The same buzz of voices, but there were inflections now—culminations of sound when groups got fresh intelligence of disaster, and short, sharp expressions of surprise in features and movement; bubbles, so to speak, above the foundered firms. Many a rich argosy escaped shipwreck in the shelter of the Barbary Coast of three per cent. a month, and sailed a long voyage afterward with its signal of distress, a usurer's heart sprouting vultures' claws. The pinched "drags"—bodies pea-green, and wheels daintily picked in red and brimstone—of horsey-looking men who dealt in dry-goods were not seen of afternoons upon the road. Elderly citizens, uxorious no longer, rebuked testily Madame's propensity to gad when she proposed the sea-side or Saratoga, declared these were contrivances for the encouragement of heat, racket, dust, dysentery, and mosquitoes, and that, contrarily, the city was an elysium of freshness and ease. Poor women, nurses, seamstresses, and schoolmistresses, with their little all hoarded in stocks, bore anxious hearts, in which every rumor roused a pang. The blind and bed-ridden annuitants full of years, stripped of their small support—let us trust that heaven made of their adversity a blessing, and sanctified their crust and cruse as were never Splinter's sapid viands by grace episcopal, uttered in the bishop's most mellifluent manner, and bodied with turtle and Green Seal.

Among others, Mr. Horton's failure had been announced, and had occasioned a little stir in the great world of traffic. His property was hastily attached. Brentlands, near Wilton, was seized. The village lawyers were busy and blithesome, and the sheriff was a happy man in view of fees. There came, however, a lifting of the clouds.

Brentlands was a productive estate of fifteen hundred acres. Under the skilful management of Mr. Horton it had furnished a yearly revenue equal to the interest of more than twice its market value, and even that value, because of the financial distress, perhaps for a long period would be depreciated. These considerations tended to abate the eagerness of a few who were sordid, and who stood for a speedy sale of the lands and chattels, and prepared the way for an arrangement. A call, to effect this, appeared in the *Commercial Register* for a meeting of the creditors of Clement Horton at the offices of Lytell Jowl, Esquire, Attorney at Law and Solicitor in Chancery.

Many phases of character were presented to amuse the spectator pleased with variant views of human nature in the assembly at Jowl's. There was the venerable Bliggs who contradicted nobody, whose lips distilled honey of Hybla, while his head was a perpetual ambush for the unwary; Glump, whose moral nature oozed in rigorous sentiments of piety, and at whose approach his children feared and trembled; the manly Duncan; Jacob Bloker, of the firm of Bloker and Ball; the fair-minded Larned; and Rapin, extensive "operator" in salt fish, who knew by heart the British peerage, and wore a moustache of such unparalleled ferocity that it suggested gunpowder rations and trainings before Sebastopol. There, too, luminous " emongst the lesser lights," beamed Bartimeus Scroggs.

The vanity of Scroggs would have scouted less than a separate and especial paragraph. A solitary feat of his babyhood was preserved by tradition, the habit of closing his fist upon a coveted object with a singular obstinacy of grasp. The builder of his own fortune, he began and continued life with a purpose—the acquisition of wealth; and he was successful, for his energy cropped from a rich sub-soil of self-esteem. Assiduously he prosecuted his aim, holding crooked courses to be rather unsightly, but necessary to the aptitudes of business. He deposited, perhaps sometimes with disrelish, his eggs of contrivance in any carcass, satisfied if they returned plump and early maggots. Unprofitable in the end, if Scroggs but knew of any other world than that of tare and tret. And it has been well said that "he who destroys confidence murders the generations." By others, Scroggs was styled an infidel; he called himself a spiritualist, and talked glibly of an inevitable disembodied progression, an assured development and exaltation of the soul hereafter; of which, averred the scoffers, that of Bartimeus would stand in urgent need. The heaven into which he looked to enter was a mixture of Mahomet's paradise and the elysium of classic paganism. Such being his creed, it cannot surprise that his cherished maxim was, to live entirely in and for this world; while he contemplated the next as he would a Chinese puzzle, with curiosity but without concern. With inordinate ambition, wealth, and a consciousness of its power, and without any spiritualizing faith, there was to be found no check in this man's life higher than the opinion of the mart to assure it just. In politics he was a fierce Republican, not from the impulses of a benevolent nature, but from jealousy of the educated and arrogant aristocracy of the South, whose pretensions, seldom temperate and sometimes thrasonical, offended his enormous vanity. Yet he had some sense of equity in the abstract—as Alexander Carlyle's carousing and wenching Scotch lairds had of religion—which supplied him with a basis of semi-sincerity. It was his vanity which kept him steadfast during the weakness and unpopularity of his party, and impelled him to aspire when it had acquired strength and power to offices and honors for which he was unfitted either by nature or cultivation. To secure place and its profits, although generosity was not the method of his blood, he opened his purse to infirm newspapers, and kept in pay a crew of pothouse politicians. Even in this selfish bounty he recompensed himself by a more selfish provision, and while claiming full credit for a gift, exacted a promissory note. When Wriggle of the *Bugle*, who coaxed from able writers of the party editorials in charity, and ostentatiously claimed them for his own, was unprosperous, he offered inky incense at the shrine of Scroggs, and settled his weekly bills. One two-column biography, intensely seasoned, of which ten thousand extra copies were forthwith scattered broadcast, Scroggs in areas and doorways, until the town, as with an Egyptian plague, was Scroggs-infested, supplied the *Bugle* with wind enough for several months of tooting. Perfect temperance in drinking, and toleration of the shortcomings of others provided neither his prejudice nor interest was invaded, were among his sources of strength. Yet with all his advantages Bartimeus was not Machiavel, and was sometimes surpassed by abler and shrewder men. In person he was robust—"alimentiveness large," said the phrenologists—his hair was red, and his gray eyes, from which diverged busy wrinkles, would have been hard but for a tendency to moisture scarcely emotional. For his occupation, he was a heavy dealer in brass.

It was the last of several meetings to discuss Mr. Horton's affairs, Jowl presiding, and looking, with a stretch of fancy, as if he had plunged into all the commentators and was present to be wrung.

"Any of our friends gone up to-day, Mr. Glump?" asked Bliggs.

"Not that I have heard."

"Wait till the first of the month," said Rapin: "Houses will go like a row of bricks on edge when the end one tumbles. Never knew such deuced kite-flying. Paper on the street is as hard to move as lead—gilt-edged and short at that."

"Things will settle, perhaps, after that," observed Glump.

"Dunno. Is this Hulger's fourth or fifth stop, Larned?"

"Uhm—I forget. He fails as regularly as a Dutch almanac in its predictions of the weather. Ninety thousand this time, I'm told; but he'll be right again in a month. Can't afford to lose him on 'change; he makes more business than any three men there."

"He's living fast, though—drinks hard, and will go off yet with a Frenchman. I saw Mrs. H. on the street to-day, not sombre and sorrowful, but fresh as Aurora and beautiful as Aphrodite," said Rapin.

"Not his wife—not married!" exclaimed Glump.

"I never asked to see the certificate," responded Rapin.

Duncan laughed, and thought he had heard that Hulger had left it at Cyprus in his travels.

"Nothing can exceed the thoughtlessness of our young men in these trying times," reflected Bliggs. "There's Sherrard Timmins—breadstuff Timmins's son —who, I'm told, has actually taken to writing poetry; and I saw him myself carrying a switch cane in business hours. Ah!"

Just then there was some cross talk about a sale of building lots on the line of the proposed Slowcut railway, and Scroggs, who had been sitting with closed eyes in a highly developed state of fat smile, it was supposed communing with spirits, relapsed to mortality with this sententious offering to the general fund,

"Wouldn't give it—there's no money in 'em at that price!"

Finally, the conclave rose, the attorney rung in his man Scipio with a bundle of cigars, and Rapin solicited subscriptions to procure a silver spanner for the Phœnix.

CHAPTER IV.

Thanks to the human heart by which we live,
Thanks to its tenderness, its joys, and fears,
To me the meanest flower that blows can give
Thoughts that do often lie too deep for tears.
        WORDSWORTH.

AN invalid with a sprained ancle, Mr. Horton was stretched upon a cane settee in his piazza at Belair. In reaching to thrust aside a bough which overshadowed the dial, he had slipped upon the gravel walk. In this little, though painful accident, what embryo vastness of casualty. "A simple sprain!" quoth the reader; "anything short of a luxation is a personal affront, and a heroic nature would have given us a compound fracture." Alas, that the conscientious historian cannot make events at pleasure, like the writer of mere fiction, and rise superior to flannel and opodeldoc.

Quiet rested upon the merchant. Afflictions spiritualize virtuous men; and there was nothing obsequious in the now subdued bearing of Mr. Horton in his intercourse with the world; he walked invested with the dignity of gentleness. The old roughnesses were rasped down, and the old bluntness was swallowed in a new benevolence.

Emily, seated beside her father, was plying her needle. Since she knew of his difficulties—she first heard them from his lips under the elms in the serenity of a bright Sabbath—her attendance upon him had been tinctured with those nameless graces and subtle amenities which make much of the charm and even strength of domestic life—so blossoming trailers make fast the rifted crag—the delicate Corinthian combined with the chaste, fixed Doric in the family structure when Cultivation and Love are the builders. Resting, she picked from her work-basket a rose, and surveyed it musingly.

It was surpassingly beautiful. Its petals where they started, from a stem dark with excess of green blood, were in color alabaster faintly incarnadined, which gradually deepened to a glow of gorgeous crimson spread below pollen-laden stamens of blush-tinted amber. Emily embraced its splendor and inhaled its fragrance with sensuous delight.

"All the poetry it has occasioned, from the smooth lines of Waller to the exquisite conceptions of Elizabeth Browning, is not worth five minutes communion with this September flower," she said.

"'Sultana of the nightingale.'

And a right queenly look it has."

"Fit, father, to have inspired the memory of the blind. Aunt Dinah, by the mill, will talk to you all the hour of her old-time garden treasures, with, What a season that was for dahlias! recalling their various colors, exhaled a score of years, and painting now—more poetry—perhaps the plumage of rare birds, or Brazilian butterflies, or strange shapes of tropical bloom; and famous double hollyhocks, that ran out at last, and tantalize her in dreams."

"So, my dear, our great poet regrets, in that pathetic apostrophe to Light which has moved many hearts, that to him returned not the

'Sight of vernal bloom, or summer's rose.'

If there be aught spiritual in us, we find our surest and purest satisfaction, under God, in contemplating nature. It is then toil is thankful in its strength, and pleasure penitent."

"Often in delirium," said Emily, "the mind wanders in mazes of flowers; and sometimes to the dying they color the dawn of the great change. Nature's fashioning of these glowing, graceful shapes from the common clod and the impalpable gases is a daily miracle which warrants the belief in a higher transfiguration. Can such impressions be glimpses of *arcana cœlestia?*"

"Are like appearances produced by narcotics? I forget, and De Quincey sleeps to no earthly awakening."

"He could have told—perhaps he has," said Emily. "My recollection of the 'Confessions' is like that of a dream—a rigid countenance ghastly in the play of laudanum lightnings from dark, cavernous eyes—a gleam of candles falling upon a decanter and revealing its ruby contents, which, distilled through a singularly subtle brain take spectral similitudes of faces terrible or grotesque, fear-stricken fugitives from disaster, majestic processions, wreak and wretchedness, and all the pageantry of triumph. Never poppies amid the friendly corn outglowed his pages."

There was a pause.

"Every manifestation of the beautiful," urged Emily with enthusiasm, "which is a blessing here, may be such intensified hereafter; and the meek violet acquire to our heightened sensibility a supernal effulgence infinitely surpassing the glory which we now acknowledge in the august lily of Surinam. And who shall say that color *there*, where there is 'no night,' is not an exquisite musical expression."

CHAPTER V.

As some men gaze with admiration at the colors of a tulip, or the wings of a butterfly, so I was by nature an admirer of happy human faces.
VICAR OF WAKEFIELD.

ERY enjoyable were the soft, dreamy autumn days at Belair. September would yet a space recline upon his stubble and listen to the low fretting of the crisp corn blades, the blackbird's call, and the whirr of the startled partridge, or saunter with his lazy zephyrs in the groves; then give place to lustier October clad in russet, who brings no wrinkles to the year, but is fragrant with the mow, full of bread, and jolly with cider. The orchards were heavy with their pride of spheres, golden and garnet-freaked; and from wall and trellis drooped the clusters of the vine, a repose of sunny purple, such as pretended by the old Greek on his canvas drew the festal clamor of the birds. More enjoyable to Emily that she had much of the society of her father, who for a time could only move in a chair on castors, and then with stick and crutch. Besides, Caroline Mellen was spending several weeks at Belair.

Time owed no spite to the wholesome lasses. They rode, drove, angled, trespassed upon the domain of the old Scotch gardener to his undissembled disgust, gathered fruit and made bouquets for their friends in town, laughed over their schoolday frolics and recounted and conjectured the fortunes of their former mates, stringing on the thread of memory which they held in common, as it happened, beads black and white. Among the odors of the boudoir could be recognized the aroma of new books, and scattered paper-knives might have been collected in piazzas, arbors, and other retreats. In the evenings they played the last music for Mr. Horton's pleasure as he reclined on a sofa; or a social gathering was made happy by the exuberant gaiety of Mellen.

Sometimes they drove to the city, and mixed with the blithe throng of the world. But their regard was not exhausted by the sprightly and modish. On one of these occasions Emily called on her mother's friend, Mrs. Allen, and carried her some pears. Everything about the modest house was neat and well kept, but the decayed fortune of the family was to be seen elsewhere than in the faded widow's weeds of the lady. Mr. Allen had been a merchant of worth and standing— it was the old story of bankruptcy, unvaried by impressive incidents, but not therefore the less pathetic; a syllable of that solemn monotone of our busy American life. The thoughtful face of the widow was still delicate, despite the wear of more than fifty years. It was a Christian's countenance—calm, resigned, and sweetly benevolent. They found her in her little garden with a neighbor, who was lifting from its spot of soil a luxuriant shrub. Her husband had planted, and for many years she had nurtured it. She turned to greet them, with tearful eyes and a constrained smile, but their presence jarred the chords of association, already tense, and her speech faltered. "It was his," she said, "but I cannot keep it; there is no yard where I shall move." And bowing her head in a burst of grief, she passed with them into the house.

Emily's birth-day occurred in Indian-summer, the vintage-time of Solitude, when, robed in a tranquil glory of sun-sublimated haze, she quaffs her wine among the hills and is glad. Mr. Horton insisted, so a small party was arranged for the occasion.

There was cream to be got for freezing at Farmer Gregg's. This worthy agriculturist toiled and worried through the seasons on his fruitful acres, such champaign as the tiller loves, which skirted a bend of the Tarnell. Andrew, the gardener, cheerfully consented to row the ladies. The fresh morning lay upon fields of grass, and stubble, and shocked cornstalks, where beads of dew trembled like quicksilver in the cobwebs.

"'Tis a pleasant lift the day. Miss Cawroline, gie me your hand, and step light upon the gunwaul."

The oars thumped in the row-locks and the boat sprang forward, with Emily at the tiller.

"Luff! luff a-lee, Emily, or you'll shipwreck us on that sand-bar, and consecrate it forever to the elegiac muse. Think of our becoming newspaper naiads in one of Max Heyhurst's effusions! There goes my umbrella!" and the lively "Cawroline" reached overboard.

The boat dipped sideways quick and deep, releasing Andrew's port oar as he was bending to the stroke, and sprawling him on his back. With the bound of an athlete the old gardener was again upright. He contemplated the vivacious Mellen with a look of solemn wrath. His sense of decorum had been outraged in its entirety. Slowly he spake: "Seat you, Miss, anent Miss Emily, and hold your freeskyness, or it will be a far cry to Belair!"

The culprit answered nothing, and sat an edifying spectacle of contrition. Presently she burst into song, and the ploughman paused afield to listen to "Ettrick banks."

"Aweel, weel," murmured Andrew; "'tis a bonnie sang," and for a moment he beheld the smoke curling above the heath-thatched shielins.

They found Farmer Gregg in tribulation concerning a dead horse. Quite a group—the farmer and his men, with two or three sympathizing neighbors—surrounded the defunct quadruped. The doctor also was present, a practitioner without a coat, in a broad-brimmed white hat, gingham cravat, and an undue proportion of suspenders. His thoughtful style of sucking a straw, as he contemplated the bearings of the case, was a triumph of art, and hinted at illimitable hoards of veterinary wisdom. All seemed duly impressed with this appearance of profundity, except the horse; so lately most interested, but now a breathless bulk of muscle.

"Jeemes!" said the farmer, "take off his shoes. I know'd it war'nt no use."

"He'd be a live hoss now if I'd been fetched in time," remarked the doctor, with decision.

"Think 'twas the kolery?" asked a hand.

"Too much fever," replied the doctor; "it was a disease of the wital innards."

"Bots, mebbe?" pursued a speculative neighbor.

The farmer scouted the idea.

"It was all along of the shootin' of the fish-hawk down in the river-field," he declared, and there was unshakable conviction in his tone.

"What had its nest in the old hickory?" asked the speculative neighbor, brightening with new light.

"Yes, Billy. There was some strange men gunning there a week ago, and I haint seen it since. It kind o' worried me to miss it; and when Mike was taken with a gripin' like, I knowed it warnt no use: it allus happens."

Aunt Becky, as Mrs. Gregg was commonly called, was in the act of a family baking. A brisk lass was raking the coals from the ample oven, and puffed batches of dough, pies knobby where slices of apple bulged the crust, inchoate rusks, pippins, and gingerbread sweating molasses at every pore, were ready to be shoved to its hot inclosure. Then there was a churning in the background—twelve or fourteen pounds, Aunt Becky said, as she nudged the handle of the well-scoured barrel. After that, and dinner, and the moving work, our housewife would put on her heavy silver spectacles and ply her needle on the

4

"men folks" clothes, inspect and feed her poultry, and look up in the almanac the changes of the moon, or copy with slow labor from the county newspaper, prudently anticipatory of the afflictions, a speedy cure for cancer, and a remedy for the bite of a mad dog, which was never known to fail when rubbed in well. Aunt Becky was hugely pleased to see her favorite, Emily, and in the exuberance of her spirits poured forth such a multitude of orders and expostulations that the bewildered "help" looked wild in the eyes and showed symptoms of derangement. She would have them with her to the dairy to see the goodly files of bright milk basins that dripped coolness and showed a thick, unctuous surface of contents, so different from the pellicle which mantles the lacteal supplies of city cellars. Then, to survey her cheeses, a tawny store of curd; the hives and their busy architects; the sleek young calves with their blundering heads, clear, full eyes, and bright nozzles; and her fatting turkeys, glossy and plump with a plethora of mush, and happily ignorant of Christmas.

While they were seated in the rustic porch listening to Aunt Becky's large discourse, a horseman came racking up the lane. At the runlet midway, in the shadow of a beech, he drew bridle that his beast might drink. The horse, a stalwart sorrel, shone like satin with good grooming, and as it stood at ease with fore limbs flexed and stooped neck, quaffing the stream, it was a study fit for Rosa Bonheur. The rider was stout, full-bearded, seemed faultlessly attired, and sat well in the saddle.

"Who on earth," pondered Aunt Becky aloud after a prolonged survey, "can that be? Law sakes! if it aint Mr. Bloker."

"Who lately bought the Smise farm?" inquired Emily.

"Yes, darling, a rich merchant in the city, with ships that trades to the Ingies; and they *do* say," continued the old lady impressively, but with some reservation in her tone implying doubt, "that he owns an indigo mine."

"He is an acquaintance of father's," remarked Emily to her friend, "at whose request I have invited him to my birth-day."

In a little time the visitor, having finished his business, sauntered to the house. The disconsolate Gregg, plucking his wristband diffidently, performed the introduction—

"Mr. Bloker, mother and ladies."

"Your servant, madame," responded Bloker, raising his hat,—"Miss Horton's, and her friend's,"—pausing interrogatively.

"Miss Mellen, sir," said Emily.

"I had the honor, Miss Horton, to receive your invitation through Mrs. Klett, and I shall surely not forget it."

Deportment composed, tones bland. His unrumpled dress was an agreeable result of cultivated taste. Linen purely white, uncreased patent leather boots of a refulgent jet, a brown silk cravat tied *neglige*, a vest of unblemished marseilles, ample trowsers of light cassimere, and an olive-colored frock, constituted it—

a costume which was well displayed on a muscular figure.

"The builders at my bachelor's quarters deny me possession, and I am at present on the bounty of Mrs. Klett."

"I suppose, sir, you intend great improvements."

"I mean to make the place snug, if I can—a sort of box, you know, with comforts."

"Folks all about is talking of your water-works," remarked the old lady. "I think it will be a grand thing on wash-days in a drowth, when you have to haul, and lose half on't by jolting in the ox-cart."

"Mrs. Gregg alludes to a fountain I am contriving," he explained with comical serenity.

"Of course you will christen your new property—what may we learn to call it?"

"Really, Miss Horton, I shall be fortunate if you make me your debtor for its christening." An unpleasant gleam about his mouth.

"It is impossible, sir, from my slender resources to oblige you suitably; Miss Mellen," laughing and gesturing toward her friend, "has a quicker genius."

"Now I call that a cowardly shifting of responsibility. I dare say Mr. Bloker would gladly empty his bottles over a failure in izzard from you. But stop—'tis wise to withhold. You confess to being a bachelor, sir, and for aught I know you have all the faculty of fancy and satirical temper of Bachelor Benedick, and can do better a dozen times than our best, which would only whet your sarcasms. I grow quite afraid; you shall have no naming from me."

Hospitable rites were not forgotten by the kind hostess. Upon the little spider-legged table in her parlor she spread a spotless cloth, and placed regalement of currant wine, rusks, and honey.

"Aunt Becky, I will turn beggar for one of your nice baked apples and a bowl of milk," said Emily.

"Bring a plate of 'em, mother," said the farmer, "mebbe the other folks would like. They ought to eat greedy for they've got a road before them."

"Seems to me there's no apples nowadays will bake as they used to when I was a girl," observed Aunt Becky, as she placed the dish before her guests. "I mind a tree on father's place, that bore the fullest; a goodish-sized, reddish-streaked apple, that come out of the pan coated with a thick, rich jelly, sweet as sugar. I often think things don't grow as they used to, owing to the seasons I suppose; and I'm sure people was a deal honester in old times, as I told Jed'diah only yesterday, when that swindlin' peddler took me in with the vail."

"How did he cheat you, Aunt Becky?" asked Emily.

"Why, he offered it so cheap, considering it was real lace, that I thought I'd buy it for Sairey Ann. He said he got a lot of 'em in some damaged goods from a fire by mistake, at auction in the city, and it cost five dollars apiece to import them, and he'd let me have one for two dollars and a quarter, and warrant it. So I took it, and after he'd gone we was examining it, and Sairey Ann found a big hole in one corner gummed over with blotting-paper where the ticket was. I called out to Jed'diah, who'd just come in, to follow on at once to the river and make the man take it back; but all the horses was out ploughing, and when Jed'diah got to the ferry it was too late."

"Well, mother, no such doings can come to a good end," remarked the farmer, consolingly.

The guests partook with heartiness, though Mr. Bloker's face was thought to gloom as he sipped the wine, which might have wanted the relish of Verzenay Perhaps it was only an intrusion of the indigo mine.

"One sprightly and clever; *the* one, charmingly shy," thought Jacob Bloker, as he rode away.

"Freezingly formal," summed up Caroline.

"Something more disagreeable than that, I think," said Emily.

CHAPTER VI.

> —— like the elements,
> That know not what, nor why, yet do effect
> Rare issues by their operance, our souls
> Did so to one another; what she liked,
> Was then of me approved; what not condemned,
> No more arraignment; the flower that I would pluck,
> And put between my breasts, Oh she would long
> Till she had such another, and commit it
> To the like innocent cradle, where phœnix-like
> They died in perfume.—THE TWO NOBLE KINSMEN.

IT is happiness to contemplate the attachment of two pure and lovely women. The friendship of women who live in what is called "society" is seldom so sincere and enduring as is that of those who have been reared and are resident among the scenes of nature. In cities are jealousy and fret, the growth of a forced rivalry of beauty, manners, wealth and position. Nor is it possible for even persons of exalted culture, unless they are vitalized by religion, to rise entirely above the influences of a highly artificial condition of life, in which "envy and deceit glare through the flimsy mask of complaisance, and strengthen in the buzz of vanity and hate." The early education of country girls is pursued at home, and in comparative seclusion. They are morally and physically strengthened by innocent zests and employments. Less exposed to rancorous strife for ephemeral distinction, they are as far exempt from the pangs of rivalry, and untempted to entertain its spites and practise its subterfuges. The country girl does not regard her companions as obstructions to her shining, but as enliveners of her quiet and regular existence. Her healthy impulses are not sacrificed to the tyranny of etiquette, nor is her personality lost in the pageantry of fashion. Her sound body is a spring of cheerfulness; and her mind, though happily ignorant of pasteboard pomps, is not uninformed of life's loftier purposes. The girlish joys, disappointments, and movements of country life have been in common—the children have learned and played together at the school-house in the grove, and the maidens have slept and risen together under the farm-house roof. The gay world is a stir of strangers in which events lie thick, and those separate impressions are choked before they strengthen to durability which in their sum constitute friendship. While, then, the pleasures of intellectual intercourse are fullest and freshest in the metropolis, the affections find kindliest nurture among fields and woods. The civic best of social bloom and fruitage is fed by country roots. The staminal collapse of cities is constantly counteracted by an infusion from God's wide domain, and the mothers of the belles who languish in concert rooms and blanch at midnight routs, were cheered at their labors by the sunrise choir of robins and challenged in their cheeks the orchard's bloom.

Emily and Caroline had been trained companionably, like kindred shoots, from childhood; though the nature of each had taken its proper shape of development. Their lives had been nourished generously by the same scenes and sympathies—they had read the same books, felt an ownership in each other's household surroundings, enjoyed together the same natural prospects, hummed together the same new airs.

Caroline was the daughter of a physician whose fortune permitted him to decline practice and devote himself to scientific investigation; one of that honorable class who "live laborious days," giving time and sacrificing pleasure to the pursuit of physical truth—by which the world is profited so much, and which it thanks so little. The imagination of Dante would have made of her an etherial vision. She possessed, rarities it has been said among American women, a classical bust and well-rounded arms. Her head reigned exultant above the luxuriant loveliness of throat and thorax. The black tresses which were shed from her brow timidly returned to dally with the flexure of her white neck. Her eyes were not wells of tenderness—as they should have been to satisfy an orthodox rapture—but as the humor was, sparkled with mirth, or flashed with scorn in glances that trooped forth beneath an ample arch of forehead, which rose from the shaft of a Grecian nose. The eyelashes were flickering filamentous shadow. The contour of her cheeks was best displayed when the heart showed emotionally in their soft carnation, and the chin, fairer than a turning in ivory, just trembled responsive to their emergent flush and the compression of her coralline lips. In her unusual strains, the joyfulness which dimpled round her mouth was more jubilant than victorious trumpets.

CHAPTER VII.

Capulet.—Nay, gentlemen, prepare not to be gone;
We have a trifling foolish banquet towards.
ROMEO AND JULIET.

THE tenth of November came to teem with placid merriment. Away be Meditation and her sober lessons when Beauty celebrates birthday or bridal—stay for a happy space the hours that wear us out, and make them rich with lights, and glad with garlands, and sounding with harmony!

A gay company was assembled at Belair. Gentlemen long and lean, galiants short and solid, tesselated the group with ladies of equally various appearance, though not so common-place; Mr. Brown was simply fat and perspired, but Miss Julia's rotundity was *embonpoint*, and—"A fan, sir? it deserves my best curtsey; I protest spirits are contagious here, and put one in quite a glow."

"'Through Coron's lattices the lamps are bright,
For Seyd the Pacha makes a feast to-night.'

—How are you, Dolman?"

"Shark-hungry, Max."

"'Sirrah! go hire me twenty cunning cooks,'" exclaimed Max Heyhurst, with an affectation of generous earnestness, as he half-turned toward an astonished servant. "Ah!" he continued, "you should try the virtues of your 'true Sherris', which means at Belair, Horton's. It is liquid amber infused with the sublimation of all delicate pungencies, 'pon my taste!"

"Can't; it would plague me next morning."

"A sad case, truly—I feel for you. 'Headachey myself after milk-punch."

"Milk-punch is it you're discussing?"

"Imputatively, doctor."

"Incalculable amount of sustenance in milk-punch. Heard of a sailor who was marooned on a desolate island with a tame goat. Captain relented at the last moment so far as to ask if he could do anything for Crusoe at parting. Got a request for a puncheon of Santa Cruz out of the cargo, to be charged against wages for the round voyage. Skipper acceded. Limes were indigenous, and Crusoe got sugar from sweet grapes. There passed two years of rum, milk, and meditation—of choicer draughts than the Amalthean that nourished the infant god on Ida. Then, goat tumbled from a cliff into the sea and was drowned. The hermit thrown upon Santa Cruz neat, went off in delirium tremens. Before he died, however, missionary ship arrived. Last words were, 'More punch!'"

"If that unfortunate seaman had but lived, with grizzled hair and glittering eye!" ejaculated Max; and, as he wiped a damp optic, he murmured, with reflective pathos,

> 'It is an ancient mariner,
> And he stoppeth one of three—.'"

"You enlarge upon sherry with so much gust, Max, that I am almost persuaded you are descended from one of the critics whom Cervantes tells of," said Dolman.

"Which one?" inquired Max, gravely.

"Well, there were two, called to pronounce upon the contents of a butt of celebrated Xeres. One connoisseur lingered at the brim of the glass, and immerged his mind in the liquor at every sip. The quiet bystanders watched the process, and glanced from the taster to each other admiringly. But when it was announced, with emphasis, that instead of the true vinous aroma there was a tang of iron, they thrust their tongues into their cheeks and shrugged in derision. The other judge, put to his mettle, deliberated long, while the juice with pleasant titillation lapped the edges of his tongue, or he marked with upraised eye its transparency. The spectators looked expectant, as they would say—Now for an opinion which will make the reputation of the vintage! It came. 'Yes, I am dead sure,' blurted number two, 'the flavor *is* of leather, if there be a side in Cordova.' Everybody now laughed outright, and one or two tapped their heads as intimating lunacy, and winked aside. But when they pumped the wine from the cask they found a thong looped in a rusty key."

"That sherris sack, at least, had a 'two-fold quality,'" commented Max.

"The veterans are gone," said the doctor, as he mopped his purplish visage; "you rarely meet even a two-bottle man now-a-days. The present generation drinks negus, and thinks itself heroic; the next, I suppose, will stagger under the nutmeg-grater."

"I admit your wit, doctor, but I object to the sneer," said George Dolman. "I like good wine well enough, short of being brought to grief, but I hold that so far as the age is more temperate, it is not only more virtuous and happy, but it has more humor, mirth, and genuine gaiety; for the larger part of your vaunted maudlin humor is downright profanity, or grotesque conceits, lacquered often with bawdy. I know well that English literary history is full of tavern life; and I grant that the wit which everywhere scintillates about the Mermaids and the Mitres, the Apollos, Will's, and Button's, attaches a fascination to the localities themselves. And it is the consecrated associations of letters which prejudice so many educated men against modern temperance—which, as it is preached, is sometimes intemperate enough—but the wit of 'Rare Ben' and his compotators never grew from the Canaries or gin; the drawers never brought it from the cellar; it was only too strong for the malt and juniper, and—as the asp-wreathed arm of Cleopatra was still a limb of beauty—was wit in spite of them. By-the-by, a little less brandy-and-water would take nothing from the flavor of some of the most genial and humanizing of our modern fiction, which has no need to hiccough its way to posterity.

> '——the lore
> Of mighty minds doth hallow in the core
> Of human hearts the ruin of a wall
> Where dwelt the wise and wondrous—'

So those old taverns are open still. While we listen to the talk of Templars at the Grecian, or of Garrick and Foote at the Bedford, we cannot hear the 'barbarous dissonance' of the common carouse, and it is impertinent to ask us to sign the pledge. Yet, valuable as they were, appointed though erring almoners, the world could have better spared the tipsy poets and the tipsy Porsons than the fair imaginations and capacious intellects which they have blighted. Pagan society fabled the drunken inspiration of Silenus, and produced the temperate philosophy of Socrates. I believe, sir, to ring a change on a famous saying, that hell is nebulous with empty bottles."

"Newfangled notions crop so thick in these latter days that I dare say we are on the verge of the millennium," declared the doctor, testily. "Even our poets have got a mythology with Ganymede abolished. There was a kindly thirst in friendship before the old serpent wriggled all his iniquity into the cork-screw;" and, playing with his glass ribbon, he sauntered to amuse with conversational whimseys another knot of talkers.

Caroline was looking over some plates of Audubon, Imperial in vigor and fidelity were those representations of the beautiful in nature, bird-pictures gathered from a thousand miles of wilderness to delight, amid the appointments of luxury, fair women clothed in fine textures—and such is a single aspect of civilization. Conscious of a presence, Caroline raised her eyes. It was Bloker.

"Now, there's a duck, Miss Mellen, to gladden a cook's heart. With green peas, say, of tender age, and an apricot tart?"

"Yes—a cook's. I fancied it nestling its glossy breast in the desert waters of Labrador. You are right, sir, an irreproachable bird for larding, and delicious with olives."

"Better worth is a voyage from Europe to know it by the palate," and Bloker passed his hand with unconscious complacency along his expanse of waistcoat, "than a voyage thither to know the Rhine and its scenery, the marvels of Rome, which I am told is a tumble-down place, or the bepraised pictures and skies of Florence."

A beetle which had been buzzing about the sconces plumped upon Caroline's neck. The young lady beside her recoiled, with a little scream—she was at the Lalla Rookh period of maidenhood, and sighed for Bendemeer bowers and nightingales — and Bloker, with praiseworthy promptitude, sought his pocket-handkerchief. Caroline calmly grasped and withdrew the insect, its barbed feet vexing her white flesh to a ruddy blotch, and dropped it in a vase, which she covered with some sheets of music.

"Lay you there in sepulture, and dream of old Egypt. Is that your chivalry, Mr. Bloker, to a damsel in distress!"

"Really, you are unjust."

"Urgent, you mean. Were you merely thinking of a vinaigrette for Miss Grayson?"

"You don't seem to stagnate here. I hope, Mr. Bloker, you find these ladies entertaining," said Emily, who joined them.

"Charming."

"You hear that, *bella donna?*

'How dangerous is it, that this man goes loose!'"

Bloker coughed.

"I think Mr. Bloker's sincerity needs no vindication when he compliments Caroline Mellen and her friend."

Miss Grayson's pleasure perched very prettily upon her lips.

"Exquisite, Emily; but I will disappoint you; you shall have no delicious little speeches in return, however much you may deserve them—we will burn you no incense," replied Caroline.

"It would be but just homage," said Bloker, ardently. Then, suddenly recovering himself, he added, "if homage were possible among peers."

"My dear Miss Horton"—it was brisk little Doctor Pledget—"take the word of a patriarch, who has no account in flattering when he declares you to be as blooming as Hygeia, and is ready to meet in mortal combat any recreant knight who disputes it—with a thumb lancet," and the doctor put himself ludicrously atilt.

"I am proud, doctor, to have such a formidable champion—it completes my happiness," replied Emily.

"If he were less like still Champagne to-night; I

don't question the bouquet, but we miss the effervescence," urged the mocking Caroline.

"Miss Mellen will impute my gravity to a sermon I was forced to listen to this morning as a director of a charity, and which was *not* in the manner of Jeremy Taylor; and to too much roast beef at dinner to satisfy exhausted nature after the effort of attention. Melancholy meat, if we believe Galen."

"For a contrite countenance, now and then, I would pension you liberally with dull sermons."

"Abandon the intention, my dear Miss Mellen, and I will never transgress to levity again. But there is enough in contrast here to make an old fellow like me a little sad. The exultant teens, and the crowning triumph of twenty," inclining toward Emily, "and sounding life before, like a majestic march of heralds. Even the hurried flow of my shrunk veins reminds me of spent forces by the feebleness of the wave. I am a long link between knee-breeches and the electric telegraph. Like a quaint old coin slipped from a bankrupt collector, I show odd among the bravery of the new mintage, but I have lost fixed rate, and they higgle about my value at the shops. My 'babes of memory' are now children of the wood, and each year adds to their covering of dead leaves. But what last-will-and-testament stuff is this! Fill my snuff-box and shut me up with the beetle, fair gaoler, for I believe I am only fit to sneeze away my remnant of life."

"I thought, doctor, when I saw you the other day at the steamboat pier with a lady, that you might be looking to matrimony as a refuge from your 'sea of troubles,'" observed Bloker.

"Steamboat pier?—old lady, with two bandboxes?"

"When the pedler nearly jostled you into the river."

"By the libeled Cupid! spinster aunt—Israelite, who wanted me to buy a watch—made her debut before the last war with Great Britain, in the time of turret head-dresses, and part of the beauty Packenham threatened at New Orleans."

"A striking group for an artist," said Caroline. "How should you name it, now?"

"'The Finding of Moses,' I suppose. Am I so very gray, Miss Mellen?"

"Just white enough in your beard to sanction your *role* of the venerable—and, doctor, permit me to say it is a beard worthy of a Bedouin. I fancy you a sheik, scouring the desert on a fiery barb, and followed by a band in burnoozes."

"Perish every hair if I must be conjured to such an unseemly shape. No: patriotism forbid; to say nothing of religion."

"Apropos of beards. What becomes of the trade-fallen barbers, doctor?"

"I hardly know. They don't take to suicide, and cut their own throats: though I have noticed a tendency among them to go mad, and open wide ways with their razors for the lives of other people. Perhaps they emigrate; or get prudently run over and go into hospitals; or, as a last resource of garrulous destitution, edit the Sunday newspapers. Ah! Mr. Davenport, I am glad to see you. Well out of your ailments, I hope?"

"Why, no, doctor; there's still a sinking here;" and the old clerk placed his hand upon his stomach.

"An excellent symptom, my dear sir, if you sink enough there," responded Pledget.

"You don't think it pulmonary? Ours is a cancer family."

"No, my dear fellow; no bellows to mend," and the doctor, with a nicer regard to anatomy, tapped Davenport above the bulge of his buff waistcoat.

"Perhaps, doctor, Mr. Davenport's disease is of the type of inward bruises apt to afflict middle-aged bachelors," suggested Mr. Horton.

"Eh, love?"

"The lady is'nt invoiced yet," sententiously averred the patient.

"So, so, when the article is wanted we will order a creole beauty to be forwarded, with a cargo of sugar, from Porto Rico or Barbadoes," said Caroline.

"I have known two or three of those expensive exotics, Miss Mellen; who were proud as Lucifer, capricious, and pretty enough to the turn of twenty-five, when they ran to gamboge complexions and ear-rings, and delighted in monkeys and macaws."

"It's odd how likings differ," philosophized Davenport. "I knew a bookkeeper of a romantic turn of mind, in the China trade—we called him Nankeen Fortescue, because in warm weather he always wore trowsers of that stuff, and pumps—who would get quite hot asserting the charms of the female portraits on the tea-caddies. I saw him the very day he died, of an apoplexy, opening some cases of crapes in August, the windows shut to keep out the dust," continued the old clerk, with a touch of pathos in his tone.

"Talking of love, doctor; how will you define it?" asked Mr. Horton.

"One may spend a great deal of fine talk in trying, and know less of it at the end than his cook and coachman. It is in the mind, and, free of all other control, is servant to its own conception, which it holds precious beyond all other values. It is, when at its purest, the highest placidity below that of heaven diffused about an imperial image, which creates, and in which is concentred, hope and happiness. It is a pervading something which is electrical, exploits, and explodes."

"And, like lightning, never strikes the same people twice the same day?" demurely questioned Caroline Mellen.

The doctor continued.

"Love working in the blood may be a spell of tameness, or of turbulence. The same passion which made Max Piccolomini, in Schiller's play, long to exchange the crimson laurel for the first March violet plucked in familiar fields, when distorted to jealousy, has pointed many a stiletto. You remember Gibbon's description of his Lausanne flame, the excellent Mademoiselle Curchod—afterwards Necker's wife and the mother of De Stael—it is in the same stately strain which he employs when depicting the Antonines—

and how his love was 'the union of desire, friendship, and tenderness, inspired by a single female;' yet its disappointment does not seem to have at all disturbed the evenness of his after life. If Coleridge's love was up to the measure in 'Genevieve,' what a long reach was it above that of the historian! Indeed, the poet sings his own rapture;

> 'You stood before me like a thought,
> A dream remember'd in a dream.
> But when those meek eyes first did seem
> To tell me, Love within you wrought—
> O Greta, dear domestic stream!'"

"The sudden transition in the last line is natural and pleasing," said Caroline.

"An instinctive criticism," observed Mr. Horton, banteringly.

The doctor smiled, and continued.

"So, with women the climate of love may vary.

> 'They are but beggars that can count their worth,'

exclaims the impassioned Juliet. There have been, I dare say, ladies less ardent. The black-eyed of Andalusia and the blue-eyed of the Elbe woo and are won with a difference. Perhaps it is this diversity of its manifestation which tempers and restrains the passion. Emigration and conquest merge nationalities, correct the redundant characteristic of one people by an infusion of its converse from another, and preserve a general balance."

"Beyond doubt," said Mr. Horton, "the love of the sexes is the perfection of mere human bliss; that love which when wedded is pure, and sanctified before

God and angels; upon the happy bed of which the sword of the Spirit severs from all lust, and the bower in Paradise 'showered roses.'"

"You called love electrical, doctor, and you mean, I suppose, love at first sight. If it be, heaven hinder a multitude of modern marriages!"

"Yea, and amen. I don't profess to know more of the human heart than did Shakespeare. The ill-starred pair of 'Fair Verona,' and Ferdinand and Miranda surrendered to each other at the instant, and neither of the ladies stipulated for pin-money."

"But Beatrice, while inspiring with angelic visions the great poet of Italy, did not surrender to him," rejoined Caroline.

"I believe Beatrice to have been a *lusus naturæ*— she was, at least, an Italian blonde," said the doctor, laughing.

"*I* cry out with Rosalind, 'O how full of briers is this working-day world!'" jested Caroline.

"Love in the heart, though profound and hidden, is all graceful inflexions, like the wash of the lower sea in the windings of a shell." The speaker was Emily, who had paused to listen in passing.

"Splendid image!" attested Bloker, with sentimental fervor.

"Or, not to stray from the shell, love is like a coal of fire on the back of a tortoise," said Caroline.

"Or like quicksilver, which eludes the grasp of the living and will rest in a dead man's hand," added Doctor Pledget, tapping his snuff-box.

CHAPTER VIII.

"——what do ye call the place?
A plague upon't—it is in Gloucestershire."
HENRY IV.

ABOUT thirty miles from Belair was the residence of Mr. Crosby, who was well known through all the country side. A considerable estate, which had descended to him through several generations of Crosbys, was carelessly cultivated, as the broken fences, grass-grown middles, and rusty tools abundantly declared. In reality, the daughter of the proprietor, Adelaide, was both master and mistress of the premises. She bought the necessaries, household and farming, settled the accounts, cut the garments, and mixed the physic of the working people, did the business correspondence, overlooked the condition of the cattle as well as of the pantry, and gave the overseer such general instructions as he received. And she exercised this authority because Mr. Crosby was so eccentric as to be a little mad, and his helpmeet was a hippish invalid.

Walter Crosby when a young man was celebrated

for strength and comeliness; which, inasmuch as he was the inheritor of many acres, made him a favorite theme of speculation with matrons possessed of marriageable daughters. His understanding was fair, and it was cultivated to the respectable standard of collegiate requirements, perhaps beyond, for he was fond of books. A year or two of European travel enlarged his views, and invested him with gracefulness of deportment. He married, and entered prosperously and hopefully upon life. With health, possessions, an inquisitive disposition, and the invigorating employments and exercises of the field, nothing seemed wanting to promote his happiness. But man's mind refuses to conform to fortune; and perhaps a portion of adversity would have kept his in ballast. When Mr. Crosby cast loose from rational habits, he persisted in his foxhunting. A change of manners, made by a new class of population, had left among remembered things the meet of gentry, of whom some were dead and some were old; and a few small farmers and country idlers had succeeded to the sport. To join these, when he was in the mood, implied no hospitality to be received or returned. Abandoning the society of his family and his neighbors, renouncing the world and books, he lived separately with his hounds, and lavished upon them and a couple of favorite hunters the whole sum of his attentions. A hale, grizzled man, of slovenly appearance, stagnant except in physical vigor, he reigned the monarch of a kennel.

To the left of the avenue which approached the mansion was an old brick chapel, very homely, nestled in a grove of buttonwoods; the Crosbys had been Catholics since colony times. It was a quiet spot for a dreamer on a calm autumn day, where he might blow at ease bubbles of fancy, or, reclined, watch through the rifts of the half leafless trees the fleecy cumulus shifting in the blue cope above, and listen to the cattle audibly feeding around.

The grounds were well shaded, and there was a garden, which exhibited traces of former taste and care, despite crumbling terrace and ragged espalier. Still there were efforts at amendment, sincere and satirical, where a piece of ladder, masked in whitewash, closed a gap in the fence, or a decayed trellis leaned helplessly on the rough-hewn support of a rail. Even in the vegetable garden, the weediness of the spaces and rankness of the thistles, and beyond all the tardy locomotion of Ned, the guardian of the spot, an aged negro who might have been inoculated with rheumatism in his sable infancy and have never recovered, he was so cramped and gnarled, suggested slender asparagus and early peas at midsummer. The mouldering roof of the ice-house, upon which perched a peacock, was patched with a thatching of cornstalks; and its door, which hung by a solitary strap, was kept in place by props The weather-beaten martin-box, conspicuously aloft, from which the birds were gone for the season, looked ripe for the Limbo of outworn things. Nothing was needed to make this dreariness a charm but a tough-constitutioned October rain. A half-grown cadet of the family and a ragged cub of a companion were prying for rats in the foundation of an old chimney, assisted by a truculent terrier, which they alternately cursed and encouraged by the name of Brandy. Through the centre of the house ran a hall wide enough for the passage of a wagon, on each side of which the ample rooms, deep wainscoted, subsided in capacious recesses of chimneys, where had blazed many a hospitable fire. But the paint was very dingy, and the cracked panes were unseemly with an eruption of putty. The occupants expelled, ghosts might have revelled there of gusty nights to the clatter of the broken lightning-rods—it was just the building for town boys to play in and remember all their lives. At this weather-tinted mansion Emily and Caroline, on a visit to Adelaide Crosby, were now arrived.

An old negro, hight Jake, shambled from the region of the offices, and with ceremonious scraping proceeded to distribute his attentions between the horses, the guests, and his individual legs. He was much molested by fleas upon a tender cuticle, which he entrapped with twine ligatured about his trowsers, dexterously securing them at the barriers.

As no one appeared to receive the ladies, Jacob was questioned. It was useless to ask for Mr. or Mrs. Crosby, so, Where was Miss Adelaide?

"Young Missus' gwon to Mr. Steve Loyd—him child dead."

"Is there nobody at home but Mrs. Crosby?"

"Missuses aunt's yer."

"Well, let her know some friends are come," said Emily, alighting.

"Tell Susan jemediate, Missus," and, with an obeisance, Jacob was off.

Susan shortly presented herself and ushered the visitors into the house, and was followed in due season by "Missuses aunt," a shrivelled old lady in black, wearing a cap which glowed with a profusion of ribbon, and which was set in the exigence of the occasion slightly awry. The dame made a stately bow, which the visitors appropriately returned.

"We are sorry, ma'am, not to find Adelaide at home, but suppose, from what the servant said, that she will soon return."

"'Nan?" responded the old lady, with a hand to her ear.

Emily repeated the substance of her remark.

"'Na—an?" again, with a tremor of excitement.

Evidently an auricular defect. Emily, in despair, urged her friend to an essay. With a preliminary inflation of the lungs, Caroline enunciated this striking observation—

"Delightful weather to-day, ma'am."

"Yes; I've heerd of several cases—I hope it isn't ketching," replied the old lady, with briskness.

. "I hope not," exclaimed Caroline, seized with a sudden freak which she knew she could indulge in undetected.

"So the doctors say," returned the matron, with the promptness of an answering battery, "but I don't put much dependence in *them*." Her look of lofty incredulity was sufficient to crush the whole college of physicians.

The arrival of Adelaide Crosby terminated this ludicrous practise with cross-purposes.

"I have been," she said, "to see the wife of a laboring man who lives near, and whose child, an infant, died yesterday. I promised to go again this afternoon, but I will send and excuse myself."

"Certainly not; on the contrary, if you will allow us, we will go with you."

"I am to take some necessaries. I must get ice, and we have none—have suffered provokingly all summer for want of it."

"Yet, if I recollect, last winter was very cold," remarked Emily.

"Yes; our pond was frozen, but it was infested with muskrats, and the dam having been neglected they gnawed through it and let out the water, when the ice fell into the mud and was lost."

Loyd's house was in the skirts of a wood, and was a comfortable cabin of moderate size, which derived from the sylvan surroundings an air of picturesqueness. Upon the rough stone chimney which buttressed the house were hung some calabashes above a slab bench, the stand of a piggin and kitchen utensils. The well, with its low wooden curb and long sweep of pole, was near at hand. A stone's throw off the cow was ruminating in an open byre. By the door-sill a dog lay blinking in the sun, heedless of the efforts of a flaxen-haired little girl to rouse him to a sportive humor.

In a contiguous lot belonging to Loyd was an ancient burial ground, which had been used, perhaps, in the early days of the settlement by some family now scattered or extinct. It occupied a knoll which was topped by a wide-spreading walnut tree, and the heaped turf of the old graves, still marked in places by unpretending lichen-covered stones, had subsided below the general level into shallow cavities where the grass grew ranker and greener. Here, with mattock and spade, Stephen Loyd was sternly at work. Upon a swelling of root sat his eldest son, a lad of thirteen, with his thoughtful face rested on his hands. The Loyds were poor.

That night, while the mother of the buried babe lay wrestling with her grief, the schoolmates blithely lived again the past. After next day's dinner, at which was served a Brahmapootra brought by "Missuses aunt" to stock with exclusive poultry the Crosby domain, and which had been slain in the general inattention by a blundering scullion, like any dunghill fowl, the Belair ladies departed.

In a wooded dell on the grounds of Mr. Horton there gushed a hill-side spring, cool and limpid, which was bordered with rustic seats. It was a place where Retirement might nestle and pensively muse away the hours, sobered by the hue of evergreens, and startled only by the rustling of the leaves, the little stir of rabbit or squirrel, and the crackle of the bird-molested brambles. One morning the ladies were seated there after a ramble, and occupied with their respective fancies, when Caroline exclaimed, "Here is Bradley!"

Emily raised her eyes, beheld him descending the slippery path, and started quickly to welcome him.

CHAPTER IX.

'Twas twilight, for the sunless day went down
Over the waste of waters; like a veil,
Which, if withdrawn, would but disclose the frown
Of one whose hate is masked but to assail;
Thus to their hopeless eyes the night was shown
And grimly darkled o'er their faces pale
And the dim desolate deep—twelve days had Fear
Been their familiar, and now Death was here.—DON JUAN.

BRADLEY HORTON had not apprised the family at Belair of his intention to return from his travels. The omission to write was a caprice, and a happy one which prevented much painful suspense. The Icaria, in which he sailed from Europe, never reached its American port.

Sometimes in the calms of after life did Bradley mentally recall the incidents and impressions of those days at sea—the joyous company flushed with anticipations of affection, business, and pleasure; the lapse of placid hours; the grateful stimulus of new and various acquaintanceship; the serenity of sky and ocean; the discipline of unaccustomed movement aboard; the spouting of distant whales; flocks of flying-fish scudding before the ravenous bonito; and the impetuous charge of porpoises across the bows, black and furious legions, leaping and plunging, now sunk then seen, beating a long track of foam against the wind in the gray waste; the lazy regularity of meals; the dreamy satisfaction of the after-dinner cigar; music by moonlight, and books and cards in the snug saloon; and then—the sudden fury of the storm!

And *then*, eventful days and nights of fearful peril. How the brave ship struggled and shuddered in the turmoil, and still went on with "solemn face" against the angry waters! How would have sunk the din of hostile navies in that great symphony of wind and wave! The blast, misty with spray, swept upon the leaning ship. The billows, gathered in swells of hundreds of feet in breadth, bore it upon their undulations buoyantly as a cork, or broke along the bulwarks, sending a throb through every timber, and jarring to its iron heart, which still beat on in slow pulsations. Then there was a lull.

"Wild weather," said the captain cheerily, "but it has blown its worst—look to the ladies."

Anxious faces lightened; faces before serious over open Bibles retained no vestige of the text in their new assurance. Some of the most timid ventured pleasantries, and talked of hunger; and waiters stumbled about with trays of biscuits and cold meat.

The pause in the gale was short. Again the blasts burst appallingly, and goaded anew the watery onset. A rumor spread—muttered, but more distinctly heard than the shrill cordage—of a discovered leak. The few passengers who cowered and clung on deck searched for evidence of disaster in the captain's unimpassioned face, and searched in vain. Soon apprehension became certainty; mattresses and blankets for the breach were passed below. The pumps were worked to their utmost capacity. Still the water gained. Tubs were rigged, and the tackle manned by passengers and crew. Gangs, relieving each other, worked day and night unceasingly. Still the water gained. It rose upon the furnaces and hissed among the fires. The force of the engine ebbed like the breath of a dying mastodon; then, with a shiver, the strong limbs were still. The ship, but half owning her helm, wavered and pitched ominously. Men were hurled overboard with the wrecked spars which they strove to clear. As if envious of the elements, disease came, swift and fell, to its banquet. The unshrouded victims of cholera, with no funeral service but the clamor of the storm—half a score a day—were buried in the sea. Steadily—with hopeful Christian steadiness, a few awaited death; others were stoically dumb. Some were drunk with fear, wildly appealing to heaven to bridle the ruthless winds, or silent and blanched as the dead.

Once more the gale subsided; but it was plain the ship would soon go down. At daylight on the sixth morning preparation was made to launch the boats. There was still discipline, which was due to the firmness of the commander, but the moment of final test was come, and vehemence and distrust swelled threateningly, when arose an eager cry—"A sail!" and within the same hour another—"Sail ho!" The vessel which was first seen bore down upon them, and proved to be a barque.

"We are sinking—will you stand by us?"

"Aye, aye! while I can float—Men! give them three cheers."

And the brave shouts, heard above the sullen tumult of the sea, thrilled sturdy hearts with hope and thankfulness, as suddenly turned from its ebb the tide of life; and some shouted in return, and some sobbed outright. Now God bless all true sailor men!

That evening, at Belair, before a cheerful blaze—the weather had changed and rain came down in gusts—there was gathered a united family. The manner of Mr. Horton was unwontedly serene and tender; Emily was earnest and fond; and the gaiety of Caroline was subdued to a sober and silent satisfaction, for "there is a joy in which the stranger intermeddleth not."

Bradley talked of his perils on the ocean, while the wind wrestled with the trees and shook the casements. It was observed that he dwelt with enthusiasm upon the heroic demeanor of a Miss Bardleigh. When the others had retired, Emily still lingered with her brother. Leaning upon his chair-back she listened rapt, or questioned to provoke talk. The clock in the hall had struck midnight, in familiar tones which the traveller joyfully heard once more, when they separated.

Andrew, the gardener, had much horticultural history to relate to Bradley, of hopes realized, or disappointed by slug, curculio and fungus; of failures in flowering and favorable frutescence. "These be clips, sir, from your father's choice vine, the Nawth Cawrliney, which that feckless chiel Barney cut down to sling the weights for the hayrick with."

"What has become of the humorous fellow?"

"O sir, on his leaving here he hired with Farmer Gregg, and spered so anent this and thot he nearly drove the auld mon daft. One day they were emptying the pig-yard, and Barney wrought hard with the spade atop of a well loose filled, which settling sudden, took the noble descendant of the O'Keefes toward Auld Nick and brimstane rations afore his time. The mistress bro't the clothes line, and they lugged him up the matter of fifteen feet. He went off straight, and clean disappeared."

"That ending of his career, Andrew, suited well its beginning."

"Sic a steer! It was the red-faced major's wig, which he left in the swath while he tried a turn with the scythe, and which Barney found, misconceivin' it for a strange bur-urd's nest."

"A fine fuchsia."

"One I set by. I suppose, sir, you hae seen unco grand gardens abroad."

"Many. The loveliest I saw, though ragged from neglect, were in Italy; delightful without being trim, with flowers and flowering vines, the rich green of the orange and myrtle, and cool retreats fenced with shrubbery and shaded by poplars and pines, where brooks meandered among fallen statues and by broken fountains."

"And did you meet in your travels in Italee a Sandy Gillivray?"

"No, Andrew."

"He was my mother's sister's son; a pawky lad, wha became what they call a coorier. It is forty year since we played thegither, and dwelt anear by the burn. I mind the time as yesterday when Deacon Deans took him by the lug at kirk, in the first psalm, for jobbin me wi' a preen.—There's a new terrace, sir, raised since you left. The magnolias, foreby, did bad this year. Weel, weel, each must gang his gait!"

While in Europe, Bradley Horton chose his occupation. He determined to be an engineer. He was now twenty-two, and old according to the notion of many stirring and superficial Americans to be a learner. A natural fondness for mathematics and mechanics which he possessed had been stimulated by association with men of science, and by the contemplation abroad of massive roads, tunnels, aqueducts, and bridges, that combine a portion of the old Roman strength and durability in stone—we build less massively than they who laid foundations for the ages—with the lightness and grace of modern civilization, whose talisman, as was that of the rude Gothic days, is Iron.

CHAPTER X.

It was managed with proper spirit on both sides: he asserted that I was heterodox, I retorted the charge; he replied and I rejoined.
VICAR OF WAKEFIELD.

If you can look into the seeds of time,
And say which grain will grow, and which will not,
Speak then to me, who neither beg nor fear
Your favors, nor your hate.—MACBETH.

N a winter's afternoon unemployed business acquaintance would visit Clement Horton's counting-room for familiar conversation. Assembled around the stove are Scroggs, Bliggs, Glump, and a stout gentleman of leisurely appearance, who has been introduced by Bliggs as Mr. Blumenbach. The stranger's accent is German, and his talk indicates him to be a man of culture. His sense of propriety seems outraged by the closeness of Scroggs' unbooted foot, which emits an unsavory steam as it toasts at the fire, the dingy stocking being stroked the while with its owner's usual complacency. It is always the left foot which Bartimeus comforts, having lost two of the toes proper to it by a trap in his marauding boyhood; and it was this calamity which brought him his little limp. There is a quick

play of thought and sensibility in the German's face, as he listens and replies to Mr. Horton, so different from the show of narrow and oily cunning in that of the venerable Bliggs, that it is clear the association of the two men is not of affinity, but of accident. Glump's solemn visage is over the market report of the *Evening Popgun*.

"Now, do you think, Mr. Scroggs, this is a ginuine communication from Julius Cæsar?" asked Bliggs, incredulously, as he finished the perusal of a crabbed piece of penmanship on a soiled and crumpled scrap of paper.

"Every word on't; look at the internal evidence," responded Scroggs, with calm emphasis.

The querist bent his gaze again upon the paper, but failing to find the proof referred to, slowly folded and surrendered it to Scroggs, who put it deferentially in a little pocket-book, with an air of triumph.

"Well," pursued Bliggs, after a pause, "I don't profess, Mr. Scroggs, to be a philosopher, but if I'm right informed Cæsar lived in the world before the English language was spoke, I may say invented, yet you nor me could have writ that document plainer."

"Ah! there it is—the work of spiritual progression. He learnt it in the Speers," replied Scroggs, benignly.

"Would you make a time purchase on such advices, Friend Scroggs?" asked Glump over the *Popgun*.

"Would you take the ghost's word for a thousand pound?" asked Bradley.

"No; the communication *might* be a counterfeit.

There's lieing spirits. There is no money in *them*. Besides, bargaining 's for our common sense, not our higher nature," replied Scroggs.

"Mebbe this one was bogus," suggested Bliggs.

"How then could he have known John Bunyan, and be able to tell all about him when he was in this state of existence, living, as they did, so many hundred years apart?" responded the unperplexed Scroggs.

"Well, it *is* a little curious," admitted Bliggs.

"More credible, Mr. Bliggs, than some of the wonders of the Bible in which you believe. I dare say you never doubted the Jewish passage of the Red Sea?" said Scroggs.

"Which you disbelieve?" asked Mr. Horton.

"It is all a fable, sir," answered Scroggs.

"Yet you contend that tables and chairs can be lifted by supernatural forces, and held in mid-air. If the law of gravitation can be suspended for such trifling, why could it not have been for a momentous purpose?" urged Mr. Horton.

"Spiritualism as a human faith is new, and we don't know yet its capacities. I won't undertake to limit them. A spiritual army, for instance, divested of the incumbrance of flesh and bone, which is so much dead weight to be overcome here, might do amazing things."

"'—— so soft
And uncompounded is their essence pure;
Not tied or manacled with joint or limb,
Nor founded on the brittle strength of bones,
Like cumbrous flesh—'

Thus runs the epic measure," said Bradley.

"Exactly: Epic was a spiritualist," responded Scroggs.

"I must deny, however, the novelty of spiritualism," continued Bradley. "It was believed in Pagan times, a score of centuries ago, about as it is now, Spheres and all. If you want easily consulted evidence, I shall be glad to lend you, Mr. Scroggs, Old Burton, mine Author. And was it not also the reservoir whence Simon of Samaria, and Elymas of Paphos, and the soothsaying damsel of Philippi drew their inspiration?"

"That rather s'prises me; I didn't think it dated so far back," pondered Bliggs. "The Carthagenians was Pagan, as well as the Philistines; I expect we Americans ought to be more enlightened than them."

"It is nothing but the wiles of the Enemy," remarked Glump, with decision.

"We liberal people are prepared to encounter the prejudices of education," blandly observed Scroggs.

"Mr. Glump has certainly warrant for that 'prejudice' in the Gospel and the epistles to the primitive church," remarked Mr. Horton. "Perhaps he was thinking of Paul's warning against 'seducing spirits and doctrines of devils,' which he foretold. But, apart from that, what evidence have you—I mean proof, in the rigorous sense of the word—to establish the authorship of these communications and manifestations, granting that they are not produced by earthly agencies, in the disembodied spirits of men. How do you know they are not utterances from Jupiter, say; of superior intelligences, if you please, to ourselves? If this supposition is sufficient to account for them, how will you prove that it does not?"

"Jis as like as not—or Hushel," said Bliggs, contributing his quota of astronomy.

"Extremely improbable," insisted Glump with some asperity, as scorning an abandonment of the diabolism hypothesis. Scroggs made no response, but lapsed into his fat smile of serene compassion. Unfriendly cavillers contended that in these fits of abstraction, which seemed to radiate placidity and innocence to such an extent that his very eyes were misty, Bartimeus planned doubtful schemes of profit. But others, who knew him to give respectably of his substance to projects of philanthropy when they were not evangelic—for they had seen his donations conspicuously set forth in the newspapers—disbelieved the imputation, as they surely ought.

"But grant," continued Clement Horton, "that these tapping propagandists are the disembodied spirits of men; what kind of spirits are they which are so affectionately familiar with the worldly and wicked? Goodness does not thus easily mingle with evil—the spice-laden ships do not steer for the icebergs, be the treacherous sea about them never so inviting."

"The spiritual bodies of men have been seen by the endowed in the process of formation," said Blumenbach.

"Thomas Jefferson Spriggens, the seer," added Scroggs, impressively, "saw the spirit of G——, the distinguished scholar who was executed, form. It was awakened in the Speer by soft music. And what corroborates him is, G—— was very fond of just such music in this life."

"Was Spriggens, Friend Scroggs, the seer who saw so many people without souls in Boston?" asked Glump, scoffingly.

"Seven hundred and thirty-two he counted; many of them highly respectable," was the tranquil reply of Scroggs.

"Now, though I'm no philosopher, I expect spiritualism is only the national genius on a new shoot—that it is being smart in a new shape, which pays by making people stare and spend. If that seer could have invented an improved steam-engine I reckon he wouldn't have seen spirits," said Bliggs.

"There's clearly a spark of 'the main chance' in the new 'religion.'" said Clement Horton. "The thaumaturgists who receive regular mails from Hades, take care, I am told, to collect the postage in advance of delivery; and the great American miracle-monger, who puzzled the kings and councillors of Europe, married a princess, or somebody of the sort, the other day. Much I fear that the bland bishops who dispense the stirabout of spiritualism for gospel meat are given to filthy 'ucre."

"As to spirits, Mr. Bliggs, the mejeums see 'em constantly, walking up and down, and sometimes can't distinguish them from us," said Scroggs.

"Then it's the kingdom of Beelzebub displayed—What's the use of seeing them?" growled Glump.

"The elevation of human nature," replied Scroggs, with an air of contempt.

"I don't perceive that; nor how a perpetual motion of ghost-traps is to lift it a peg," said Glump.

"Because you're a supralapsarian, sir," retorted Bartimeus Scroggs, with lofty commiseration.

"Mebbe: But the straightest Calvinism is something more than a mixture of sorcery and twattle," said Glump.

"Dr. Pledget, sir," remarked Bradley, by way of a diversion, addressing his father, "objects to spiritualism on conservative ground. A ghost used to be an event—something creditable to have in a family. It stuck to the pedigree, and gave it a smack of mysterious importance. This is over since the unpolite Smiths and Joneses have taken to walking out of their winding-sheets."

"We are certainly entitled to ask, what's the use of hearing the spirits, when we consider that which they are declared to utter. It is melancholy to reflect how the intellects of Erasmus and President Edwards have dwindled, and what a Miss Nancy's warble the muse of Milton is become in 'the music of the spheres;' nay, even Satan himself is shrivelled, and no longer stands

'Like Teneriffe or Atlas unremov'd,'"

said Mr. Horton.

"Sir, you say true," assented Blumenbach, with energy. "Very much of the inspiration is miserable, what you will call atrocious, abominable—such as the schoolgirl may despise. Most people have little brains in this world, why should they have more in the next? The pretence of such cheap intercourse with the spirits of great thinkers and scholars is one humbug. The philosophers do not much know the mountebanks here, when they are together; why should they seek communion when they get out of their company? Fudge! Yet the grand subject of spiritualism is sure and not fabricated."

Scroggs referred to his watch, as he rose to leave.

"As well doubt that there is mon—morals—she's stopped: the work of some mischievous spirit," he said.

"Permit me?" asked Mr. Horton, reaching his hand. He held the watch a minute in his warm grasp, gave it a vigorous shake, and returned it ticking.

"The work of Jack Frost rather; the oil in the movements was congealed," he said, smiling.

"Though I don't profess to be a philosopher, I shouldn't wonder," acquiesced Bliggs.

"To believe such doctrine evinces a low order of intellect," said Glump, when Scroggs had departed.

"Spiritualism has converts who are much desired for wit," replied the German, curtly.

"Yes," said Mr. Horton, "poets, and persons of imaginative power. To them the soothing revelation of Madame, 'who died o' Wednesday,' to her surviving spouse, seems no more inappropriate than the consolation which Creusa gave to Æneas; and they do not care to inquire too curiously if it be simulated. Yet Shakespeare makes Hamlet, who is one of them, doubt if the Devil in the shape of the spirit be not abusing him through his melancholy. *They* can frame from the commonplaces of the creed the architecture of a sensuous and intellectual paradise—but how unsatisfying!"

"Why say you so?" asked Blumenbach.

"Because man's moral nature is far above his intellect, and the highest development of that nature impels to self-denial, which produces a purer and more exquisite happiness than sensuousness."

"Not alone poets, but philosophers, from Socrates to Swedenborg, have believed in the spiritual existences," asserted Blumenbach.

"Surely you cannot claim that the Greek and the Swede were in any wise identified with the spiritism of to-day. Granted the 'infernal' theory of Mr. Glump, and the old partnership of the Witch of Endor and the Devil renewed, with an extended connection, would be more in point," said Mr. Horton, pleasantly.

"You cannot so suppress the strange story of Saul, grand and wayward man, from whose nature every element in that of your Shakespeare's Othello might have been drawn—courage, credulity, jealousy, fiery passion—with a sneer. Spiritualism is the belief in hereafter, and cherished knowledge of the wise few of the ages, aggregated at last into a religious system; just as the Church is the complement of Christianity: and the great, queer Athenian is its Paul," asserted Blumenbach.

"Concerning the 'dæmon' of Socrates, his 'prophetic voice,' of which he talked familiarly, it is enough to say that he believed it, that to him it was a revelation, whether true or false, which originated beyond himself and the operations of his intellect. That such a faith should have been professed by the first of the heathen sages, a faith which was a virtual confession of his own insufficiency, is the sharpest satire upon empty carpers at the element of revelation in Christianity, and an argument by implication against the ablest objectors. Of the belief of the pure-minded Swede we are fully informed. He held, that on their separation from the body the good become angels, and the unregenerate spirits; their conditions respectively being celestial, and infernal; and unchangeably fixed. He declared, that both good spirits and evil spirits are attendant upon every man. That the former live in the good affections, or the internal and spiritual man; and that the latter live in the evil affections, or the external and natural man. But the internal spiritual man may be and continue so closed as to admit of no communication with heaven; which is a kingdom established in the hearts of living men, as well as a disembodied condition; and which is only attainable by prayer through the Lord Christ, who is the fulness of the Divinity. Your spirits give lessons in good morals, you say—'teach the morals of Jesus,' I believe is the phrase—yet all the time they deny his divine competency, by which those 'morals' in their great results are recommended to men; they pretend to accept the doctrine while they degrade the authority. 'Satan himself,' says St. Paul, 'is transformed into an angel of light. Therefore it is no great thing if his ministers also be transformed as the ministers of righteousness.' It is simply temptation in the garb of virtue—the wasp in the peach.

Accept Swedenborg, and modern spiritualism would indeed seem to be the invisible Satanic *en rapport* with unregenerate natures in this world."

"In such sort, I can conceive your credulous man mistake dyspepsia for temptation from his evil spirits: the devil is fond of the liver, and hates calomel worse than holy water," said Blumenbach.

"Well, not accepting for an argument that which is only a sarcasm, compare the practical results of Christianity with those of spiritism in this world," urged Mr. Horton.

"You will!" exclaimed the German. "War, despotism envassaling the mind of Europe, Paris barricades and Naples dungeons, Frenchmen roasting Arabs and Englishmen mangling Hindoos?"

"It is true that the French Revolutionists who beheaded Louis were infidels, but the English Puritans who doomed Charles fought their battles between a prayer and a psalm; and while the end in the one instance is a self-perpetuating military despotism, in the other it is constitutional liberty, vital with possibilities of beneficent development. And as to war, hateful as it is, Hobbes had the countenance of history, at least, when he declared it to be the natural state of man. You can verify Hobbes in the next street. Go watch unsanctified human tendency in the riotous rancor of boys at a stone-fight, or see Hogarth justified by a crew of young ruffians cruelly hunting to death a harmless cur. It was always pleasant to destroy, and nothing but the Christian Church, corrupted as it was, curbed the impulse short of a resulting anarchy—a

European Jacquerie—in the rude ages of social oppression; and preserved, even advanced, the civilization of the world."

"The one germ in all human tendency is order—you will behold it in a street mob," interposed Blumenbach.

"Certainly; there is an order of infernal force. Hell is organized; and the damned of that 'dark monarchy' tempt men—nay, limitedly, perhaps each other—with systematic subtilty. In new societies, where there are no established laws, assassins and gamblers will combine to hang a burglar. There is nothing in your spiritualism which stimulates to virtuous actions here; for if a man is convinced that he will be virtually the same hereafter, a shadowy duplicate of himself, or probably better, he will be apt to be better at his leisure: and still more unconcerned will he be if he believes in a certainty of amendment; for then he will surrender his sense of responsibility to the law of development. I cannot think that the aspirations of a creature who may possess the heart of David united to the brain of Shakespeare will end, if you will pardon me the phrase, in this horse-heaven business. Wisely may atheism crave its annihilation if the innate longings of man, the tribulations of the race, are to terminate only in the unsubstantial projection of the present, and a mountebank ghost."

"Could we make what is, from an ideal pattern, everybody would prove a master-workman. By speculative perfections you will not change the universal humanity," observed the German.

"Now, that's very true," said Bliggs. "Human

nature is a strange thing; though I don't profess to be a philosopher, if I could afford to quit business, I've often thought, I would turn my attention to the study of human nature."

"You refuse all moral truth and beauty which spiritualism can render. The painter who sees angels, can put them on his canvas; the man of meditation can bless his soul with a glory from the vast and perfect spiritual order; the composer will hear unearthly melodies, ravishing, and utter them for earthly ears. Spiritualism opens our obstructions here; therefore it is knowledge—wisdom, if we will, and joy," said Blumenbach.

"It is not in spiritism that this capacity of enjoyment exists, but in the painter, the meditative man, and the melodist; that is, in the imaginative faculty of each under stimulation. Let us be exact. That which in the pagan hind of Greece or Italy was a debasing superstition, in the pagan poet is an alluring allegory. The purer and higher happiness of Christianity is the boon of the humble and the dull," insisted Mr. Horton.

The German replied with a shrug.

"I will tell you a case," he said, "which I can avouch the fact. It is of a friend, very near, the experience observable. He was a composer, and had got much esteem for his works. He gave all his earnest nature, a strong love, to his subjects. He was producing an oratorio, and inspired himself with the grand Hebrew prophets, and thought his music day and night—it was always, always in his mind. The brain was made sick, and for two weeks life was one weak light behind your hand in the wind. Again he rose from his bed; but with memory no more. He could not even read. It was very sad, the strong man, in mind grown feeble as a babe; sitting still and alone in his chamber day after day, dumb between his cryings. At a time when thus drooping, on a calm, sunny morning, he fell asleep. Then he saw—*saw* grand spectacles, which told would cause smiles and be called dreams. I shall not tell them—only this: He lay tranquilly looking at the light which flowed through the colored windows of an old cathedral. An atmosphere of subtle poison subdued all his being but consciousness—a pleasing poison which it was bliss to breathe. The Titian-like figures of dusky pictures brightened gradually into exquisite shapes of beauty, and faded again into indistinguishable cobweb grey. Then the pent air shook with the vibrations of the organ, and his own lost music was reproduced. The organ ceased, and for a space he was unconscious. Then it was midnight in the cathedral, and he lay in a coffin, and the moonlight streamed through the painted panes upon his shroud. Out of the darkness of a distant aisle was raised a pedestal crowned by a wreathed bust in pure white stone, which rested on a scroll. As if drawn with phosphorus, shone characters upon the scroll, and, behold a resurrection of his own brain-child—the score of the oratorio, traced by a luminous finger!"

"Though I don't believe in ghosts, there *does* seem sumfin supernatural about that," said Bliggs.

"No doubt the phenomenon was the result of brain

fever, and the recovery a good providence: when the impressions were received the disease had spent its force, and the mind was reassuming its wonted clearness and harmony," remarked Mr. Horton.

"Did your friend go on with business afterwards, or had he made enough to give it up?" asked Bliggs, with sudden vivacity.

"He came not to want, sir," replied the German.

CHAPTER XI.

Having often received an invitation from my friend Sir Roger de Coverley to pass away a month with him in the country, I last week accompanied him thither, and am settled with him for some time at his country-house, where I intend to form several of my ensuing speculations.—SPECTATOR.

RADLEY HORTON'S shipboard acquaintance with Miss Bardleigh was continued, and he became a familiar visitor at The Cedars, her father's seat. Judge Bardleigh was a jovial gentleman, with a big waist, a big heart, and a face which glowed in laughter purple as his wines. In the line of paternity the Judge had a well supplied quiver; and he so abounded with geniality and benevolence that he might have set up creditably as a stepfather besides. And a very pleasant place was The Cedars, the broad, fat acres of which bred no anchoretic tendencies. You could read savory plenty in the sleek red flanks of the straight-backed Devons, as they browsed with slow content the juicy herbage. Better mutton never sheltered under fleece than was killed and dressed at The Cedars. The ducklings there illustrated the peas; and the peas, ravished from their pods in the adolescence of early marrowfats, were creditable to the ducklings. The good cheer was appreciated throughout the country side, and as the judge, who was at once a hospitable host and a hearty talker, had beneath his roof-tree a rout of frolicsome boys and sprightly girls, there were frequent merry-meetings at The Cedars.

On a warm, sullen day in early June, Bradley Horton and Lydia Bardleigh were pacing a shady walk which skirted the garden at this rendezvous of good fellowship. A few large drops of rain which pelted through the leaves overhead drove them to shelter. In the earnestness of their conversation they failed to observe the close of the shower. A peal of laughter drew their attention, and looking forth from the cool retreat down a lane of sun-glistened shrubbery, they beheld, at an old well nestled beneath a noble English elm, a couple in playful altercation.

"Your brother Charley," said Bradley.

"And Rose Stuvesant," added Lydia.

"Pshaw! sir; you can never catch it; let me try," said the young lady at the well.

"Look out now, Rose! Like as not the little beast will jump your way," expostulated the youth, as he made sudden dashes with the tincup into the well-bucket.

"What monster have you got?" called Lydia.

"A little fellow in Lincoln green, and more than a match for us," returned the young lady.

"Yes; jolly green to get himself in this fix," exclaimed Charley, as with a jerk he brought up a frog by one of its convulsed hind legs.

"You began your gipsying to-day in other company, Rose," said Lydia, as that young lady and her escort entered the arbor.

"O yes—Luke Bardleigh. He was stupid enough to get a fish-hook in his finger; so, when he went about cutting it out, I left."

"Now would you think, Lyd," said Master Charles, "that I've been betting against you?—Beg pardon, Mr. Horton, I didn't notice your foot."

"But I do your head, sir, and will take the liberty to remove your hat;" which Rose proceeded to do, regardless of an appealing look from Lydia.

"Quite right," exclaimed Bradley, flushing; "I declare I was so absent that I forgot—"

"The presence of ladies. Well, your forgetfulness is atoned for—there," tapping smartly with a willow switch the placed hat.

Bradley amusedly assented, with a penitent bow.

"You see, Mr. Horton," said Charley, "I've been improving Rose in the practice of the saddle, till I think I can count on her against our brag horsewoman in these parts, Miss Lyddy, here. Rose says she's not afraid to try, on my Cricket. Come, don't back out, Lyddy!"

"I can't think of humoring your nonsense, and risking your cousin's neck," replied Lydia, laughing.

"What charming consideration!" mocked Rose Stuvesant.

"That won't do, Lyddy; Rose is not a baby, you know, to be nursed. You can't escape that way—challenge still open!" said Charley.

"Well, Charley, perhaps I wouldn't refuse Rose a chance for victory and applause, but this is her last day at The Cedars," said his sister.

"Then what is to hinder the trial coming off this afternoon in our ride to Cranberry Beach? You know we are all to go," urged Charley.

Cranberry Beach margined a bold curve of the bay, some six miles from The Cedars. It was a road, which gradually shelved sideways, of compacted sand with here and there a little shingle, where at the height of the tide several horsemen could ride comfortably abreast a long reach, with the beasts of the inner at times fetlock deep in the yeast of the encroaching waves. In the ample cove, at the season, fishermen cast their seine; and their squat, weather-beaten cabins, deserted now, seemed very lonely and desolate as one listened to the melancholy plaint the water, in slower or quicker measure, beat upon the shore. Under a rude shed were some empty barrels, a few scattered float-corks, and a broken pitch kettle. The skeleton of a boat lay just beyond the tide-line, where the wash had left its edge of scum—chips, weeds, dead crabs, and the dart-like remains of the gar. The wheatfields and groves of the remote opposite highlands now looked gusty in shadow, and then the spreading sunshine swept away the frown, and gaily chased it over the water, where a flaw of wind wasted itself in a feeble show of white-caps and shivered in the slanted sail of the shallop, from which the creak of the jibing boom came to the ear with sharp distinctness.

They had turned their bridles homeward and ridden

together a few hundred yards, a party of four gay ladies and their cavaliers, when Rose Stuvesant, twirling her riding-whip defiantly, cried, "Now, Lydia, for a gallop!"

Their horses were nearly neck to neck when they started gallantly from their companions, who, catching the enthusiasm, spurred after them.

A young and gentle woman in a jaunty, feather-festooned hat, which scarce half conceals her waves of hair; in trailing drapery of skirt which depends from a *petite* mould of creaseless bodice, upon a horse of mettle, is a pretty picture, though a common. The charms that belong to it are heightened by rapid motion. The doe which, startled from its lair, clears at a bound the crackling branchlets, nor pauses till it gains the neighboring crest, and then turns its faultless neck and looks behind with pleading eyes, is a type of Beauty in action, which spells you to compassion. A ship before the trade-wind, ploughing a phosphorescent sea on a soft tropical night, her full sails straining, while her leeward bulwarks lean and dip as she glides swiftly through the long swells that heave to meet her —her full sails straining, still steadily straining toward Tahiti asleep beneath a purple sky, is Beauty in another shape of movement, which lulls you like a delicious dream. Your lady in the saddle, Sir Knight, sans helmet, with her bridle free, her flexible body, forward face, and glowing cheek, surpasses mountain deer and trimmest yacht that ever wooed the gale—is a display of loveliness at once graceful, tender, and impetuous.

A cloud of dust and a clatter of hoofs. An easy-going countryman who is jogging in his dearborn behind "Betz," the sleek old mare bushy with wild indigo to keep off flies, hears in a doze the approaching cavalcade, cranes out his neck to reconnoitre, and draws up to the fence. Rustics in the fields lean upon their plough-handles and gaze stolidly. Dogs at the infrequent farmhouses bark, and housewives pause at washtub labors in the shade to look. Colts at pasture catch the congenial spirit of the scene and frisk at speed the length of their enclosures. Even the stage is civil and makes room, though it carries the mail and runs on its official dignity. Lydia and Rose are before; Charley Bardleigh and Bradley are close after, gallantly curbing their horses.

As they were passing a cornfield in which were scarecrows, Rose Stuvesant's horse shied. Perceiving the start, Lydia made a quick movement to seize the bridle of the frightened animal. In her anxiety for her cousin she lost her own seat, failed to recover it, and was flung violently to the ground. A shriek from Rose announced the accident. The men were quickly dismounted, and beside the fallen lady. She was carefully lifted by them, found to be insensible, and carried to the roadside. From a wound in her head, where it had struck upon a jagged stone, blood freely flowed. At Bradley's desire, Charley Bardleigh, half frantic with excitement, rode off to summon the doctor to The Cedars. Other members of the party procured near by a mattress and a country wagon.

Judge Bardleigh sat in his piazza, smoking and chatting with a neighbor, when the party with his injured daughter approached. Instinctively he divined disaster in the array, which he started down the avenue to meet. Shocked and solicitous, he insisted on removing his child in his own arms to her chamber. Nor were his restless attentions diminished until the arrival of the doctor, who calmly examined the case, and after due, and, it seemed to the judge, tedious deliberation, said, in a tone where matter-of-fact and sympathy were oddly commingled, "Badly hurt, sir, but not fatally, I believe—I have known worse damage got over." And then, from an alarm in which he regarded the speedy death of his child as probable, the mind of the father was incongruously moved to an earnest concern at the ascertained seriousness of her injury. The doctor kindly undertook the organization of the sick room, and prevented Rose, in her inexperience and perturbation, spreading a mustard poultice on her lace-edged handkerchief.

For a week the situation of Lydia Bardleigh seemed critical indeed, and scarcely to warrant the not unfavorable prognostication of the physician. That excellent man was placid and assiduous; welcome alike at bedside and board; for, strictly professional duties done, and well done, his acute and informed conversation, cheerful conceits and pleasant gossip, dispelled for a time the household gloom, and imparted to the judge a breadth of satisfaction which he would sometimes acknowledge by an approach to his customary inclusive laugh.

Doctor Grow was a stout, wide-chested gentleman

with a stoop in his figure, the wear of over sixty years, a bronzed complexion, and a full white beard. In creed he was a devout presbyterian. His innate vigor had fruited variously. He had invented and modified surgical instruments, produced a seedling strawberry of rare merit, performed a successful amputation of the hip-joint, and published an ingenious essay on the civil polity of Moses. At much trouble and cost he had contrived to import a pair of Peruvian llamas, and he eloquently urged their adoption by the agricultural interest; but the sturdy farmers stuck to their Morgans. Ancient females were terrified by the exotics, associating them mentally with jungles and an escape from a menagerie, and horses were incited by them to run away upon the road; whereat a feeling of public injury was aroused which culminated in a suit at law, when the doctor gloomily gave up his patriotic undertaking. By the rude poor his science was reverentially extolled; it was generally confessed that he knew more than the celebrated Indian who practised with herbs; and, upon the whole, that he exceeded in a knowledge of remedies old Black Baltic, who was infallible in the treatment of worms and famous in the line of fits. By the cultivated, he was cherished as much for his feeling and manly nature as for his acquaintance with the pharmacopœia. Scores of men sit in cabinets and senates, even among those who have not attained conspicuity by low artifices, or have not been thrust upward on a little distended rhetoric, with far less of the intellectual fertility, promptitude, energy, patience and courage which are sometimes possessed by the unpretending country physician.

At the request of Judge Bardleigh, Bradley remained at The Cedars, and made himself serviceable as a relief to his host. For some days, except a few moments once or twice, the rigorous proprieties of the sick room forbade his presence there; and these glimpses of a pale, unobserving, half-conscious face, which he had so lately seen aglow with health and vivacity, inexpressibly saddened him. At hours when callers were not expected—for he represented the master of the mansion, whose unavoidable employment and vigils compelled him to sleep much of days—Bradley would saunter alone in field or wood, and partake of that peculiar enjoyment which characterizes the brief respites of the watcher who is gloomed in the presence of sickness and of care. For such occasions blow fresher zephyrs—then added incense rises from the landscape; the little stir of man and his events subsides in the confident calm of nature, which seems to say, "Cling to me; *I* am steadfast, and remain!"

It was a warm and quiet summer afternoon. Enveloped in a light *robe de chambre*, the fair invalid reclined in an extension chair wheeled to present her wan face to the shadow of the room. At a jalousie, vainly wooing a breeze, Bradley Horton was seated, book in hand. Upon a servant rustling at the door, he rose softly and received a plate of ice. When he turned toward his companion he saw that her eyes were shut, and that she seemed to doze. He stood for a moment and gazed upon her, and felt that there was an expression of tranquil rapture in her face very exalted and lovely. Then he musingly resumed his seat and book, glancing through the blinds occasionally into the effusive sunlight without, where a humming-bird at the casement balanced with a musical flutter, or a load of hay drawn by panting oxen straining on their yokes went up the dusty lane. Then the midsummer stillness was enthroned again in the arid air. Awhile, and a brisk patter of approaching footsteps was followed by the joyous exclamation of a child, as she burst into the room regardless of Bradley's monitory gesture.

"O, see here what nice Mr. Cole made for me— Fanny Spot. He calls it, 'Pet Asleep.' I must show it to Aunt Lyddy, and its just like her."

"What is, Kate?" asked the lady.

"Make haste and look at it, sir, and let me take it," said little Kate, impatiently reaching for the Bristol board.

It was a pencil sketch of a kitten sprawled on a kitchen floor, sleep-overtaken in the act of playing with the strings of an apron. It laid on its side, its ears perked forward, its face turned half upward, and its upper legs still flexed as in the final pat.

"Aunt Martha thinks it's beau-ti-ful," said Kate, "and I wanted Mr. Cole to make the old cat too; and Mr. Cole said, I must catch and hold it, then; and I found it in the wash-house, and it tried to scratch me—it's very vicious, and I don't like it a bit."

The child seated herself on a stool at Lydia's feet while the picture was examined and commended. The lady passed her thin white fingers through the golden ringlets that fell upon her robe. Sobered by the tone of the place, the child sat long quiet. The picture lay unregarded beside her as she watched a radiant concern in the thoughtful eyes of her aunt. "Suffer little children," the lady gently repeated. After a pause, she turned her head toward Bradley and addressed him.

"A poet, I suppose by the blue and gold of the binding?"

"It is Tennyson; and I have been reading that gusty lamentation, 'Locksley Hall!'"

"I remember it—a story of disappointed love, told in a strain of keen distress?"

"Yes."

"Do you think there are many such griefs, Mr. Horton?"

"Many; of which the world is mostly ignorant. The anguish of unrequited love is not an affliction to be hawked in the market-place. Perhaps its history will end undivulged before a battery, and be buried in a trench—perhaps it will be buried in a mad-house. It is an English malady. Miss Edith's Roman nose is inherited from a Norman pirate, so she is constrained to be a social purist.

'She was sprang of English nobles, I was born of English peasants;
What was *I* that I should love her—save for feeling of the pain?'"

"The prescriptive sundering of natures which were created to approach, and which are worthy of each other, is a cruelty of British caste as abhorrent, I think, to reason, as is any assumption of Braminism," said Lydia.

"The English Bramins hedge their lives with arrogated social sanctities to the very threshold of eternity and nakedness; and hoard poor butterfly dust as though it were gold of heaven's own minting, seven times refined—cherish their narrow conventionalism to the last punctilio, to make grim merriment for waiting ghosts, that laugh at the fools whom they welcome," said Bradley.

CHAPTER XII.

Overreach.—I am of a solid temper, and steer on a constant course.
A New Way to Pay Old Debts.

THE house of Bloker and Ball was one of the most substantial in the city. It had survived a half dozen "panics," and had not been known to ask for even an extension. Ball, indeed, was no longer in the flesh: a gaunt, ambidextrous quaker, he had gone out of the firm years before, and disappeared with the fashion of smallclothes, to which, including buckled shoes, he had adhered staunchly to the end of his earthly career. Jacob Bloker's was the brain and bank-account of the house of Bloker and Ball.

The counting-rooms of Bloker and Ball were light, airy apartments, aristocratically aloof from the region of warehouses, in a solid and ugly brown-stone building of the bastard Egyptian style, which they shared with a popular insurance company—the Diddlum Mutual, with ample assets in wild lands and the notes of kindred corporations—a bill engraver, two or three brokers, and a stationer. Bloker and Ball's clerks never presented themselves to the public gaze hurrying in inked jackets, but were notable for club-house movement, spotless linen, the neatest of neckties and boots, "nobby" hats, and in general a pick-the-teeth air of deliberation. They could put one up to a move or two in billiards, give all the fine points, operatical and occult, of that magnificent creature, Calypso Tuberose, and talk "dog" acceptably to the veterans at the "Sportsman's Bag." Yet the affairs of the house were administered with system and courtesy, and even bilious people were known to have declared it a pleasure of existence to do business with Bloker and Ball.

"Of course, Mr. Cripps, you have brought home Captain Warner's effects—I wish you would let his wife know of his death, if she has not already seen it announced in the marine intelligence; I hate scenes," said Jacob Bloker.

"Well, I won't skulk a dead man's message, and I am charged with one; but I'd sooner face a pampero," said the first officer of the merchant's ship Swan.

"Good weather and run from Rio?" asked Bloker, examining some papers.

"First-rate, sir, till we got in the stream, except squall off Pernambuco."

"How long was Captain Warner sick with the fever?"

"Ten days in hospital, and they took him ashore the second day."

"It kept you back with cargo nearly a week, it

seems. Um!—bad; but it can't be helped," said Bloker.

"It went hard with Warner to go—on account of his helpless family, he said."

"Helpless?—yes—I believe so," said Bloker, slowly, while making a memorandum on the back of an invoice. "He always kept close drawn."

"He had been in your employment fifteen years, I think he told me," said Cripps.

"About that time. A careful man, and wide enough awake—seldom lost a spar.—How many vessels were waiting in port when you left?"

"Eight Americans, and more North of Europe craft than I ever saw at once at Rio," answered the mate.

"Freights will rule low, then.—Captain Warner got three dozen fowls at Marseilles, I see; yet I believe he took out four pigs," remarked Bloker.

"We had a passenger from Marseilles.'

"So—yes: well, the accounts, on the whole, seem unobjectionable. I'm glad you are here at last, for coffee has taken quite a jump, and I don't think it will stay up," said the chief of Bloker and Ball as he gathered the papers for his bookkeeper.

The following day Jacob Bloker's private office was he scene of another conversation. A sorrowful woman, of middle age, addressed the merchant.

"He was a tender husband, sir. I had something heavy on my mind, but I was not prepared for such a blow."

"My dear madame, it is only a question of time with us all," said Bloker.

"True, sir; but that consideration lessens little the bitterness of our loss," replied the lady. "Our poor Frank is worse again with his spine, and he is expecting his father daily; I have not dared to break the news to him, though I think he guesses that something is wrong—my poor, patient child!" and the mother wept.

"He has been an invalid for several years? I remember to have met you two or three summers since crossing him on the ferry-boats for the air. Does nothing help him?" asked the merchant, civilly.

"It is but too likely that nothing ever will—the doctors give no hope," said Mrs. Warner.

"That is discouraging. Perhaps, Mrs. Warner, this is hardly the time for the formality of a settlement, but I have by me the balance of your husband's account, and will give you a check at once. At the time of his death there was one hundred and sixty-one dollars due him. There were some expenses, which I will not mention. I will make the check two hundred dollars, and ask you to accept it," said Jacob Bloker, in a tone large with generosity.

It is not probable that the widow had thought of a gratuity just then, but as it was offered—thirty-nine dollars to represent the appreciation of fifteen years of faithful service in a responsible station—and in a manner which said plainly, "This is final," she was bereft of all power of utterance.

"But, stop!" exclaimed the merchant, arresting himself in the act of handing the check to Mrs. Warner, and summoning a clerk, "how thoughtless I am; I will have it drawn for you, madame—Charles, get gold for this."

When the widow recovered from her surprise at Bloker's offer she flushed with indignation; but she was a mother; she thought of her bereaved and dependent family; of her stricken, helpless boy; and she stifled her anger. In anguish of heart she dropped the yellow pieces into her purse, and went to her desolate home.

Yet not altogether desolate. The God of the widow is bountiful of compensations. Poor, patient Frank, though a cause of solicitude, was also a source of comfort. Thin and wasted, his pale, meek face seemed to have taken on a fore-look of spiritual glory. It was surpassingly pleasant to mark the electric glances of affection which passed between mother and child. They were a language in themselves—the voiceless communing of sympathetic souls. Week after week, all day, the lad laid propped with pillows on a lounge, reading his story books, watching and listening to his canary, or, his couch wheeled to the window-seat, cleaning his few pot plants of insects. A feeble, misshapen child, but dear to the family heart, and precious in the sight of angels; with the town's tumultuous tide sweeping about him the fortunes, strifes, and crimes of men, quiet, thankful, and heedless of its roar. Two other steady boys received scant wages in places where they looked for advancement; and Jane, the eldest daughter, taught at a rural seminary.

Upon hearing of her father's death, Jane Warner came home to mingle her grief with her mother's.

When told of Bloker's gift, she kindled at once to a decision:

"The thirty-nine dollars must be returned to this man, mamma; my father's memory shall not be thus insulted—I will send the sum out of my savings."

Shortly afterward, among the merchant's correspondence was a letter which contained a remittance of seven five-dollar bills, and four gold dollars glued to the sheet. Its written contents were concise and conclusive.

MR. JACOB BLOKER, Shipowner.

SIR:—You will receive, here inclosed, the benefaction which you graciously bestowed on my mother. In a condition of mental uncertainty, produced by sudden and deep distress, it was mechanically accepted by her; reflection, which has occasioned a proper sense of self-respect in the living and a just regard for the memory of the dead, has determined her to return it.

The probity, carefulness, and energy in a responsible station, which you have freely confessed characterized the services rendered to you by my father during many years, can hardly, in the most stringent estimation, be requited by the inconsequential sum of thirty-nine dollars. If you should urge that the current wages received from you by the deceased were adequate payment for his exertions in your interest, there is no room in equity for a gift. In neither case ought the money to be retained.

Your humble servant,

JANE WARNER.

Perhaps while Bloker was angrily pouching his rejected bounty, a person, as the world goes, with a very different social stamp, was cheerfully surrendering his little fortune in acknowledgment of an unrecorded favor; for the abstraction of five-and-twenty dollars relieved a rare turgidity in the purse of Terence O'Rourke.

"And this is how it was, ma'am," explained Terence to Mrs. Warner; "I'd wrought for the captain—God rist him—years ago at stavadoring, when he kept from saä—bad cess to it—and he know'd me for an honest, hard-working, industhrious mon; when one shudderin' winter there was no thrade, and not even odd jobs, and Biddy and the childer wanting the bit to ate. It was then the good captain—rist his soul—gave me the manes to live; saying, 'Terence, whin you get foremist the wur-uld with the loike of this sum, I will recave it; if you niver do, it don't matther—use it with aconomy.' And, ma'am, it was the good that money did me that can't be tould! But, somehow, I could niver make it convænient to return it, till racently a society of which I was a member, the Hoibernia Bineficial, broke and divoided the funds; and Father McGuire says, 'Terence, as you don't requoire that sum for the present nades of your family, is there no old obligation on your mind you would wish to attind to?' And thin, ma'am, I thought for the first of the captain's ginerosity, though, in troth, I hadn't forgot it."

CHAPTER XIII.

> Saint Cupid, then! and, soldiers, to the field!
> LOVE'S LABOUR'S LOST.

A SMALL party surrounded the mahogany at Belair, drinking claret and eating the September peaches.

"This melocoton, Mr. Horton, is easier to take than was Sevastopol," observed Jacob Bloker, essaying a harmless joke.

"You must thank Mr. Davenport then, who budded the tree."

"I like them best in dumplings, with the right sort of dip," said the old clerk, modestly avoiding the arborary sponsorship. "Fortescue— Nankeen Fortescue we called him—in the India trade, a very sensible man who died of apoplexy, always stood up for cherry pie in preference, with good farmhouse milk, but I never agreed with him."

"You will have choice fruit, Mr. Bloker, in a year or two. Bradley tells me that some of your Van Mons pears are rare in Belgium. I should be glad to exchange grafts with you," said the host.

"Of course—when you please. By-the-by, Horton, that gray colt which I was about to sell, and you thought of as a saddle horse for Miss Horton, wants exercising—he's perfectly broke, and I'll send him over," said Bloker.

"You didn't fix on a price, I believe."

"No: try him awhile, and you can judge better of his value. There may be some defect unknown to me—we won't close the matter just now."

Presently they joined the ladies, Emily Horton and Caroline Mellen, and sauntered about the grounds to enjoy the beauty and freshness of the approaching sunset.

"You shall take charge of me, Mr. Davenport, and teach me botany," said Caroline.

"Should be glad to, but I'm not well advised on the subject. Yet my family has, I may say, a botanical genius. My mother is counted very skilful in sickness to make herb teas, and I recollect my grandmother would talk by the hour of plants, and could describe a half dozen sorts of snakeroot alone. The old lady had a drawer in her bureau full of valuable receipts for almost every complaint, which she left to mother. She had been all her life collecting and writing them out, but, as they were mixed together and she was a slow reader, it would sometimes take nearly a day to find a particular one, which was inconvenient when a neighbor was taken sudden."

"I suppose bachelors are fond of flowers, for I find, when they don't smoke, that they carry in their clothes a smell of lavender," said Caroline.

"I like them when they are bright-colored, such as roses and sunflowers. And I like to watch the bees about them. When I was a youngster, next to our warehouse yard there was a drug-mill, the owner of which, a low-spirited man, kept a hive, and in the season I bought bouquets of the market-women that I might draw the bees and see their pleased and busy movements. More than once, thus occupied, I have fallen asleep on a packing-case at the open window, and done my letter copying at night," said the old clerk.

As they went leisurely down the walk they heard shouts before them, and upon looking in that direction they perceived a violent ripple in a growth of shrubbery, and then a heifer in headlong rush toward them, with Andrew the gardener and a bawling lad hard after. There was a summer-house close by, and, gallantly seizing Caroline, Davenport made for the convenient refuge. Having thrust her in, the old clerk was entering with elastic step, when his hat struck the lintel and rolled away on the gravel walk. While he turned to recover it, the cow charged upon him. The situation had been suddenly sprung, the brute was unfamiliar, and Henry Davenport had heard of hydrophobia in rampant cattle. He ran; and coursing fleetly down a side path only halted when he reached a tree with an accessible fork, nor then until he was sheltered in it. As he mopped his face in this place of safety, he was pleased to behold the incensed gardener punch the head of the boy, whose carelessness he accused as the cause of the mischief to his horticulture.

"You wullin!" exclaimed Andrew, "will you mind the heck next time?"

Then, turning to Davenport, "Hoot, mon, come doon!"

"Certainly;" said the fugitive, as he dropped with difficulty to the ground, "I was just going to. If only I had my fowling-piece! A cow did you say! By Saint George! I took it to be a bull."

"Disobedience and heedlessness, lad," said Andrew, in a strain of moral reproof, "is foreby the deil; and if ye nae mend, you'll howl and greet worse than thot. Gin it was nae for patience, which is the wale of a' virtues—there's the head of yon Ageeptian lily bit clean off!" and at this fresh provocation the gardener made a threatening movement toward the culprit, by whose superior agility it was eluded.

Caroline welcomed Davenport from the window of the summer-house with seasonable banter.

"I don't believe, sir, a more masterly retreat could have been executed—but, what's the matter with your hat?"

"I accidentally put my foot on it."

"Had your head been in it, it had been the better for your hat, Mr. Davenport."

"You may laugh, Miss Caroline, and I like to hear you, though it is at my expense; but he would be a desperate man who would stand before an infuriated animal with horns, without even an umbrella for defence. I've known cattle to go through plate-glass windows, and in hot weather the hospitals take in a number of tossed people. Many years ago, an acquaintance of mine—Tarbox, salt provisions was his line—was shook up awful."

"You did quite right to run away, Mr. Davenport; I should have done the same," said Caroline.

"Tarbox," continued the old clerk, musingly, "didn't recover short of an operation, and then it was a tedious case."

"'Twas only a woman's raillery, Mr. Davenport; I don't think you a bit nervous."

"Yet if I wasn't, I would have spoken my mind about some things long since," replied Davenport, with confused briskness.

Seeing that her companion regarded her appealingly, as if to emphasize his remark, Caroline responded to the look with respectful attention.

"It must be a hard thing which staggers your frankness, Mr. Davenport."

The simple reply of the lovely woman, half sympathy and half compliment, touched the old clerk sensibly, and emboldened him to proceed.

"It *is* a hard thing for me, and I can't keep it longer—Miss Caroline, I am your devoted admirer!"

She flushed and started; but in a moment, when she had conquered her surprise, she answered with affected misconception,

"And I am your admiring friend, Mr. Davenport; I hope we shall always feel for each other, even if chance should permanently part us, a cordial esteem."

When Caroline began to speak in her kind accents, Henry Davenport's face mantled with eagerness; when she finished, he drew a long breath and was silent.

"Night will catch us playing truant if we stay longer; the frogs in Cattail Marsh have been practising this half-hour, and there's the first lightning-bug," said Caroline, pleasantly.

Bloker and Emily Horton are standing where the ground is mossy by the poplars.

"So you know Mrs. Warner? A very worthy lady; though, I am bound to say, a little imprudent—that is with expensive tastes," said Bloker.

"Because she refuses proffered bounty?" replied Emily, with a tone of sarcasm.

"Ah! I see you have been told a certain circumstance, and that, doubtless, in the telling I have been treated without mercy. I suppose my slight gift was represented as final—a closing of the account?"

"As you urge me—I believe it was so regarded."

"Now see the mischief of misconception. I assure you that it was only an instalment of what I intended to bestow. It was my desire to serve Mrs. Warner in the amount, who, to be plain, has no just notion of the value of money. The captain's ample salary was always needed when it was due."

"With some chances for observation, I have not noticed extravagance in Mrs. Warner's housekeeping. There were a half-dozen children to rear, and some of them sickly."

"The last is the most distressing feature in the situation of the family," said Bloker, with an attempt at commiseration. "The condition of that poor boy touches me deeply. I spoke to Dr. Conium, who stands at the head of our faculty, about him, and requested his attention to him."

"Yes; they told me—the doctor sent. Poor Mrs.

Warner is so weak as to have an unconquerable aversion to clinics; fearing the effect upon her long secluded child of three or four hundred inquisitive, noisy students."

"You surprise me. That proceeding is Conium's, and I am not to be held answerable for it. Love of science, amounting to a passion, I suppose explains it," responded Bloker.

"Perhaps, sir; good manners don't, in the light of your statement."

"I hear Miss Jane Warner is praised for a fine understanding," said Bloker.

"And justly."

"When I saw her, several years since, I thought her rather pretty."

"About that opinions may vary; she is certainly not the reverse," said Emily, with womanly noncommittalism.

"One of my clerks tells me that she was a belle at Leasowes, last summer—very amiable and gay," said Bloker, dubiously smiling, though not obtrusively. "Garth was rapturous about her; I overheard him depicting in the counting-room the happiness of late dances and moonlight drives. But Garth, I believe, is fresh at watering-places, and like enough mistook the young lady's toleration for favor."

"Her friends consider her discreet."

"O, I dare say she is. No one who knows the world will regard the rattle of a smitten and prating boy. I hope that she will make a good marriage."

The *deshabille* conversation of the Belair ladies,

while they were arranging their hair for the night, among other topics, touched upon Jacob Bloker.

"I can't think so ill, Emily, of our fastidious bachelor as you do. I grant that he might be thawed to advantage, but predominating duplicity I don't discern."

"That Warner business?" asked Emily.

"Shabby, if you reject his explanation, but not that I see deceitful."

"Well, Carrie, I can't translate tone and manner into words, but to me they are reasons; and if I had no reasons, I have an instinctive dislike to him."

"Life's a battle, in which such instincts are sometimes conquered," said Caroline, merrily, as she took her candle and bade her friend Good-night.

CHAPTER XIV.

Snug.—Have you the lion's part written? pray you, if it be, give it me, for I am slow of study.
Quince.—You may do it extempore, for it is nothing but roaring.
Bottom.—Let me play the lion too. I will roar, that I will do any man's heart good to hear me: I will roar, that I will make the duke say, Let him roar again: let him roar again.—MIDSUMMER-NIGHT'S DREAM.

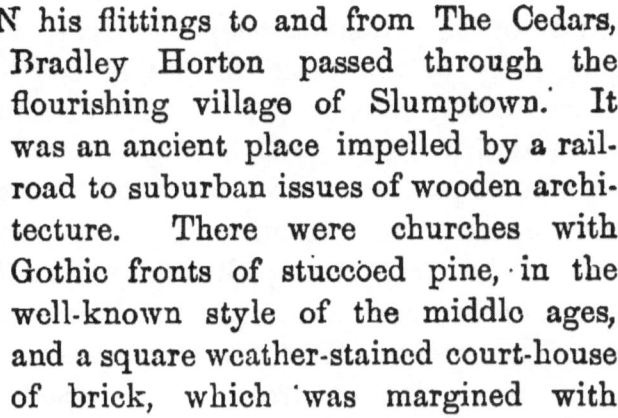

IN his flittings to and from The Cedars, Bradley Horton passed through the flourishing village of Slumptown. It was an ancient place impelled by a railroad to suburban issues of wooden architecture. There were churches with Gothic fronts of stuccoed pine, in the well-known style of the middle ages, and a square weather-stained court-house of brick, which was margined with maple trees and flanked by its attendant jail. Slumptown had its lawyers, who preyed on the politics of the region, or passed their vulturine lives in scenting for lean retainers in assault-and-battery cases, and, with rapacious wrangle, in gorging their maws from the carcasses of encumbered estates. Of course Slumptown was blessed with rival editors, who maintained a state of chronic hostility; and it was an exquisite display of reciprocal unconsciousness when the *Palladium* passed the *Spirit of Jefferson* upon the street. There was an opulence of "store goods" on Court-house square, the trading and professional centre of the town; an open air arrangement about doors and porches of hay-rakes, pitch-forks and scythes, brooms, rolls of carpet, crockery, horse-collars, and straw hats; and at a heavy dealer's, perhaps, there was placed an empty sugar hogshead conspicuously in the way; while two or three "Cheap Johns," with city-made slops, kept the native tailors at their wits ends and half-starved. There was a bank at Slumptown, which held mortgages on half of the county farms, and which occasioned in the minds of very distant people a lively interest in the geography of the place, for its bills, illustrated by a couchant dog before a prodigious iron chest suggestive of bullion in every knob, stuffed the wallets of drovers on Illinois prairies and were carried by lumbermen into the forests of the Atlantic slope. At the lyceum, in weekly debates, Young Slumptown shaped that eloquence which was to rouse from the rostrum and captivate the senate. Nor was Slumptown unknown to literature. One or two of its parsons had written books which were printed, and it boasted of a sweet poetess who invoked a sappy muse over three initials and an asterisk.

But the reputation of this prosperous borough was subordinate to that of a neighboring locality. Figuratively, the glorious eagle of our country still screamed in triumph over the battle-field of Hickory Hollow. Eighty years of peaceful tillage had, indeed, obliterated every trace of conflict; the rural historians who had repulsed, in willing narratives over their cider on winter nights, the English grenadiers, slept with their fathers; but the surrounding population sometimes assembled among "the embattled corn" to sustain their patriotism with the reminiscences of a martial anniversary. On such occasions in the olden time, a citizen read the immortal Declaration," and an orator, usually a fledgling of the law, anatomized the British lion; whereupon the people gravitated in content to roast ox and rum and water. But at length these celebrations became the outcries of political parties against each other, either of which, in turn, was the orthodox exponent of the temper of the purer days of the Republic, and its opponent hostile to every moral and material interest of the country.

And so it was, that as Bradley Horton and the anniversary of the battle of Hickory Hollow came together, they found Slumptown in a political ferment. The fences were eloquent with posters that had exhausted in their production the typographical resources of the *Palladium*, invoking the "Men of the Old Guard" to assemble

"Like the winds in their hurricane wrath,"

and ratify the nomination for Congress of "that incorruptible patriot and zealous champion of the people," Adoniram Slossom. Long before noon the village barrooms were thronged with sovereign citizens who devoted themselves impartially to cocktails and controversy; and the streets and stable yards had grown populous with groups of disputants, that suddenly scattered, from time to time, in the very crisis of argument, when the thick coming vehicles laden with fresh patriots rattled bravely up, or a couple of inebriated wranglers passed from polemics to pugilism. There came, in disciplined array, the Slumptown Invincibles, and the Slossom Irrepressibles, with their bands. Then followed the Carthage Cadets, and the New-Egypt Look-Arounds, with their bands. There was marching and counter-marching; huzzaing and flag-flaunting; and a showering from female Slumptown of wreaths and bouquets. A traveling menagerie, adroitly arranged for, excited to a higher pitch the interest of the populace.

There was to be a "mass meeting," a presentation, and a barbecue during the day, and at night a torchlight procession. A platform in an adjacent grove, decorated with banners, upon which were inscribed inspiring watchwords and appeals, was surrounded, in due course, by the multitude, which was rigorously excluded from an inclosure containing hastily constructed tables of rough deal, destined to receive great lumps of beef and pork cut from the spitted carcasses. A corpulent gentleman with a moist and red face, at the appointed time, elbowed forward among magnates of the day, newspaper reporters, and a swarm of political fry, who were upon the stage, and proposed an organization:

"I nominate, fellow-citizens, for president of this meeting, Algernon Sidney Briggs, esquire. Those who are in favor, will say, 'Aye.'"

There was a general affirmance; whereupon the

names of sixty-four vice-presidents and thirty-two secretaries were similarly submitted. Then, Algernon Sidney Briggs, esquire, introduced Expectation Biles, esquire, to read the resolutions, which were very full, and very fierce.

Expectation Biles, esquire, was to one of his auditors a new appearance of an old acquaintance. Bradley had met him on the Paris boulevards and in the cafes, usually with profuse Americans, whom Biles contrived to know, and, perhaps, to serve, for the gains that flowed from their generosity; the nature of Biles being parasitic but not prodigal. And here he was again on the Slumptown boards, as self-important and bustling as ever. In the many parts played by Expectation, one consistent result was always held in view—Biles. And thus it was that opinions—and there are people of leisure who will form opinions of anybody—differed concerning him; one observer designating him a blusterer, and another insisting that he was a sycophant and a sneak. Biles was possessed of a passion to write for the ephemeral press, and for its sort of scribble his was the best of styles, florid and floaty, which never took the reader's breath below the surface. His translations, conspicuously claimed in the head-lines, of French tales for the Sunday newspapers, were among his happiest efforts, and gave harmless satisfaction to the milliners' apprentices. As a Secretary of the Central Republican Concatenation, pitying the incapacity of his associates, and fearing for the national welfare, he appropriated the correspondence list, and magnified the cause by means of this patriotic larceny in an epistolary profusion over his own proper signature. In the enumeration of his "literary distinctions," to employ the language of his friend Wriggle of the *Bugle*, his famous Reports of the decision in the great Split Pea case, (Podde *vs.* Pulz,) and on the interdiction of the *East-Manse Review* by the Anchorsmiths' Atheneum, must not be omitted. As an inventor, too, he was conceded a reputation for having given to the culinary world an improved gridiron, and to the agricultural a patented double-action dog churn. He had been a conservative, but was become, since it was likely the political tangle would untwist that way, a high-seasoned Republican, with his own little reel to make fast to the public skein; though he held also the "popular-sovereignty" knot while there was any doubt. He believed, on moral principle, in empty treasuries for parties out of power, as preventive of corruption; so his nummary contributions to the Concatenation were small and infrequent. Articles of utility, indeed, he held to be innocent gifts, and he presented to the club a new coal-scuttle of galvanized iron on the day after the party carried the State election by a large majority. Expectation Biles, esquire, read the resolutions.

Several distinguished "speakers" from abroad addressed the assemblage, among whom were the "War-horse of the West," and the celebrated "Converted Blacksmith." The latter, having renounced the errors of Democracy, was on a mission for the propagation of the true faith, and he made a horse-shoe with imposing exactness at a forge beside the stage to authenticate his vulcanian pretensions—Expectation Biles, esquire, officiating spasmodically at the bellows.

But the most interesting event of the day was the presentation to Senator Sparhawk of an exhumed cannon-ball, which, after having lain imbedded for three-quarters of a century in the memorable soil of Hickory Hollow, had been produced by a curious well-digger to serve as a public testimony of that eminent statesman's efforts in the cause of compromise and conciliation. The ceremony, though simple, was impressive. Mr. Mordecai Dabster, aglow with inspiration and "Bourbon," made the presentation speech. He was elegantly attired in a blue coat, scarlet waistcoat, and trousers of a delicate shade of sorrel, made somewhat scanty to display a crural symmetry, since Tully himself would have been nothing without legs. At either side of him, mounted upon candle-boxes, were his friend Biles and the editor of the *Palladium*, upholding at much personal inconvenience the national flag in the most classic canopy style. Close by, and facing him, stood the Senator, practising with little success an appearance of meek indifference. At the critical moment, when the silence of expectancy was most profound, Dabster began.

"Venerable Man! When I behold this surging sea of upturned faces; in each eye the fire of moral dignity and civil freedom; when I contemplate the memories summoned by this consecrated place; when I see, in fancy, trooping ghosts of heroes clad in the battle panoply of other days; or behold Liberty herself, divine goddess, lingering fondly to inhale these Hickory Hollow breezes, I find it difficult to realize fully the sublimity of the scene; and in this dilemma I expect I am not solitary and alone.

Sir: What shifting spectacles are presented in the panorama of our history! First, the aboriginal red man of the forest, with his bow, his wampum, and his bark canoe. The startled deer flies no more before his unerring arrow; his withering whoop rouses no more the echoes of the swamp; his picturesque prow has long since ceased to glide over the glassy bosom of the lake. In the beautiful language of your fair Slumptown bard, in her poem of the 'Disconcerted Tomahawk,'

> ' Like a girdled tree in the arms of the blast,
> Wampanocussit has shrieked his last!'

Suddenly the kaleidoscope changes. Serried ranks of marshalled veterans appear. The mercenary minions of despotism these, and above them floats the red cross of Saint George. From our rock-bound, ocean-lashed shore our country's eagle descried the approaching host, and screamed defiance. Then, from valley, and mountain, and the gloomy recesses of the wilderness, our forefathers rushed to the tented field, to the inspiriting strains of 'Yankee Doodle.' Senator! this ball was shot from a British gun; and is a trophy of that perilous and immortal time. (Sensation.) Cherish it in your heart of hearts! Bequeath it unimpaired to your remotest posterity!

Time rolled on, and there came another tussle with the presumptious tyrant of the seas. History will tell you, sir, how it eventuated. In defeat; after the smoke and carnage of battle; by flood and field; England lowered her haughty crest, crowned with a thousand triumphs, to the Young Giant of the West, aching with his strength. But, if we are a great and glorious, we are a modest people, and will not exult. Though we can be cantankerous, thanks to our enlightened institutions, we are not conceited. Nor, although a military, are we a rileable people. Terrible in our anger, and full of poison as a mad bull of the prairie innoculated with rattlesnake bites, we are slow to wrath.

But it is also the triumphs of peace which we are assembled this day to celebrate. We are here to rejoice that our boasted heritage is to be rescued from the debauched, demoralized, diabolical, and rapacious party to which we are opposed. That miserable conglomeration, too long permitted to prey upon a confiding people, is destined to simmer out before the irresistible onslaught of the great Republican host. The craven who contents himself with skulking now, instead of breathing the air of God's blue welkin, might manage to exist, and to fish out of the miasma of his own degradation a disgusting subsidy, like the rag-pickers who filch a livelihood from the alleys and sidewalks of life, but he will go down to posterity unmourned and unsung.

Fellow Citizens! The bugles of our advance are sounding to-day in Slumptown! Our slogan rouses to-day the echoes of a continent! Hickory Hollow shouts to the great lakes, and from their joyful bosoms bounds the patriotic thunder to the absolute and applauding sea! Europe, benighted Europe, hears it in her Tuileries and Saint James's Park. The hour is come—where is the man? (cries of 'Sparhawk!' 'There he stands, old hoss!' and tremendous cheers.) For the auspicious result which awaits us, no one, Senator! has labored more efficaciously than yourself. A nation honors you; a nation too long betrayed, but never dismayed. When it has rid itself of the foul faction which oppresses it, in the day of its supremacy it will remember and reward its Sparhawk!"

The eloquence of Dabster stirred the pulses of the multitude, and when it culminated in the peroration the applause was uproarious. The bands played "Hail to the Chief!" and the Senator responded. The popular estimate of the distinguished gentleman's oratory was not flattering; in comparison of the brilliant rhetoric which had preceded it, it appeared very tame and common-place, and hardly superior to the talk of an educated and sensible person. There was in it no impassioned invective, mellifluent portrayal, nor apposite imagery, like Dabster's. This man who sits in a curule chair and is oracular in the Capitol, follows Dabster's pinions on these poor pin-feathers!

As Bradley was passing to his room in the Slossom House, a human head, cautiously protruded into the hall from a half-opened door, attracted his attention. At a glance he recognized the globous summit of Scroggs, and saluted him.

"You here!"

"The very man I wanted—come in," said Bartimeus

"I didn't see you at the meeting."

"No: the fact is, I'm not expected till the night train, when they have arranged to serenade me, so I keep close."

"And very judicious of you not to draw off the enthusiasm prematurely," assented Bradley.

"I'm preparing a speech for the occasion, and I can't make it suit me. Lord Brougham, I am told, recommends writing out your speeches beforehand. A deal of trouble to take, but its a duty, even if there is no money in it. How did Dabster come off—was he pathetic?"

"There was more of the sentimental than the tender in his harangue, I think," said Bradley.

"If you can spare the time to look over this rough copy, and touch it up a little, you will greatly oblige me. Supply any flourishes that strike you—you know. I prefer a plain, fundamental style, without many big words; though you may put as much fire in it as you please," said Scroggs.

"Some of the Demosthenian vehemence?" asked Bradley, laughing.

"I dunno," replied Scroggs, dubiously. "Demosthenes might say what he chose; there was no scrub reporters to make fun by telegraph in the morning newspapers."

"I'll take it and do what I can, willingly," said Bradley.

"Half a minute!" cried Scroggs into the passage. "Couldn't you contrive a slight touch of the pathetic?"

CHAPTER XV.

The harbor-bay was clear as glass,
So smoothly it was strewn!
And on the bay the moonlight lay,
And the shadow of the moon.
     THE ANCIENT MARINER.

IT was one of the last of the night excursions by water in the season, and upon the ample deck of the Arrow there was assembled a polite company. The bracing temperature of early autumn, moonlight and music, produced an exhilaration which manifested itself in the merriment of the promenaders, and the sprightly measures of the dance. The dusky waiters in white jackets, emerging from darker back-grounds with trays of ices, grinned their enjoyment over their gelid offerings. Even the ponderous man, who flung himself upon the chain-box in emergencies to give the boat a list, and who passed a life of meditation and shirt-sleeves, relaxed to a taciturn approval, and looked on.

"Yes, the ripple's gleam is pretty, to be sure," said Doctor Pledget; repeating *sotto voce*,

"'And on the bay the moonlight lay,
And the shadow of the moon.'

Had we only the Mellen here to help Miss Horton outsparkle it! I owe neuralgia a special spite, and shall take care to accumulate the aconite in the very next case."

"We must be content, doctor, to take our bliss as the Fates allot it; and I confess it comes in pleasant parcels," said Bloker, glancing at Emily Horton.

"I venerate wisdom, for it was my grandam's—dear old lady! there was something a little foxish in her knack at undervaluing a grapy altitude—for the rest, I think, if it's not immoral, that water Mellens are seasonable," replied the doctor.

"How fresh a smell of the soil the breeze brings," said Emily.

"I believe few climates have weather which surpasses that of our first two fall months. You have got past the summer's glare and languor, which make you think too much of your bodies, the air is a tonic, and you are pervaded by a *sans souci* feeling," remarked Mr. Horton.

"Apropos of that," said the doctor, "I got a letter to-day, from a friend in England, which contained a request for a box of our October leaves. I sent her some last year, and she thought them painted. I wrote her that the artist was a Pre-Raphaelite, and that the coloring was laid on in oxygen."

"They will make pretty head-dresses," said Emily.

"O yes; Bull will drop from his short-horns to patronize the glory of our Indian Summer in all its bright diversities as seen by London gaslight," grumbled the doctor.

"Your barren leaves, like barren lives, will don a gay wardrobe—but 'tis a stale moral," said Emily.

"Do you see! there's somebody overboard," exclaimed the doctor, who sat next to the rail.

There was a wild cry on the forward deck of, "Stop the boat!" and general confusion. The pilot's bell tinkled peremptorily, and the engines ceased their motion. The headway of the vessel, however, could not be instantly checked, and some time was consumed in lowering a boat. In the track of moonlight astern a swimmer could be plainly seen, seemingly hampered by a burden, but bearing bravely up. It was calm, and the tardy rescue was in time, and just in time. A black waiter had saved the boy of the black cook. That was all; and the engineer, having expressed himself with an oath, started the wheels again. The captain did not swear, but he was very peppery at the outrage.

"A pretty piece of presumption, I admit, in a fellow who is only a vulgar fraction of the curse of Ham; yet, after all, the rascal plunged for the drowning lad something like a white man," observed Pledget to the incensed skipper.

"I don't mean to say here isn't a worthy fellow, but a New-Foundland dog would have done it," said Bloker.

"The better for the dog, then. Perhaps, though, the dog practises an instinct without estimating values or chances. The dog will go overboard as soon for a duck as for Dives, and we wouldn't, you know, my dear sir. The ethnologists who trace our resemblances in ebony to an improved gorilla with an exceptional brain-knob, don't ascribe to them aquatic tendencies, that I hear—while they justly insist on the whole heel, and even insinuate the plantigrade, they do not warrant webbed toes."

"O! a very creditable act," said Bloker, observing the ladies to be much interested; "Nature sounds us all with the same plummet, and it will dip deep in the dark. It would be quite right for somebody to start a subscription."

"Let Doctor Pledget tell us a merry story to calm our nerves after this horrid fright, and then, Mr. Bloker, you can collect a purse."

"Yes, yes; give us a composing draught for our nerves—a draught on your imagination, doctor—a story!" was the cry in concert.

"Story, my beautiful and beloved, I have none to tell. If a little authentic biography would suffice—."

"That would be rare, indeed!" they exclaimed.

"Then you shall have a narrative of the sufferings of

My Nervous Patient.

"My friend and patient, Mr. Jeptha Bullwrinkle, was a bachelor. Whether he had ever solicited or been sought, I know not; I am too incurious to pry in the private cabinets of my acquaintance for stray arrows from the quiver of the beetle-headed son of the Paphian. After this confession I need hardly assure you that I am regarded as a bungling charlatan by the ladies of our Dorcas society. When I first saw my friend Bullwrinkle—I had been hastily summoned to visit him at midnight in my professional character—he was a mild-mannered person, on the hither side of fifty, with a large bald spot on the crown of his head, restrained leg-of-mutton whiskers of a faded sanguine hue, and an aquiline nose; and he was a bachelor. It was in the cholera time. He felt uneasy, and judiciously dreaded spasms. I prescribed with appropriate promptitude. At my next visit he informed me that he had detected the odor of asafœtida in the physic. Had he not recovered, this narration would be impossible.

My friend Bullwrinkle hated noise and novelty. His grandfather, by the maternal side, had been blown up in the explosion of a powder mill, and had involuntarily introduced a new sensation into the family. There was also a tradition that a near collateral relative, an Arkansas gentleman of some property, had lost with chivalric resignation an ear by the teeth of a fellow-citizen for declining to vote the Democratic ticket. Whatever influence these incidents may have exerted upon the characters of the Bullwrinkles, it was commonly observed that they were either all lion or all hare, and that there was nothing hybrid about them. So, there was an aëronautic Bullwrinkle, oftener complimented for courage than veracity; and a marine Bullwrinkle, who for moral and physical toughness might have competed with Captain Kyd on his own quarter-deck,

'—— when he sailed.'

The reticent and retiring members of the family were best described by negatives. They were never proclaimed "public-spirited citizens" in the blare of newspaper trumpeting; they never were among the "distinguished gentlemen" who consented to address political meetings; they did not affect the militia.

Within a year after my nocturnal introduction to my patient, his estimable uncle, Hezekiah Bullwrinkle, died at the Italian town of Avellino of a slow fever, which was aggravated, it was thought, by unpleasant telluric rumblings and a sudden eruption of ashes from Mount Vesuvius. He bequeathed to his nephew Jeptha, in the testamentary language, "because of the strong sense which he exhibited when a youth in accompanying me to fish in the country on the occasion of the arrival at —— of General Jackson and Black-Hawk, in their fussy tour of 1833," his spacious mansion in our pleasant city, its library, pictures, and furniture.

When I next visited my patient he was installed in his newly-acquired domicile. I found him in dressing-gown and slippers superintending the placing of some padded double-doors. He seemed in good spirits, and cheerfully observed that there was a case of concussion of the brain near by, and that they had laid the street with tan the previous day. Remarking that he was glad to notice in the tables of mortality an absence of contagious diseases, but that it was early yet for small-pox, he invited me to partake of luncheon. When I had regaled on cold tongue and a temperate glass of Madeira, and was whisking with the napkin the crumbs from my waistcoat, chatting the while in a contented tone, he interrupted me with a request that I would tell him, after auscultation, if I thought his heart a little wrong; and gravely appealed to my candor. I solemnly assured him that his cardiac mechanism worked well, and recommended him to the country for a taste of the fine autumn weather.

It was in February that I was again summoned to see him. He was bedridden with catarrh, and quite ill. When I asked him for the history of his sickness, and he replied with indignant energy, "desdeeple." I thought him a little delirious. As, however, he insisted on an architectural origin for his ailment, I requested an explanation. The congregation of the church of Mount Zoar, it seemed, had quarreled about the qualifications and orthodoxy of a new pastor, whom a majority of the magnates had called to its pulpit. The contention was of that unappeasable kind characteristic of differences in the same communion. After two injunctions had been obtained from the courts, and all the iniquities of the deacons who took sides in the controversy had been made to appear, the flock separated. The seceders, intent on the erection of a new church, hit upon a lot of ground opposite to my friend Bullwrinkle's, and bought it. Now, here was a carpenter's shop, which, as a precautionary measure against racket and fire, my patient rented. It chanced that the good people of the Mount Zoar exodus had riveted their purchase before he got wind of their preference. His chagrin thereat was great, but unavailing; all that remained to him was barren invective, and a view of the progress of the enemy. There was at first a hope, which sprang from the emptiness of the seceders' treasury, but it was illusive; the society set up a plea of persecution, and the mites, offerings, and subscriptions increased amain. Then, there was an obstinate irruption of water, which flooded the cellarage and threatened the foundation; but the offshot Zoarites got a patent pump, and dug below the sponge. A stuccoed structure rose, in brown and speckled ugliness, like some huge fossil toad of the Pre-Adamite world. There were minor disputes concerning a clock and the color of the interior, and there was a strong party against an organ, but all disagreement ceased at the steeple. It was unanimously determined that it should illustrate superior doctrinal soundness, and exceed in altitude that of the parent church full twenty feet. It was of fragile construction, and put up rapidly. As it ascended by daily jumps, toward the sailing birds, apprehension entered into the mind of my friend. The spire, at length, was finished, and—it swerved from the perpendicular! My patient's perturbation gushed into protest. He introduced the matter to the notice of the grand-jury, by which sagacious body it was overlooked. He wrote alarms to the newspapers concerning it, and was answered by counter-communications of blended denial and sarcasm. When storms howled and tempests blew, the steeple shook. My friend Bullwrinkle expected to be indecorously buried, on some windy night, in its ruins. It was while outwatching, in thin apparel at an open window, the constellations, and trembling at every blast from the unruly West, that he became a subject for deliberation and drugs.

Jeptha Bullwrinkle let his city residence to a flourishing biscuit-baker, who had sprung, with the agility of an Egyptian frog, out of the kneading-trough, and whose three unmarried daughters in ringlets were possessed with cravings for fashionable society. Gathering his penates, he retreated to a lonely district of country on the Chesapeake, the chief productions of which were intermittent fever and canvas-back ducks, and where he owned a sterile property. Here he wooed retirement, and dallied with its charms. But fate was stronger than the rural fascination. As he sat, one day, on the stump of a hill-side chestnut, and surveyed in a meditative mood the expanse of cattail in the marsh below, a stranger approached and accosted him.

"Don't know me, it seems? A Bullwrinkle—your cousin Ignivomous, author of 'Satanhoof: A Story of the Dark Ages.'"

"Of course; how dull I am. Yet you are changed, and I did not dream of seeing you—a pleasure altogether unexpected."

"I have run down here with an object; to be frank, I want to make a sensation. I have a new book in press, 'The Cadet of Carthagena, or the Terror of the Spanish Main,' and I am on a mysterious disappearance."

"A—what?"

"You don't see it, eh! It will be in all the journals of the country to-morrow—telegraphed everywhere. 'An inscrutable mystery! Foul play suspected! That accomplished gentleman and popular author, Ignivomous Bullwrinkle, esq., has been unaccountably missing since—' and so on. The mayor will probably offer a reward, and all the detectives will be apprised, and furnished with a description of my appearance. I was shot at only three months ago—you might have chanced upon the item, for it was widely copied."

"Shot at! Bless me, how was that?"

"It was the result of a business arrangement with Scurfee Lake, the artist. I gave his 'Descent of Pluto with Proserpine' a column puff, and in return he put a bullet through my hat at a lonely place among the rocks, and then testified to the occurrence as a naked fact apart from the pistoler's personality. Confirms public suspicion—twig?"

My friend Bullwrinkle went to bed that night a panic-stricken man. His *penetralia* were no longer sacred; his prospect, lately so serene, was clouded with terrors. His guest would be advertised—tracked, and detectives would swarm upon him. He himself would be published for complicity; perhaps arrested. Mount Zoar would be jubilant. He would be deposed from his position of vice-president of the Numismatic Society. His days became spiritless, his nights restless, and his meals insipid. Even autorial readings of "Satanhoof" failed to refresh him. Finally, at break of day, when Mr. Ignivomous Bullwrinkle was in a salubrious slumber, he left a hastily written note, and fled the country.

He fled the country for such security as might still be found in a city street. He took comfortable apartments remote from his old neighborhood. For awhile the current of his life was placid in its flow;

there was nothing more serious than a brief fit of neuralgia, or a slight decline in stocks, to disturb his composure. But evil days were at hand. His landlord was a politician, whose time was generously given to the affairs of the nation and the municipality. These, under the stimulation of oft-repeated "nips," and ward-house and kerbstone polemics, he contributed to settle. There was wanted an open-handed candidate to complete the ticket for the common-council, and Jeptha Bullwrinkle was inveigled into an acceptance of the nomination; which was easily "engineered," with a profusion of whiskey, in the back-room of Mr. Terence O'Flaherty. Then came the annoyance of a canvass; a daily depletion of the purse, unseasonable conferences with free-and-easy "roughs," plotting and counter-plotting, and an importunate mob one night at his street door, who, to his speechless terror, demanded an harangue, and were only diverted from their purpose by a liberal banquet hastily supplied in the parlors. The day of election arrived, and he proceeded, in a state of tremulous dignity, to the precinct poll to deposit his ballot. He took his place in the *queue*, and was replying blandly to a short-haired, thick-necked citizen in a red flannel shirt, who with beery fervor solicited him to "vote straight along and go in for constertootional liberty," when a cur, which was hard-pressed by a pursuing crowd, suddenly turned the corner upon him, and with a vindictive snap at his obstructing legs, glided away through the scattered throng.

They said the dog was mad. They profanely

bawled his rabidness, and attested it by his capture and execution. I was absent at a country consultation, and my friend's summons did not at once reach me. When I returned, I found him in agony of mind, surrounded by sympathizing acquaintances with the woe and resignation of distinct and several funerals in their faces. Water he abhorred; they had even taken away the suggestive washstand and foot-bath. There was no lack of advice regarding the treatment of the case, though the majority agreed that recovery was impossible. One believed in lobelia and steaming; and another in homœopathy and two tumblers; and a persistent old lady, with more than Roman firmness in her aspect, insisted on giving a bark. I dismissed the company with brief ceremony, and was defied by a parting look from the Roman of such "grim appearance" that it might have lineally descended from that of Coriolanus when he met Aufidius at Antium. A scrutiny of my patient's condition satisfied me that it was not hydrophobia with which I had to deal, but rather an approach to hysteria. After some preliminary soothing, I dexterously recalled to his memory the salutary potion which I had exhibited to him in the cholera time. It struck his vein, and he declared that he thought it the saving remedy. Immediately I ordered it to be prepared by a neighboring apothecary, and waited to administer it; keeping my patient's mind the while free from fancies by a continued strain of discourse. He took the drink at a gulp, without the faintest quiver of a spasm; and I left him, having much diminished his solicitude for the result. He was out again in time to receive condolements on the election of his competitor to the common-council, and to pay the price of a surprise-serenade, kindly arranged by his landlord, which was never performed, for the celebration of his own.

> "The man recovered of the bite;
> The dog it was that died."

Nevertheless, his sympathizing acquaintances resolved that he was far from being safe. Appearances, they said, as they shook their heads ominously at each other, were deceptive. The poison—*virus* they delighted to term it—they declared would lie latent in the human system for years, to be unexpectedly developed to the fatal fit. They were curious to know if my patient felt, at times, an itching in the suspected part; if he was troubled with crawling sensations on a ferry-boat; or recoiled at the sudden showing of a horse's teeth. Those possessed of delicacy of feeling would habitually inquire when they met him, in a sepulchral voice, whether he was getting over it?—were there any symptoms? Others said that he would have to wait for assurance seven years, when, for better or for worse, his constitution would undergo a crisis. A few pestered him with congratulations. To travel was the only way left to escape this inquisitional and compassionate persecution, and my patient determined to visit Europe.

The procuring of his passage-ticket was succeeded by a period of irresolution. He had too lightly considered the perils of the deep, and, inopportunely, a steamer had just gone to pieces in a Newfoundland fog. While he was reconsidering his purpose, an official missive was handed him. He cut the envelope and extracted a fresh-minted commission which designated him a brigadier-general. He came at once to a decision, and sailed the following day. He grasped my hand at parting, as we stumbled among a chaos of luggage upon the steamer's deck. 'My dear friend,' he said, 'I shall remember you. We shall ramble together, though apart; the quaint old streets of the Flemish towns, and behold together Mont Blanc rise out of his 'silent sea of pines' with a morning greeting to his sovereign the sun. No! I shall never forget your kindness and your skill; and—you do not think that possibly the dog was mad?'

When I last heard of Jeptha Bullwrinkle, he was drinking still champagne and studying the pictures at Florence."

The dance went blithely on. Bloker and Emily Horton sat apart, he beating time with his fingers to the music and making occasionally a sterile remark on the saltatory scene, which she acknowledged in a monosyllable, withdrawing for the moment her gaze from the vivid and frequent flashes of lightning which played along a bank of cloud risen in the west.

"Do you know that lady with the rosebud in her fine black hair?"

"No, sir."

"They call her Julia. I noticed her earnestly congratulating our hero of the night. The generous emotions show fittingly in a fair woman. Without compassion, for instance, I think a woman's nature is incomplete."

"The sensibilities, I suppose, were intended for human nature, irrespective of sex," said Emily.

"To us, the rough requirements of our artificial life well nigh prohibit them. And there is less fine feeling than there seems. The world is full of spurious philanthropy, put on to jockey the world. There's our friend Pledget, now, who isn't a hypocrite, because he is a satirist."

"If a man's heart is not calloused by covetousness, I think his rougher and wider experience must daily educate it in benevolence, even if it loses in susceptibility.

'He chid their wanderings, but relieved their pain.'

A man knows more of the uncertainties of life, the strength of temptations, and the fallibility of opinions."

"It is a melancholy admission, but I fear the commerce of the world inevitably makes us selfish," said Bloker.

"It is not strange that weakness and want, which are needy and apprehensive, should be selfish; but self-reliance, which is full and fearless, should be liberal."

"Some people with no conscience to speak of, are yet too proud to be stingy," said Bloker.

"I suppose that in bad men of capacity, penuriousness is sometimes overcome by self-esteem, or by a more refined selfishness which would escape the miserly cares."

"Yes, there *is* a luxury in doing good!" exclaimed

Bloker, with sudden enthusiasm. "Perhaps it isn't modest, but as a bit of experience, I may say that now and then I try an open hand at disinterestedness, after business hours—that sort of thing comes in the way of every man of the world, you know—and, at the least, I fancy I find afterwards better claret, and more cheerful company at the club."

Bloker's tone of composure and impersonality, as if he were stating a curious discovery in natural science, was a triumph of audacity. And what was the meaning of his deference for Emily Horton? Was it anything akin to love, or was it even a strong liking, which prompted him to prepare his way to the position of a suitor? Conjecture might have ventured in several directions. With good management, Mr. Horton's estate, heavily encumbered as it was, could be freed, and would then become of great value. There was a love of domination in the man, and a capability of a keen enjoyment of conquest after repulses. Perhaps, sordidly shrewd, he would not disdain to employ a virtuous and accomplished wife as a shield for his own shortcomings. Who can tell? He assailed the lady of his desire perseveringly, and yet not with overboldness. He invested alike in his approaches, her moral convictions, her filial affection, and her personal tastes. His dissembling was various; sometimes transparent, but generally managed with tact. He was not so clumsy as to pretend to be severely virtuous, and, thereby reaching too high, to overreach himself. His heart, as he displayed it, was a well-arranged organ of the conventional consistence—a respectable hollow muscle not extra pulpy.

The suppressed rumbling of thunder, which for the last half-hour had proclaimed the approach of a storm, was succeeded by a startling crash directly overhead. Then came a sudden burst of wind, which forced the steamer to heel. When that was spent, there was a minute or two of calm, during which the only sounds were the straining of the machinery and the plunging of the boat through the ruffled water. A few large drops of rain, shot pattering upon the deck and hissing into the tide, followed. Another great explosion, lengthened in reverberations—then others in shortening intervals—and all the tones of the gathered gust pealed in exultant diapason along the gleaming vault of heaven.

The storm had settled to a steady rain when the Arrow reached her pier.

"Cab!—carriage, sir?"

There was a small supply of vehicles for the company, and Doctor Pledget, who lingered, was cut off from his companions by the interposition of a stout lady terrified from a rival chaise."

"O no, the old lady needn't git out—by no means. Let the gent in, too; don't you see he's standin' in the rain. There's precious little danger, as they ain't oats, of their being run away with!" from a sarcastic charioteer.

"Keep the place, ma'am, and I'll find another somewhere," said the doctor, in reply to an offer to vacate it.

But the carriages that remained were all filled to the

boxes, and literally and figuratively there was a dull prospect. Just then a trap clattered around the corner gaslight down the street.

"In time to take you home, sir!" exclaimed the driver, in a rather patronizing tone, seeing an umbrellaless old gentleman with a west-end look alone on the wharf at midnight.

"But, my friend, you have a fare already," said the doctor, looking into the coach.

"Plenty of room, sir; it's only a gentleman with a telescope."

"A what?" asked the doctor, in some perturbation. He knew he smelled whiskey, and thought he saw a carbine.

"Mr. Smithers, who I took up at the 'Salutation;' the gent what shows the heavenly bodies," explained the cabman.

The short colloquy aroused the astronomer from his slumber, and he demanded peremptorily the cause of the delay—

"Hallo! what's broke?"

"Ony another passenger a comin' in, Mr. Smithers," soothingly.

"Is he wet? I'm not going to have a drainage on to my instrument, and that's the whole of it."

Finding that the doctor was not wringing-wet, thanks to the shelter of a freight shed, the contemplatist of the firmament admitted him.

"I beg your pardon, sir," said the man of science when he could survey his companion in the light of a street lamp, "for seeming bumptious, being woke up sudden—these hackmen are monstrous aggravatin'."

"Don't mention it," replied the doctor.

Mr. Smithers, he observed, was a spare man with white whiskers, a nose which outglowed the dog-star, and a bird-like way of carrying his head, which might have been due either to the telescope or the "Salutation," or, as was most likely, to a combination of the two.

"These storms, which is frequent of late, spoils business, sir," said Smithers.

"By shutting up the planetary system?"

"Yes, sir. It cuts into Jupiter bad, which is in season, and commands quite a run."

"We had a fine moon in the early part of the night," said the doctor.

"That's stock, as I may say; but the view was good. The mountaineous surface was mottled as perfect as I ever seen it—the regular castor-oil in coffee."

"I suppose a good many people look?"

"When there's novelties, and the common shows aint a-drawing—no fool a-blowing of himself up, or walking on his head on a wire. It was a hard pull through for Saturn, last winter, agin the horse-drama."

"I thought you always have Saturn in the ring," said the doctor.

"Ha! ha! capital. A real professional joke. I must remember that. I stop here, and if you'll take a nip with me, there's a night-cellar a few doors off I can recommend. Rather not, eh! Well—evening, sir."

CHAPTER XVI.

An orphan's curse would drag to Hell
A spirit from on high,
But oh! more horrible than that
Is a curse in a dead man's eye!
　　　　　　　　　THE ANCIENT MARINER.

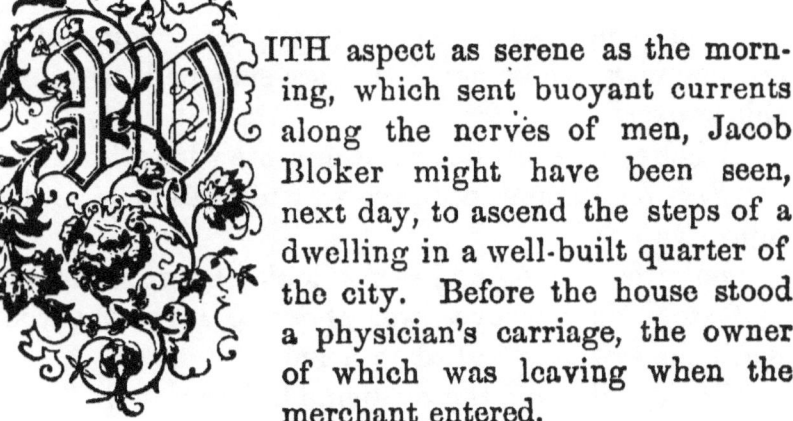ITH aspect as serene as the morning, which sent buoyant currents along the nerves of men, Jacob Bloker might have been seen, next day, to ascend the steps of a dwelling in a well-built quarter of the city. Before the house stood a physician's carriage, the owner of which was leaving when the merchant entered.

"Good-morning, Doctor Conium. How is your patient?"

"Tarries; and that's all. Running down fast—can't survive a month."

"Think so," said Bloker, musingly.

"I am certain—he's in the final dropsy. Splendid day. By-the-by, how did you like Vitalizio t'other night at the Academy? A superb contralto. Prefer Contrayerva! Don't—do not agree with you. Ta—ta."

The half-darkened chamber into which Bloker was ushered was scrupulously neat, and betokened the presence of the searching eye and ready hand of affection. In an easy chair, a wasted man past middle life, with the puffed, doughy countenance indicative of a diseased heart, was carefully pillowed.

"I'm glad to see you looking fresher this morning, Mr. Howell. All you want is a few weeks of country air at this bracing season, new milk, and farm-house quiet," said Bloker.

"You surprise me. I'm sure I couldn't stand it," replied the invalid, slowly.

"You would soon feel stronger, sir. Some of the doctors now recommend the sea-side and bathing at this season."

"I believe I shall not want anything long."

"You really must not give way to such fancies; they injure you."

The wife, forcing a cheerful look through the tears that stood in her eyes, was about to leave the room, when the sick man called to her:

"Sophy, give me the medicine before you go."

Her bosom heaved with a suppressed sigh, and her hand trembled as she measured the drops. Then, when he had swallowed the dose, she took the spoon and lingered at his chair. Looking upon him fondly, and with her fingers gently brushing back a lock of hair upon his forehead, she said,

"His appetite grows better, and a great deal depends on that, you know, sir. He eat quite a meal of tapioca this morning;" and having arranged his pillows, she went to endure a solitary grief at her household labors.

After a pause, during which the sick man's troubled thoughts writhed in his face, and the merchant sat decorously playing with his watch-seals and gazing upon a pattern in the carpet, the former spoke:

"I have sent for you, Mr. Bloker, to take a weight off my mind. The doctor encourages me, but I know that I cannot last long. Our old business relations embolden me to ask a favor of you. In ten days my time in this house will expire. I know you expect the premises, and having warned me, if you insist, I cannot stay; but I must honestly tell you that we have made no preparation to move. Our means are straightened, and when I go," and his voice faltered, "my poor wife will have to live in a more narrow way." Here he quite broke down; but added directly in a hurried manner, as if he lacked nerve to utter the fear which oppressed him, "If we move at the time fixed, we must have a sale of the furniture, and, though I hope that God would sustain me, I feel it is more than Sophy could bear."

There was a minute's silence in the chamber before Bloker composedly replied.

"Mr. Howell," he said, "I would like much to oblige you for old acquaintance sake. We have had large, and I trust mutually satisfactory dealings together, running through many years. To be sure, I hold your due-bill for a hundred dollars, but I shall not press it against your household goods. There is a small fire-proof of yours at my place which will cover a part of the amount, and the remainder I forgive. But in this business I cannot yield to my feelings. I have arranged for some alterations in the house, and the builders will be ready to begin in a fortnight. I am sorry that I can't—that it is impossible to accede to your request."

"God's will be done!" exclaimed the invalid, faintly, as he closed his eyes.

There was a flickering of compassion in Bloker's face as he surveyed his old associate, but he quickly rallied.

"Mr. Howell, you mustn't be despondent. If Conium encourages, you may rely upon it he has grounds. If you want my carriage when you move, command it. It is a quarter of an hour of 'Change, and I must be there. I hope this fine weather will improve you—Good-bye."

It was the daily meridian of the mercantile congress, and the hall was resonant with the buzz of traffic.

"There's Bloker," remarked one admirer of moral goodness to another. "He made a big outside thing, yesterday, on tallow—got early news, somehow, of the fall of Sevastapol, and sold in time."

"He's a sharp one, is Bloker," was the reply, liquorishly emphasized, as the speaker followed with eyes brim-full of esteem the advancing and sprucely attired figure of that acute hero.

CHAPTER XVII.

> Now the cock with lively din
> Scatters the rear of darkness thin,
> And to the stack, or the barn-door,
> Stoutly struts his dames before:
> Oft list'ning how the hounds and horn
> Cheerly rouse the slumb'ring morn,
> From the side of some hoar hill,
> Through the high-wood echoing shrill.
> L'ALLEGRO.

HE sunrise prospect at The Cedars of surrounding stubble fields and woods garbed in russet, with here and there the dogwood's red and the dark green of the hemlock, was felt to be very cheerly by Judge Bardleigh and Bradley Horton, as awaiting breakfast in the crisp, appetizing air, they paced the grounds and accepted happy auguries from the kitchen.

"See you the frost, Master Bradley? This will be a glorious day to trudge for rail. You must get into stouter boots, for we shall find few dry places except gravelly hill sides."

"You have such a powder-and-shot reputation,

judge, that I am confident you will cover my shortcomings."

"Aha! don't rely too much upon the brag of old fellows. I've seen the day, sir—at it again, by the great Orion! No. The shooting exploits that I ventilate happened in my youth, away toward

> 'The good old colony times,
> When George the Third was king—'

though my teething post-dated Tarleton;" and the judge threw back his head with military briskness—he was a brigadier-general in the militia, and had planned a score of successful musters—and merrily stroked his full beard, in which the hazel still predominated over the grey.

"Hedging, I see; but I reckon it will be well to take a hamper, and a boy to pack."

The judge's eyes twinkled.

"O, for that matter," said he, "I always fire to take the heads off the birds; it saves portage."

"Here comes Steve Trencher. He steps briskly, spite of his rheumatism," said Bradley.

"With that dreadful death-dealing gun-barrel of his. The old fellow's timeing himself to the stimulus of prospective bacon," said the judge.

"Good-morning, Uncle Steve!"

"Mornin' gents, both—the top of the mornin' to you; though I dessay I beat you there. A lot of them plaguey circus chaps come along a spell afore day, with an elephant what had gin out somewhere, and beat and banged at the door, and axed for a light. I expected to see the fence go every minute, and warned 'em off, but they kept on till the old woman like to have went in 'isterics. I put the end of 'Proclermation' out of a corner of the window, and drew a bead, and give all hands due notice, and they cleared out sudden. That's solemn."

"No wonder the old lady was flustered," said the judge.

"I had a leetle apple-jack in Gineral Washington, as I call my bottle with the picter, and I give her a few draps right off. It helped her desperate. It's better than camfire, which is good enough for bruises, but don't warm the innards like the rael sperits."

"And had you any left for yourself, Uncle Steve?" asked the judge.

"Wal—a taste like; hardly enough to keep off the ager."

"We'll see, then, if there isn't a little in the sideboard. And there's Kitty calling to breakfast—come along before the pot cools."

The three sat down to some substantial fare, after the judge had provided Uncle Steve with the promised prophylactic, when, had he not turned his back, he might have felt flattered by the dainty appreciation which it manifestly aroused as it glided over the avuncular palate.

"I've heern, judge, you cure your bacon with sweetenin'," remarked Uncle Steve, as he received from the host a fresh supply.

"Yes; with sugar and salt, and without pickle."

"Its proper nice meat. 'Pears to me the sile makes

the pork, when you once git the right breed, and a kinder than The Cedars was never nuzzled."

"Now, if we're ready, let us tramp," said the judge, when they had collected their pieces, pouches and flasks, including "Proclermation," a gun which might have been relied upon to circumvent any known manual. "In which direction shall we go for the best sport, Uncle Steve?"

"Wal, I seen pooty considerable birds about Cox's Meadows, two days ago."

"I don't believe there has been as much gunning there as on the creek marshes; its more out of the way," said the judge.

They were travelling on the causeway, a raised road straight across the marsh, which spread to a great distance on each side of it, an expanse of rank reeds and clumps of sedge overflowed periodically by the tide, which was diffused from and sluiced to the serpentine channel of the creek.

"Do you see that sloop in the spatter-docks?"

"That's the Muskrat, judge," said Uncle Steve. "I seen the captain to town at Claxton's store, yesterday, a-buying a pair of gallowses, and he told me she was stuck in the mash."

"I've got a couple of bushels of prime oysters planted in her, and there we'll dine, lads—I've brought along the knives."

Occasionally they shot with good success where a rustle of stilted legs and flutter of wings in the sedge showed the presence of birds.

"I never knowed but one man tame a rail," said

Uncle Steve, "and that was old Kurnal Cox—but there was something unyearthly about him. Folks believed he'd sold himself to the divil, who had took his shadow to make sure, beforehand. Leastways, nobody ever seen it."

"If the colonel was always as thin as when I knew him, Satan got slim security," remarked the judge.

Uncle Steve was scandalized by the judge's tone of banter, which he deemed little short of irreligious frivolity.

"Wal, he's often seen to walk about the homestead. Kiah Crocker seen him one windy night, the winter of the great sleighing, a-ridin' on a grey horse full gallop over the old sanddam. It was about four o'clock in the morning. Kiah had been to a dance at the Pole tavern, and seen him plain. I've often heern him say he was ready to take his davy on it."

"I wonder if the same birds come year after year to these feeding grounds," speculated Bradley.

"Bless you, no. They bury themselves in the mashes every winter and turn to frogs," replied Uncle Steve, with pitying promptitude.

At a reach in the fen of the corn-land the gunners came to a mud-plastered hovel fenced with a medley of pickets and brush. Strings of scarlet pepper and bunches of herbs dangled outside. Beside the hut was a patch of hoed ground which contained straggling simples and vegetables—comfrey and tansy, remainder beets and broken files of cabbages. A cow, with a baggy application on one leg, looked from a stalk-thatched shed, and shook lorn music from a neck-bell when she nosed from her brisket the flies. An aged negro, white-headed and very bent in figure, sat sunning himself before the door. There was such an accordant air of primitive make-shift, and yet coarse sufficiency by hook and by crook, in the parts of the picture, that the *tout ensemble* could not be easily forgotten.

"Mornin', Grandaddy Baltic!" Uncle Steve, who was foremost, accosted.

"Sarvent, gentlemen," replied the old man, saluting the party with one hand to his grizzled forelock, and with the aid of a stick tottering to his feet.

There was a smouldering fire of green chips, the smoke of which the breeze blew straight toward the cabin door.

"Do you have to keep a smudge all day, my friend?" asked Bradley, as he tried with tearful eyes to decipher some cabalistic characters scratched about a horse-shoe which was nailed to the lintel.

"Yes, young marster. Skeeter dreffel thick here; wus place on the mash for him."

A not untidy woman bustled at her household occupations within the cabin, and a callow brood of brats grinned from the narrow window and peeped through crevices, while one adventurous wight of six years old, clad in a loose, lone garment of coarse cotton, was seized upon appearance by a dexterous movement of the patriarch and summarily spanked. Their sleek condition seemed to bid defiance alike to insects and intermittent.

"Your grandchildren?" asked the judge.

"Yes, sar. Ise got a lot of 'em, and bressed is dat man whoms quiver's full. You Jim! clar right off, or I'll guv it you. They isn't used to quality, sar."

"I suppose they all know how to eat 'possum and pone, old man?"

"Yah, yah, sar; possum and ground-hog don't stand no chance with dem critters."

"Grandfather, what use do you make of these herbs?" asked Bradley.

"Dem yarbs useful in many tings—snake bites, rheumatiz, tender hoof, biles, cancer, yaller janders, bloody flux, fits, worms, colic, breakins out, poll evil, straightenin' bones—mose all kind sickness."

"Houndstongue, sut, and a leetle of the fat of a blind puppy, make a master eyntment for runnin' sores," remarked Uncle Steve.

"Yes, sar. That salve don't keep its strength tho', less its mixed in de full of de moon. To fotch dem shu-ah, ole man Baltic adds another ingrediem."

The patriarch's curative resources, it was understood, were not exhausted upon legitimate ailments. He was renowned for knowledge in the occult sciences, and practised a good deal of quiet *diablerie* for the benefit of a confiding connexion.

"I'm curious to know, old man, why you wear that bag at your neck," said the judge.

"Dems charms, sar."

"Against Apollyon—the Evil One?"

"Gin de witches, and sperits dat trouble de air. Dey do heap of harm, marster, if dey're let alone, so people come to Baltic to put spells on 'em. Dey dries up the cows milk, and stunts de corn, and breeds snakes in the stumuk. Baltic's charm makes um show umself in de shape of an owl; den, when him shot, de plague's gone. Sometimes good while afore him show; den Baltic has to make the charm strong agin."

"Could you let us see them?"

"Don't do to 'spose 'em in de daytime—bring mischief on eberybody."

"Aroynt! thou arch-magician!" exclaimed the judge. "This is dangerous, and we were best going. Have you a dime, Bradley?—Here, my girl; 'tis for the spring-water you toted."

As they trudged away the hours, the reports of their fowling-pieces startled the otherwise silent walks, upon which the sun shone mitigated at times through a lucid veil of clouds, or pouted sullen behind a denser cumulus, and then burst joyously in beaming splendor. It was high and hungry noon when they reached the Muskrat and got at the mollusks. The softer hands of the judge and Bradley compelled them to circumspection, but Uncle Steve's knife was swift and sure. "I never lets 'em stump me, nohow," he observed, in the pendulum-like pauses of deglutition; "I *kin* take 'em out without scratching their beards."

And thus, right pleasantly, the merry day wore on to

"——join the past Eternity."

The lightning-scathed poplars at The Cedars seemed to gesticulate of home, as they basked in the waning afternoon. The chimneys crowned with smoke intensified the welcome; warmer, Master Shenstone, than that of the best inn which ever showed a bush or bred a Boniface.

CHAPTER XVIII.

Thus do they talk, till in the sky
The pale-eyed moon is mounted high.

BOUT a quarter of a mile from The Cedars mansion was situated the farm-house of the estate. Sometimes, enamored of rural sights and sounds, Bradley Horton and Lydia Bardleigh —they were much together—took it in their evening walk. Ere yet the tints of sunset had given place to slate-colored twilight, with a tossing of horns and crowded trampling of hoofs, the herd was seen upon the dusty road. Following the cattle, a flock of sheep, less frisky than in the morning pastureward, was driven to the pen. Loud was the importunate sty. The fowls on the branches cackled like ancient human gossips serenely censorious about a neighborhood scandal; while the geese, crop-full and vigilant, stood sedately in the way on one leg, or scattered with craned necks and shrill alarm when disturbed by a trespassing horse, at whose heels the gander spitefully nipped. The milkmaids shifted from Brindle to Suke, emptying the swollen bags in sharp,

wiry spirits, that bubbled to warm froth in their lactean lodgment. Then, the teams rattled home to the clank of shaken chain-gear, and shouldered eagerly to the water-trough. Anon, came the wagoner's whistle from the mow, and the sound of currycombs struck on manger and stall-side. Gradually quiet succeeded in the darkening scene, undisturbed except by the fluttering of bat and beetle, and the house-dog's answer to the barking of the distant fox; while the moon queened it over all in tranquil beauty.

"Many of your good city people, Mr. Horton, think country life hum-drum," said Lydia.

"But it is a question if you know real country life where there is elegant hospitality and much coming and going. The madding, or gadding crowd follows you, if not the ignoble strife."

"Nobody, I suppose, believes in the superiority of rural life when it is cramped to the illiberal level of boorishness; but the well-doing, intelligent farmer's family has more and purer sources of enjoyment than are open to people of the same social condition in cities, where so many suffer the torments of vanity by being ashamed to live within their means," said Lydia.

"Ah! the rural manners are gone. Simplicity keeps from the hay-field, and the farmer bolts his front door at bed-time—the very bees forsake the clover for the syrups of the village apothecary."

"This complaint of the decline of rural manners is common to all actively civilized countries and periods. It was Goldsmith's in the 'Deserted Village,' and Cowper's in the 'Task,' as it was Wordsworth's yesterday.

The rustics whom Sergeant Kite recruits are different from those Shakespeare painted, yet they are full as good Englishmen," answered Lydia.

"When nature shows in such fascinating shapes, one supposes that the sordid tendencies in man will be abashed, and there will be no flunkying to the hypocrisies and fopperies. I think I see some vanity, however, in the angular, packing-box houses built on the barest and highest spots, and with no inconvenient trees to obscure their stateliness," said Bradley.

"The country has features for every humor, whether rugged, sprightly, or subdued. You will find the contrast of this autumn evening scene, stirring with animal life, racy and radiant, in the unnatural silence and ghastly beauty which prevail about these homes on a winter's morning after a snow-storm."

"But there is no action," insisted Bradley, "in a country life. You can sum it in an alliteration—the piazza, the plantation, and the post-office, with a horse to keep up a connection. Women can adapt themselves to this, unless they are mere butterflies of fashion, but fancy a man with no stimulus between breakfast and dinner but an essay on the last super-phosphate, or a turn at higgling over fat oxen with a butcher."

"Dioclesian, I have read, forgot the purple of the world in the solitude of Salona, his horticulture, the free air of the Dalmatian mountains, and the prospect of the island-studded Hadriatic. Then, Washington was a planter, and Garibaldi loves the vines and olives of his native Nice. Sailors, whose lives are adventuresome"—

"Change to farmers naturally, as tadpoles do to frogs; and pardon me for finishing your sentence with an awkward similie," said Bradley, laughing.

"I do."

"Your Garibaldis' and sailors but sleep off the weariness of action—then, to battles and blown seas again. The sturdy sons of England turn from her daisied turf and 'alleys green,' to struggle with polar ice or start tigers in Indian jungles."

"To employ a thought which I believe is another's—Low gales are the best winds heavenward," said Lydia.

"Doubtless; but few sails are spread to them.—Apropos of restlessness; the 'sensation' newspapers, with their licentious extravagance and mazy marvels of vacuity, unsettle the brains of a great many weak brethren. They excite an unprofitable curiosity to know what is said, rather than what is true. They enable a multitude of silly people to while away their time, pleased with a titillating relish of empty words which claim no effort of attention. It is injustice to an average human intellect to read these American newspapers. In the language of King David, 'they go astray as soon as they be born, speaking lies.' If, morally, they are less hurtful than the prurient and pyrotechnic novels, they are even more contemptible. Fertile in big words for little things, they swing perpetually between denunciation—which is often the resentment of baffled scheming, a covering of corruption, or a bait for forbearance-money—and unwholesome, unctuous puffery, the daily stimulant for somebody's vanity," said Bradley.

"You remind me of the Arabian proverb: 'They went to shoe the Pasha's horse, and the beetle stretched forth his hind leg,'" said Lydia.

"I say, the old women are predicting from the goose bones a long, cold winter, and lots of sleighing—that's a gay look out, Lyddy!" cried Charley Bardleigh.

They were flinging All-hallows-eve nuts on the embers.

"You're planning to break down the carriage horses again, I suppose," replied his sister.

"Never hurt them a jot. A clean sweat once a year does 'em good, if it does damage a trace or two. If snow comes I tell you to expect fun. Sandy Coulter's tanning coon skins, and sprucing up his jumper for a splurge—I half believe he's sweet on Kate Stedman. I mean to fetch down Rose Stuvesant, and two or three of the McCalmot girls."

"In such an array, I suppose I can't be counted," said Bradley.

"To be sure you can. Plenty of room, and a buffalo for you. Mr. Horton may come—mayn't he, Lyddy?"

CHAPTER XIX.

Yes, my dear friend! my little fortune is pleasant to my generous heart, because I can do good—no man with so little a fortune ever did so much generosity—no person, no man person, no woman person ever denies it. But we are all Got's children.
    COLERIDGE'S DANE ON BOARD OF THE HAMBURG PACQUET.

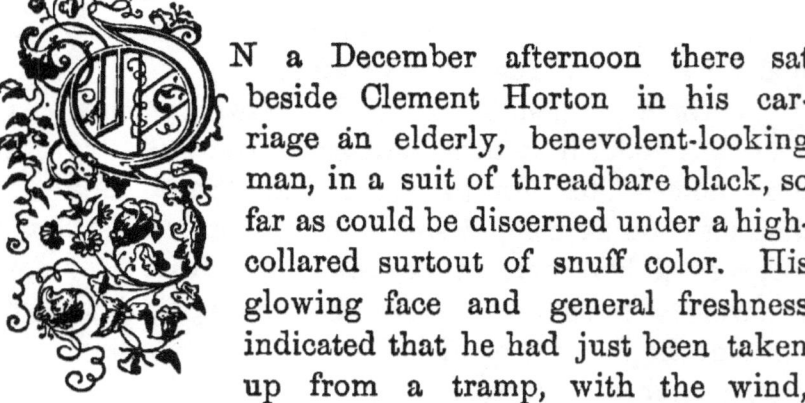

ON a December afternoon there sat beside Clement Horton in his carriage an elderly, benevolent-looking man, in a suit of threadbare black, so far as could be discerned under a high-collared surtout of snuff color. His glowing face and general freshness indicated that he had just been taken up from a tramp, with the wind, which blew free and frosty, in his teeth. He slapped his ungloved hands and rubbed his ears till they blushed, as he passed salutations with the merchant in a hearty way.

"I despaired of finding you, Father Tryon," said Mr. Horton.

"I stopped at the 'Sorrel Horse' till I got tired of the profane bar-room nonsense, not to speak of the stinking reek of liquor and tobacco, when I took to God's fresh air."

"I suspect you're a famous walker, Father Tryon?"

"Yes, my dear sir; I am kept afoot from November to April a great part of every day, and what is bad, simply in view of the creature, the heaviest work comes in the worst weather. I look like an anatomy, but my legs don't lack muscle. Providence is good to me in the matter of strength, though I am past sixty these several years, and, for the rest, I live to do my Master's will."

"I thought, Father Tryon, that we could at leisure look into your project, and perhaps devise means to advance it. I have long considered a House of Industry very much needed at Clinkers; but it will require a great deal of money, and we must go about the undertaking in a business-like way. I fear that people just now will not care to loosen their purse-strings enough for our purpose."

"If we can only get the soup department at once, it will be a great step," said Father Tryon, with ardor.

Robert Tryon began life for himself aboard a New Bedford whaler. His nature was hardy, his spirit adventurous, and often when morning broke upon the Berkshire hills he awakened from delicious dreams of going down to the deep in ships. For the lad it was a battle of sea against land, which should claim him for its own, and, in a dull age of peace, it was an unequal contest. Had there been a wolf to kill now and then, or a chance for a wrestle with a bear the paternal acres might have retained him to compete in straight furrows and tolerate slow-going oxen; but the slayer of the last of the ferine beasts slept in the church-yard, a paralytic old man when he died, mumbling to the end boasts of his youthful prowess, and grateful recollections of bounties from the State. As it was, the rural runagate picked the hayseeds from his eyes, and hastened to enjoy his imagined bliss,

> "Far as the breeze can bear, the billows foam."

It is needless to trace here in detail eventful years in the life of the young sailor. In a succession of voyages, he had deserted at Madagascar, beach-combed in South America, been shipwrecked on the island of Saint Paul, and caught the plague at Constantinople. At length the religious principle which was native to his earnest nature promisingly germinated, and in time grew to a fruitful development in the life of the devoted city missionary.

Who shall describe that Clinkers district, which was Robert Tryon's pastorate. And it was not alone a field of spiritual labor, but it was also one of secular, in a numerous and squalid, vice-immeshed, shiftless and shifting community, living by disreputable means or alms procured mainly through the missionary's appeals, and which, though scanty, were not seldom for the recipients all their bread, warmth, and raiment. Clinkers was a confusion of foul streets, and noisome alleys, and close courts, interspersed with open lots heaped with coal-ashes and the rubbish of demolished buildings, where swine and goats roamed for garbage, and the unsightly children of sottish parents infected each other with a precocious corruption. Crime and lust celebrated in Clinkers subterranean orgies, and the ear of night was vexed with the frantic gaiety of despair. Here burglars planned their expeditions in vile cribs; and wretched women, fallen to the lowest level of their sex, plied their calling, or perished by its fruits. At every corner there was a liquor-store, and dens of taverns, brothels, and lodging-cellars, in pestilent communication, sustained the horrible life-in-death of the place. The fires of fever never went out here; and moping imbecility crouched in the same chamber which rang with the fierce delirium of the dying drunkard. The coroners were rich in reminiscences of Clinkers; concerning burned and smothered infants, and bodies found in outhouses and areas ghastly with wounds from knife and bludgeon. Ghostlike, in the gusty midnight, along the rows of street lamps which flickered to the river's side, solitary sufferers withdrew, and never more returned.

In the prevailing misery there were social distinctions still. A grimy, uncombed citizen, with a reputed interest in a glue factory and a monopoly of dead animals upon the streets, the head dog-catcher, and several successful rag and bone gatherers, were, next to the chief whiskey sellers and the pawnbrokers, a caste by themselves, acknowledged magnates of the region. Though faces in Clinkers were diverse in color and airs of nativity, the predominating cast of countenance, while it presented no puzzle for the physiognomist, appealed to the feeling heart with the eloquence of rebuke and entreaty.

In one respect the importance of Clinkers was indisputable; it was a most generous contributor to the bills of mortality. Within its confines small-pox festered malignant, and, strengthening upon the marrow of misery which it found, made in its ravenousness unexpected forays into rich men's dwellings. Sometimes an epidemic came, and fastening on Clinkers, filled the town with terror. Then the inhabitants, not hurried to almshouse hospitals or pauper burial, were turned in ragged wretchedness from their infected lairs, shut out by barricades, and forced to find fresh burrows unreduced to the sanitary rule of whitewash, which, backed by policemen, as all men know is "the sovereignest remedy" on earth for any contagion which may spread from the corrupted centres of society, whether to undermine its morals, destroy its peace, or decimate its numbers. Here, for twenty years, except when cholera or fever brought boards of health to share possession, Father Tryon, wielding a moral sceptre, had dispensed the counsel and exercised the control of a single-minded Christian minister. He had watched the awful passing of the sullen or the phrensied sinner, and prayed by the pallet of the penitent till the awaiting angels received the liberated spirit and bore it to the presence of its God; and he had walked on errands of mercy in the midnight rumble of the dead-cart, with the walking pestilence.

Grateful as is the smell of hay-fields when borne by a summer evening breeze to hot city streets, is the presence of a spiritual-minded, large-hearted, and large-handed man among the selfishly busy of the world. Men behold the result of Christian benevolence, but are ignorant of the careful thought, fervent aspirations, sorrows, and prayers that prompt and precede it; for secrecy is the divine law and gauge of the highest goodness. Yet it is wisely ordained that benevolence shall increase when use has blunted the sensibility of compassion. God's blessing of bounty comes oftener through two or three gathered together than pompous convocations. Blowflies are apt to haunt the open shambles. To a fit observer, the bright faces of the merchant and missionary would have seemed more cheerful than the glow of light which surrounded them in the bright, red-curtained room at Belair. Humane tranquillity, tempered with firmness, was indicated in the countenance of Clement Horton, as some will fondly remember, who still knew it to be capable of the expression of sterner emotions. The appearance of the merchant was noticeable. He was full six feet in stature, with a straight frame, rather heavily moulded, yet instinct with nervous action. A characteristic head, with a tinge of silver in the thin, black hair, was carried with modest and intelligent dignity. A high, well-arched forehead, Roman nose, and calm, dark-grey eyes, completed the features of a grave face, which a clear complexion saved from sombreness.

"We will call on Glump, to begin—he is nearest, and shall be first served," said Clement Horton to Father Tryon, next morning, as they approached the city.

"A heavy dealer in hardware, I believe—shall we set fifty dollars opposite his name?" Father Tryon held a list, which he scanned with interest.

"Hypothetically," was the laconic reply of his companion, while a smile played about his mouth.

Aquila Glump reigned supreme in a lofty, granite-fronted establishment in Phœnix-block, Commerce street, and thither the canvassers repaired. The place was a hive of industry, where everybody was employed, from the chief to the junior boy.

"Taking our account of stock—walk in."

"As you have no time to waste on us, we will go at once to our business," prefaced Mr. Horton, as he made known succinctly and persuasively the object of their visit, while Glump listened with inflexible attention. At length, by the missionary's help, the application being squarely laid, Mr. Horton ceased, and there was a provoking pause. Father Tryon looked expectant; for who, thought that worthy man as he glanced through the counting-house window down a long storeway perspective of clerks and porters among piles of merchandise, and heard subterranean noises that would have befitted Vulcan in a pet about his thunderbolts—who with such resources can resist my friend's eloquent appeal and my own illustrations. I think, now, we may count on a hundred dollars.

Then uprose Aquila Glump, and spoke as follows:

"If I could collect as close as the charities do this winter, I'd retire next spring satisfied. Your object, gentlemen, is a good one, no doubt, but it is simply impossible to answer the everyday cry of, 'Give.' Rubies and sapphires wouldn't be sufficient. As to monuments and memorials, there's no end to them. Somebody's constantly getting burnt out. Then, there's our Dispensary; doing a heavy business and wanting aid. In the last six months it has given to the suffering poor three thousand prescriptions, more than half of them pills, with no end of tooth-pulling—the most gratifying exhibit we have yet made. Besides, there are other special claims which I can't disregard."

"Must we go with an empty-handed dismissal, then?" asked Clement Horton, urbanely.

"I must draw the line somewhere, sir. But, stop—may be I can help along your soup. Seven or eight years ago I got a consignment of beans in payment of a country bill, and there are three or four bags left. To tell the truth, I had some trouble to get them off my hands; buyers brought them back, and pretended they wouldn't boil. Give them fire and water enough, I dare say they will. I'm sure there is no mould about them, for they have been next the roof, where it's dry as a bone. Send for them when you please—Benjamin! charge Benevolence with seven and a half bushels of beans, at one dollar and eighty cents a bushel, and fifteen per cent. storage, and deliver to Mr. Horton's order."

Stimulated by this initial success, the canvassers departed to invoke the generosity of Scroggs. They found that gentleman giving audience, seriatim, to a collection of individuals whose appearance attested their independence of the industrial pursuits of this world. They were limber and slouching, bulky and mulberry-visaged men, wearing their hats in a dissipated manner, with the dull sparkle of expiring "cocktails" in their eyes, and given to an adjusted expectoration of tobacco-juice. They wore waistcoats of bright colors, glittering chains, and bossy seal-rings. There was a promise of potatory capacity in their protuberant fronts, which was often realized in bar-room arm-chairs. Tied to no family plate and napkin, they played an Ishmaelitish hand at boarding-houses, and ravaged at tavern lunches. When moneyless, they condescended to juries, but their legitimate sphere was the legislative lobby and the partisan convention. They were, in short, of that civic brotherhood which regulates the working of our republican machinery—the ward politicians. Some expected to be delegates, and about these others revolved in the relation of satellites. Bartimeus Scroggs was "out" for Congress, and scheming for his party's nomination.

"Bilkser, how goes the war?" asked Scroggs, briskly, of a black-whiskered patriot.

"We've got four precincts in our ward fixed. Sure to flax 'em there—hooks in all round. But we are dead broke—have used up the funds, and must have fifty dollars to go on."

"More grease for the machine, eh! Yes. I sent ten laborers from your neighborhood yesterday to the superintendent of the park. Don't you think a few more streets in the seventh might be repaired—small ones, you know, where there isn't too much elbow room, and the poor people won't kick at cobbles about their doorsteps, and a long job? If a storm would only come and bust a culvert!"

"I believe, with what's under way, the paving is about cleaned up," replied Bilkser, despondently. "There might be a lot of kerbstones moved in mistake, and hauled away again."

"I bought in the furniture of the United Athenians debating club, which was levied upon for rent, and donated it to the society. That ought to tell in the eleventh—it's to be noticed in the newspapers as quite in the manner of Pericles," remarked Scroggs.

"The Constitutional Carpenters is on a strike there. Two or three X's to them, on the sly, so the bosses wouldn't know, might be a big thing," suggested Bilkser.

"A good idea. I've promised Chase the printing, but keep Smellie hanging on. Chase is to do the public opinion articles—'Many Voters,' and 'Fiat Justisher.'"

As Mr. Horton and his companion were about to get an interview with Scroggs, in bustled the venerable Bliggs, and interposed.

"Mrs. Frizzleby's mighty bad; them passes haint helped her a bit. She's troubled with a dreffle retchin', and drawin' pains in the small of her back. The mejeum you sent seems non-plushed, and thinks you had better come round."

"I can't—I'm too busy. Did he make the upward passes, or the downward?"

"The motions was outard and towards the ceiling."

"That's where it is. Deuce take the blockhead! he'll pump all the magnetic fluid out of the woman's system. What she wants is witalizing. The passes must be downward, and a few touches from a galvanic battery wouldn't do any harm—they would stop the retching by easing the coats of her stomach," said Scroggs.

"Well, I'll tell him; and I hope he will relieve the old lady, for she has been sending to me every half hour since breakfast—first cousin of Mrs. Bliggs, who was a Frizzleby. If she don't get better, I reckon I shall have to shut up shop. What's spelter to-day?"

"Now, gentlemen," said Scroggs, after hearing Father Tryon, "though there may be no money in these things, I consider it every man's duty to be charitable.—Biles, how are you? Disengaged in a few minutes; sit down. —Our higher life, as I was about to say, demands the practice of charity. But no man's means is equal to every call; even Good Samaritans must have their speers in this world.—An abatement on them potatoes? We can't make it, Comly. If Green saw the rot in them, what did he buy 'em for?—I confine my charities to my own district, and if you were at work in it, I wouldn't hold back. As it is, I don't mind—are you going to publish the subscriptions? Well, ten dollars. Perhaps Mr. Biles will give something."

"Never was so hard up for money in my life—can't collect anything," observed that gentleman, with decision.

"O, they will take fixtures—they are canvassing for a soup-house. It is just in your line," explained Scroggs.

"If it's a deserving undertaking, I'll—um—say—a ladle and a meat-fork. I think they will be appropriate; and I'll send them down—when you get a going."

"I asked if you meant to publish the subscriptions, Mr. Horton, for they put everything in the newspapers nowadays. They have got my biography there—I don't know that you have seen it. No? I'll give you a couple of *Bugles*, then; they may amuse you. A good journal, by the by.—Did you think I made out a case in my letter to the *Popgun* on the extension of the public piers?"

"It was a master-piece of enlightened reasoning; I have heard it everywhere commended," said Expectation Biles.

CHAPTER XX.

We discussed the question whether drinking improved conversation and benevolence. Sir Joshua maintained it did. JOHNSON.—"No, sir: before dinner men meet with great inequality of understanding; and those who are conscious of their inferiority, have the modesty not to talk. When they have drunk wine, every man feels himself happy, and loses that modesty, and grows impudent and vociferous: but he is not improved; he is only not sensible of his defects."

* * * * *

BOSWELL.—"I think, sir, you once said to me, that not to drink wine was a great deduction from life." JOHNSON.—"It is a diminution of pleasure, to be sure; but I do not say a diminution of happiness. There is more happiness in being rational."

AROLINE MELLEN to Adelaide Crosby.

"DEAR ADDY: We are shut in at Belair—Emily Horton and myself—to grumble at the dullest and sloppiest Christmas, I verily believe, in the present century; and I think the evergreens may be doing penance for all the jollity of the past, they look so melancholy. A Spanish princess of one of the old dramatists was persuaded that Apollo, in love or envy, would scorch off her fine hair, and so kept always in the shade—how I long for the sunshine without the vanity of the story. It looks like snowing, just now, which prospect might set our blood bounding again, did we not know it will avail nothing in the mud. You must grant that nobody goes seriously about anything at this season, and as one day sufficed for the amusement to be got from the illustrated gift books and the stereoscope, with attrappes and bon-bons for the dawdling intervals, we are fallen on a poverty of resources. To the idle comes temptation, and I have yielded to it, as you will discover to your cost when you receive this infliction of my tediousness.

And why should you escape? Do you remember the unfailing correspondence we projected at school, when we should enter upon the promising land of the future, which would surely flower with new dances, new dresses, and exquisite designs of pleasure, and be peopled with troubadours and other gallant gentlemen? Some of us, alas! reached the mirage to find it a desert, with barren and bitter growths, and perished untimely in the desolation. Poor Virginia D——! Let that pass. There is so little gossip, that I must emphasise it. 'Tis my talent—so I give thanks and make no boast.

Do they toast the ladies before the clergy? I forget; but I will give the cloth precedence. Our Mr. Willey, (I belong to Belair you know,) of All Saints, has got an interesting substitute to help him through his bronchitis, which is not malignant enough to require Europe. I think he is a consumptive cleric, for I noticed a hectic glow in his cheek last Sunday afternoon when Mary Sartain spoke to him, and he looked, listening, into her eyes. For the rest, he has light, restrained whiskers—

auburn, if you please, dresses in customary black, neatly kept, and wears creased lavender-colored gloves. There is also a clergyman here who calls himself the Revivalist of America. I can't help telling you, though its shockingly profane, the odd answer they say he got from Ruffbolt, the blacksmith. It was about a subscription the Revivalist was soliciting. 'How is it to be applied?' asked Ruffbolt: 'To keep your neighbors from being damned,' replied the Revivalist: 'Then I can't conscientiously give,' said Ruffbolt.

Maggie Smith, who was one of the Langham Place juniors in our time—you will perhaps remember her prejudice against pocket-handkerchiefs—is this winter the admiration of the town. Past seventeen, would you think her? She has an untiring chevalier in Theodore G——, fresh from the shadow of the 'dome of Brunelleschi,' who serves out his Italian memories very freely, with—'When I was in Florence,' or, 'I observed in the Tuscan capital,'—a heavy pendant, I think, for a reigning belle. Caroline K—— is 'brisk as a bee,' and gathers honey from all sorts of flowers. Do the surplus sweets such people hive interfuse with existence and last through the winter of old age? They live to be old, you know; and Carrie K—— promises to, if her peach-like cheeks and ample bust mean anything but present temptation. I will venture a certain disconsolate gentleman, a city merchant, thinks there is a scornful lady at Belair. Not your humble servant. My conquests are easily told: Dr. Pledget, and Mr. Seroon, a dark gentleman from Bengal. I pity the poor fellow, and have essayed in his behalf a little good-natured remonstrance; but,

> 'This cannot take her:
> If of herself she will not love,
> Nothing can make her.'

Bradley Horton, humming 'Malbrook,' comes into the library and says a visitor we have expected, a Mr. George Dolman, is arrived; so I must close this medley. But not till I take revenge for the interruption. Well, then, Master Bradley basks periodically in the smiles of a Miss Lydia Bardleigh. He goes, again and again, 'to shoot with the judge,' (her father,) or, 'for a sail with some friends on the bay.' Do you want to see some of his rapture, my dear? A German tailor found it in a vest of Bradley's which he took to repair, and brought it immediately to me with a puzzled countenance.

MY BEAUTIFUL WHITE ROSE.

Bride of my heart! Betrothéd! look,
  And love me with thy loving eyes;
Oh! lay aside that idle book,
  And lift the drooping lids' disguise.
I know they overflow with light,
  Twin stars above a tropic sea,
Which heaving in my raptured sight,
  Makes music of the drapery!

How wide, how warm, how sweetly wild,
  The love that billows in thy breast!
And yet like dimples on a child,
  A sleeping child, it seems to rest.
So gently sways thy bosom's mask
  To strangled sighs when half confest,
Thy quivering mouth I do not ask
  To tell me I am thine, and blest!

> But turn to me thy loving eyes,
> I'll answer with an eagle's gaze,
> Till their mild radiance meekly dies,
> Outmeasured by a kindred blaze.
> The charms Cythera's goddess brought,
> To ravish from the foaming sea,
> Ne'er on the ancient manhood-wrought
> The spells thy eyes can work on me!

Isn't it dreadful?—'I pray you, mar no more trees with writing love-songs in their barks.'

The favorite bonnet this winter is velvet, trimmed with satin ribbon and rolled feathers, turned well off from the side-face and worn back. Ribbon and narrow blonde inside; with hair in full bandeau. There are some new styles of fluted mantle, very charming. I showed you once an antique garment of silk and worsted stuff, a fine vermillion in color, which was worn by my great-grandmother on grand occasions, such as riding to the city on a pillion and being chased by panthers; and which I think of converting to a Balmoral. I must break short off. Adieu.

C. M.

P. S. I forgot to tell you that I have not succeeded in sampling the silk, but I will try again. Also, that there is an angel in the house at Shellbank."

Besides the merchant, Bradley, and the two ladies, Messrs. Dolman and Bloker partook of Belair turkey and cranberry, which was followed by the inevitable mince-pie, and a delicate tapioca pudding, made by Emily, which compelled their approval.

"You see I have resolved to keep my guests sober," said Mr. Horton, quietly.

"And you are right. If a man can't do without his bottle, let him find a tavern," returned Dolman.

"Only think, Mr. Bloker, of the bins being sealed up, and snapdragon prohibited. An I am forced to emigrate, I shall go to Scheidam," said Caroline.

"I have banished the decanters from a sense of duty, without any desire to prescribe morals imperiously for others. Doubtless a conscience-restrained man may drink wine moderately without evil. Still I do not feel justified in longer promoting by my compliance an indulgence which is too commonly abused; and which, at the best, to a rational being is a superfluity. Every man's example is worth something for good or evil to a weaker brother."

"But what is to become of the wits of dull people if you take away their wine; and where are we to find that dear, delightful, romantic jollity—

'Dance and Provencal song and sunburnt mirth?'"

asked Caroline.

"Then, consider the advice to Timothy," added Dolman, continuing the banter.

"Some men think champagning customers profitable in business. I hardly know if it is, in the end. It sells as many goods as it pays for," observed Bloker.

"John Barleycorn has not been helped by the scientific nonsense of Liebig and the 'alcohol is food' chemists. And he is not to be disposed of by 'mass-meeting.' Every man, under God, must play the David for himself, and sling his own stone; with a hearty, brotherly rescue from the whole field for the poor fellows who go down in the conflict," said Dolman.

"While it is true," observed the merchant, "that no man can reform another, let us not depreciate the value of concerted effort. When you improve the poor man's dwelling, and give him room, and abundance of light, air, and water; cheap and reasonable amusements; gardens, parks, picture-galleries, and free music; schools for his children, and a well sustained industry for himself, (the province of statesmanship,) by which he may support them; and above all, to sanctify all, the gospel of Jesus, the poor man's gospel, calmly, fervently, and affectionately preached by a pure and cultivated priesthood, you strike heavy blows at intemperance."

"It is amazing that the falsehood which asserts the temperance of the inhabitants of wine-producing countries continues to be received. In Paris, where drunken men are kept from the streets, there are wine shops at which, in certain hours daily, you may find a hundred topers at a time sleeping off the fumes of intoxication; and on a smaller scale it is so throughout France. In Belgium it is worse," said Bradley.

"The only force of the cheap wine argument as a remedy for the whiskey abuse, is this: It will take more of the former to produce drunkenness than of the latter, and the excess *may not* be taken. I must beg pardon for making of no account the poetry, which is blissful with festive Falernian and sparkling Catawba. It is the difference of breaking a man's neck outright, and of his being done for by a succession of minor fractures," remarked Dolman.

"One might suppose, Mr. Dolman, that you were fresh from walking the hospitals, but for your hostility to punch," said Caroline.

"To us the individual misery inflicted by the immoderate use of whiskey and wine is apparent; the infrangible mischief which is grafted into the race—the aggregate of propagable vice and woe—can only be estimated by angels," said Mr. Horton.

"May not the world outgrow tobacco, sometime?" asked Dolman.

"It seems stretching speculation to suppose so. As an obstruction to spiritual development, it may be found by individuals the offending eye which is to be plucked out. It will never be abandoned simply because it is injurious to mental and bodily health, except by hesitating dyspeptics," responded Mr. Horton.

"Tobacco is a cherished impostor, as despotic as a Tartar Lama, and which looks grave, owns castles in Spain, and pretends to wisdom," said Caroline.

"The daily practice of alternating a stimulant and a sedative, is odd enough to be told by a traveller of some newly-discovered tribe. Yet, with brandy and tobacco, we have such a see-saw in civilized life," said Emily Horton.

"How can you presume, Emily, to criticise the reaches of the masculine understanding? Mind your crochet work."

"Ah! Don Cigarro and Mynheer Meerschaum are

not beloved of ladies. This it is to be rivalled," rallied Dolman.

"To be sure—'Ur-rur-venge!' as they say in tragedy. Can we help pining in thought for the beaux who carry our bliss to the smoking-rooms?" said Caroline.

"I knew a man," said Bradley, "of cultivation and veracity, who told me that he once shut himself up a winter to write a book, and by the immoderate use of tobacco induced the De Quincey condition, in which he saw multitudes of faces and figures. In all other respects his mind was clear. 'When I went to bed at night after blowing a particularly heavy cloud, it was either confusedly oppressive without terror—that I never felt, though I was annoyed by wakefulness—or grand,' he said. When I knew him he had quit his pipe."

At tea Bradley and George Dolman were absent. The former had been invited by Andrew to a symposium at the gardener's lodge, and had carried his friend with him. Mr. Horton soon retired to the library to look over accounts, and Caroline, regarding her presence as superfluous, or actuated by a caprice of sportive malice, found occasion to leave Bloker and Emily alone together.

Jacob Bloker's manner in his intercourse with Miss Horton, though intent, was that of a wary man, enduring but unencroached upon by sentiment. Plainly, he was not the person to take to charcoal fumes. There would be no sadness, and little fancy in his love. His passion, if such it might be called, was of the nature of an aposteme, gradually going forward and slow to point; which breaks and leaves the system without damage. Yet Emily Horton was the object of his ambition. Whoever stood in the way of his success was an enemy, to be visited, if possible, with his vengeance. Scruples were aliens to his bosom. The rebuke administered to him by Jane Warner had offended him less than the exposure of his narrowness. That, he felt, had impeded him in the prosecution of his suit, despite his own plausible explanation; and his rancor, though cunningly cloaked, rose to a measure corresponding with the force of his desire.

"I have taken the liberty, Miss Horton, to bring you 'Antonina,' which you extolled at the Forleys;" and Bloker in drawing the book from his pocket brought with it a daguereotype. He opened the case with an expression of surprise, and then handed it gaily to his companion.

"Since it is so unexpectedly introduced, I must let you see it, and tell you its history. The lady is too pretty to be given the go-by. I found it on the floor of my room, just after one of my clerks, Garth, had left me. I put it in my pocket, meaning to give it him, and forgot."

Emily instantly recognized the picture of Jane Warner.

"You know who it is?" she asked.

"I think I do. It struck me that it might be a reminiscence of Leasowes; which place, I believe, I have incidentally referred to before. A mere conjecture, however—I know nothing."

"Shall I consider it a waif, and return it to the lady?"

"You do not perceive that would be likely to compromise me. No doubt, Garth knows where he dropped it; such things are under the eyes of the happy possessors a score of times a day. I am as much the subject of misconstruction in that quarter already as I care to be. Besides, I understand that Miss Warner is at her school."

Emily resigned the picture to Bloker, who received her steady gaze with composure.

CHAPTER XXI.

*Willie brewed a peck of malt,
And Rob and Allan came to see.*

THE temperance convictions of the worthy master of Belair were not shared by old Andrew and his guests at the lodge. Three jovial Caledonians—a Murray, a Brown, and a Carstairs—had come from town to pledge the season and each other; and the rest of mankind living and dead north of Berwick-upon-Tweed, in the potent brew of "a brither Scot." The two great levellers that make all Scotchmen equal are whiskey-punch and death; and, as might be suspected, the punch has precedence. Its empire, like that of history, embraces both the finished and the faulty.

Brown, who insisted on being called Broon, was a character deserving of a separate paragraph. The broad, brawny proportions of the man indicated a tough and lasting vitality, an overmatch for any ordinary number of tankards steaming bacchanal incense to the small hours in subterranean places. There was less alacrity of perception indicated in his massive features, rugged to the hither boundary of corrugation—though here Lavater was belied—than abounding good-nature. This, perhaps, mantled at his seventh potation, when he had clean got past the hatred of Doctor Johnson which was inspired by his fourth. It was then that the old Jacobite glories rose fresh to his view. A joke once got was kept by him for ever, as another man would keep a demonstration in mathematics. His talk, sensible and ingenious, brisk enough without dazzling, and penetrated by a vein of grotesque humor, was just the staple for a company moderately volatile and a comfortable evening; for he rarely ran his share too far below the furrows of other people, and the punch did the rest. He dealt in old editions and tall copies, and catered for the book-hunters. In a narrow shop, five minutes walk from the law courts, he accumulated musty treasures, perchance—alas! the parting—from hard-pinched scholars, of black-letter, Elzevers, and broad margins, rank and file a dingy and battered array, which he would review as he walked off his morning heaviness, always short of headache, and declaimed Greek to the rickety shelves, unconscious of the weight of superincumbent dignity. He had been known to pay a whole month's board at once, to the bewilderment of his landlady, out of the profit of a Seneca; and to replenish his wardrobe, usually somewhat seedy, with the proceeds of a bundle of old ballads. But these were rare occurrences, infrequent as a stray Nashe, or a Petrarch with an Elizabethan autograph, upon his counter, and his finances as a rule were at the ebb.

"Take a weed," said Bradley, proffering his cigar-case to Dolman, "for Andrew's tobacco is outlandish, and a pipe he is sure to offer you."

Bradley and Dolman were seated by their host in rush-bottomed chairs high and straight in the backs and running unexpectedly to bulbs. There was a blaze of crackling hickory which flashed a Christmas welcome along a hospitable extent of chimney coast. At one corner of the ingle the gardener's dog was stretched, hunting in his sleep; and at the other a kettle, just taken from the crane, steamed lazily. Upon a bright cherry table, drawn within the compass of the fire, were glasses, lemons, and a canister, the contents of which were gradually disappearing in smoke and satisfaction.

"Pit some o' this into ye—it's gude as if it was illecit," said Andrew, producing a flat stone bottle.

Bradley complied, and Dolman swallowed a thimblefull.

"Ye'll alloo me to recommend it for presairvin' the constitution, tecklin' the fog out o' the throat, and preventing the destruction of tissue," said Carstairs.

"It'll mak the bluid run into your bones," added Murray.

"The good wishes of the season!" Bradley offered, nodding from the host to the company.

"The same frae oorsels," responded Andrew over a companion tumbler.

"Gin ye'd pin it in with a pipe, it would do ye mair good than gowd. Cigars are weel enough wi' cauld drinks and licht, like wines," said Carstairs, who had been in his time a small stock farmer in Australia, and had smoked his well browned dudeen, silver set at

Sydney, after tea and damper in many a savage spot of bush.

"I wad wish nae mair o' a winter's nicht," reflected Andrew aloud, while he pared a lemon with his pruning-knife, "than a flame which pits a smile on the auld beams overhead, and brings to a mon's heart a thought o' luve as it glints frae the eyes of his tyke; thot, an' a dwam or sae to uncrinkle him, an' he may lean his bock in a beguilin' cloud o' smoke and defy the winds to blaw. Buiks some folk prefer, but it's a clever chiel of them a' that's nae a wee bit daft. They e'en took to gawrdenin'," with a profound contempt in his accent worthy of a fellow craftsman of Adam, "wi' their Cyclopedias, and sic clavers!"

"Was there ever such a brooding old bird of a Zimmerman. Wouldn't you call in the neebors? Murray! give us a sang to enliven our Ancient of Tulips at the concocting of the punch," said Brown.

"After you."

"He declines; and at your amorous ditties he can outwarble Anacreon or a man-milliner. Ah!

'How sweet a singer is in Murray lost.'"

"Nae hauding off, Brown, but come forrit," insisted Carstairs.

"I've an incipient quinsy—I couldn't turn a tune."

'Gie 'Willie Wastle,' Jamie," requested the host.

'Ye'll sair repent before I'm through," said Carstairs, as he pitched his voice to sing the wabster's spouse of Linkumdodie. They all joined in when it came to the chorus, and—

> "Sic a wife as Willie had,
> I wad nae gie a button for her!"

was accomplished in a contemptuous roar, Carstairs, as the Corypheus, snapping his fingers as he disposed of the dame in an effective variety of styles. Then Andrew sang something so very Scotch and very old, that Brown opened his ears and asked him if he had ever seen it in print. Bradley was pressed and consented on the express condition that Dolman should be excused as totally incompetent to the task. Finally, Murray, insisting that Brown should succeed him with a story, and making a stipulation to that effect with the recalcitrant bibliopole, gave a rustic strain of moorland humor.

"Now, Brown, your story!" was urged around.

An Experience of Mr. Broon.

"I had lived in the city which is honored by my present abode but few months, and being of temperate and secluded habits could not in an emergency—a case of mistaken identity you understand, no other is supposable—have referred a police magistrate to many resident acquaintances, when Christmas eve found me alone, about eleven o'clock, in my own quiet shanty and riddled horse-hair covered arm-chair, cogitating concerning myself with benevolent composure. It was an out of the way neighborhood where I lived which got little of the general racket and jollity when it was at its highest, and the festively exuberant noises of the night had subsided to the rumble of an occasional cab, the shrillness of a few sixpenny whistles, and a tipsy chorus, now and then, which died away in some distant cross street. In this state of serenity I had been sitting a full hour undisturbed, since the recovery of my wheelbarrow from a crew of drunken rogues who were trundling it into the illuminated window of the confectioner at the corner—when the outer door, the shutter of which was not yet up, was slowly opened."

Here the narrator paused, looked solemn, and seemed to lapse into thought. From this abstraction he recovered, with an effort, when Murray handed him a tumbler of punch. He continued.

"The door was opened, and a little man muffled about the throat in a travelling shawl, with a hat worn at a rakish angle and preposterously tall like the neck of a hock bottle, and with a gait which I thought totty—but that might have been due to the uncertain light—approached and saluted me. When he was seated there was a restless silence of a minute or two, during which I had time to try at an inward estimate of my unexpected guest. He had removed his hat, and I perceived it was clubbed behind with crape, but so negligently that it might have been put on by an undertaker in a maudlin state at a dissipated funeral, after a rather cheerful view of the coffin. He wore large buckskin gloves, and his clothes generally had an appearance of bagginess. What could the man be?

There was a flavor of horses about him, but he lacked the true stable personality, which *will* show itself, even on a hearse-box. I had seen similar people about theatres, who posted the bills, helped the carpenters, and played second or third ruffian, at a pinch, in murder scenes; but my companion's ways were not dramatic. Then, again, he resembled some curmudgeons I had known in the usury line. Perhaps he was one of the brotherhood of Shylock mollified by the genial influences of the season to minister of his money to struggling virtue. Something like these reflections, half serious and half humorous, sped through my mind while I regarded my visitor; and yet there was an undercurrent of cogitation. *The clothes.* I had surely seen them investing another individual. Yes, that cerulean coat—instinctively I knew it to be blue, though in my shop light I could distinguish at the distance nothing more subdued than brimstone—with its queer skirt and buttons of brass, had been part of my holiday leisure and parcel of my Sunday walks.

At length the little man addressed me in a tone dashed, I thought, with a shake of grief.

'Peleg's pegged out at last.'

'The deuce, you say!' I replied; though I had not the least idea who Peleg was. 'Where has he gone?'

'I can't tell—He's dead,' responded the little man.

'Who's Peleg—dead?' I demanded with some asperity.

'Why, Stokes; as was your porter.'

I had only known him by his last name. Occasionally he had been employed by me to wheel home my purchases from the book auctions—I dealt in miscellaneous trash in those days. I got to know him well, for he lived near my shop, and I often saw him about, chiefly in his working-day aspect. I had heard of his sickness. Report said it was fever, and a bad case, caught from the ships.

'He was a good industrious critter,' continued the little man, 'as pinched along the best he know'd how, and allus managed to keep his head above water till the time come for him to go down.'

'I can bear you out there—He was a steady, honest, person,' I said.

'He was my friend. His loss touches me, but I conker my feelings. I think of the claims of the living, and it calms me to once,' observed the little man, with an air of resignation.

'He left no family?' I said.

'There's where it is—neither chick nor child, and no relations whatsumever,' replied the little man. Then he repeated with odd deliberation and emphasis, 'When I think of the claims of the living, it calms me to once.'

There was a pause, which I did not happen to impearl with any observation, and during which the little man rectified the crape upon his hat. My queer visitor was first to break the silence.

'There's an unkimmon lot of curous things, as you wouldn't think on, in the human system, what the doctors has to learn before they can cure their feller critters.'

This, though I thought it rather a bizarre remark, was plain enough to be assented to without demur.

'And yet, they tell me, they're allus a discoverin' of something new—about diseases, and sich like.'

'I believe so,' I said, as I considered if here was not a chance to sell an odd volume of Good's Study of Medicine.

''Pears to me we can't put too high a vally on science. Some folks don't like the way the doctors cut the bodies to find out things, but *my* motter is, science before feelins.'

I considered this a sensible view, and said as much; while I thought of Jeremy Bentham, and smiled at once at the agreement and the contrast suggested by my companion. There was another pause. Again the little man led the conversation.

'Peleg's as pretty a corpse as I most ever seen—Science orter have it.'

'What are you at, man?' I exclaimed fiercely.

'Strivin' for society,' he replied, unabashed. 'I'm a kind of exeketer of Peleg's, I may say—his survivin' friend. Peleg said to me as he was a going off—Abner!—Hoopes he used to call me when he was well and hearty—Abner! said he, you have been a friend in need, which, as the rhyme said on the horn handle of a knife I owned when I was a boy, is a friend indeed; I want you to take my Sunday clothes to remember me. It was affecting, and I took them. As soon as I closed my friend's eyes I put them on—this blessed night. This coat, and west, and trowsers was his.'

Here was a revelation. The scoundrel, just from a fatal case of ship-fever, and habited in the dead man's infected garments, was trying to inveigle me by artful approaches into a collusion to sell the body to the surgeons! In my wrath I clutched a quarto Dutch dictionary heavily bound and clasped. Had I thrown it with the force and precision of which I was capable, besides making costal fractures under the swallow-tailed coat and a case for the hospital, I would have carried the canting little villain clean off his chair on to my truckle bed—the last place in the world where I wanted him, bundled about as he was with contagion. So, I turned to the window behind me, threw up the sash for air, and in another moment rushed into the street, determined to hand the science-promoting Abner into custody. Watchmen were few in those days, and being usually aged and of plethoric habits, when not crying the hour, or in chase of mocking boys around the market stalls, they were to be found asleep in their boxes. I made at speed for the nearest of these, and as I passed the neighboring bowling-alley, the door of which was ajar, I heard, 'Five minutes of twelve—one game more—set 'em up!' I found the civic functionary in two overcoats, hugging a sheet-iron stove, and nodding over the precipice of drowsiness. When I roused him he inquired, 'Where was the fire?' Finally, I got him to comprehend my purpose. But when we reached the shop Abner had gone—perhaps to weep in secret—nor have I seen him since. For several years after I took an interest in the necrological record of persons who passed out of the world according to law, but my researches were inconclusive. To return—I shut the place next day, tied a badge of mourning to the doorknob, and wafered above it for the information of the literary world a written announcement of, 'A death in the family.' Then I had it thoroughly scoured, and fumigated through the back, before I ventured in my bachelor blankets and the society of Plato and the rats."

"That *was* a queer start," remarked the New Hollander.

"Rather," said Bradley, as he tossed away the stump of his second cigar and waked Dolman.

"Verawzetce, next to sobrietee," observed Andrew, essaying to rise in a style of supernatural steadiness that he might brew another jorum of punch, "is the wale o' a' virtues."

In an hour after Bradley and Dolman had departed, the dog was the most rational member of the party, for he could stand upon his legs, although he knew no Greek, and was less of a sentimentalist than his master, or some of our modern novelists. So true is it, as Charles Reade has somewhere said with his wonted pithiness, that wherever there is drinking, there is degradation.

CHAPTER XXII.

> When icicles hang by the wall,
>   And Dick the shepherd blows his nail,
> And Tom bears logs into the hall,
>   And milk comes frozen home in pail,
> * * * * *
> When all aloud the wind doth blow,
>   And coughing drowns the parson's saw,
> And birds sit brooding in the snow,
>   And Marian's nose looks red and raw—
>
> Love's Labor's Lost

Ham.—The air bites shrewdly; it is very cold.
Hor.—It is a nipping, and an eager air.

TO the willing gleaner winter is not the famine of the year. For him, Nature drops her mask of austerity, and, like the reapers of Boaz, lets fall some handfuls of purpose. There is a blue in the sky of a winter noon, which, when the winds are still and the elastic air is full of the sun's light without his fervor, is a blessing of serenity—while at night the stars shower down through the frigid quiet. These are beams from red Arcturus, sovereign of unseen worlds; and these, that glitter on the miser's tombstone, are from prodigal Capella.

Clear and calm was the February day on which

Bradley Horton rode, muffled and alone, toward The Cedars. A dazzling vestment of snow was spread upon the fields, and the forest trees shivered in lean shadows. The sound of the chopper's axe was softened by distance to a drowsy monotone. The seal of the season was half lifted from the farm-houses, though its stillness was around them, that they might breathe the balmy air. Where the warmer South streamed along the line of sheltering stacks stood patient cattle feeding at the rack of rails, or half-leg deep in ripples of fresh forked straw. In the long reaches between the homes of men, where faint and far away was heard the house-dog's bark, the only life, perhaps, would be a rabbit scudding toward the skirt of a woods, a brace of crows keeping by successive flights in the road before, an owl blinking through bare branches at the snow, or a pinched partridge in the fence.

Up and down a long, bleak hill—bleak when the north-west blows, but basking now—and on the millpond, to the left, men are gathering ice. On the margin of an opening, where the water shows treacherously smooth, some cut the limpid blocks. Others guide them afloat with hook-tipped poles to a secure landing, when they are shoved swiftly over the frozen surface of the pond to wagons at the shore, the track being shifted when the water oozes to a slop. The faces of the men are aglow, and they fetch their breath quick, as they run, or stand in the intervals of labor and slap their numb hands with a will on shoulder and side. The very horses that draw the laden wagons scarce need the crack of the driver's whip, so eagerly do they stretch to the work. Sometimes a careless wight slips into the canal, and is drawn out jeered and dripping; or an axe drops to the bottom beyond recovery. It is a scene to-day of human industry—to-morrow, the rabbit and bunting may return to the wood-belted banks, and the muskrat take his "constitutional" undisturbed; and find nothing new but wheel-tracks and the pellicle of last night's freezing.

The wind is rising. There is a chill in the roseate sunset. And now the moon is up, and the glow in the west grows dimmer and distant. Where the road dips into shadow, Bradley starts at the sudden scraping of a fiddle to meet a bumpkin going to a country dance. Here is the stone bridge with a ghostly coping, and the skeleton willows below complaining in the blast. Yonder bulges Prospect Hill, with its lone warder of a poplar, which can be seen thirty miles out on the bay. The Cedars hospitality is a league before, but the ligaments of his steed are toughened by livery usage, and the sharpened instinct of the veteran snuffeth the manger afar off. At length the lights of the mansion twinkle palely. It is the avenue, though, what with bare branches, and evergreens half snow half sombreness, it has suffered a weird and unfamiliar change. The gates are propped wide open in a hearty carelessness of trespass. With a burst, the dogs come out and bark. The wheels stop, and ostler Sam slouches forward, and keeps the pack at bay. Then, there is light, and warmth, and welcome; fragrant Mocha and savory rashers for man, and an unaccustomed extravagance of straw and oats for beast; and sleep for both, with beatific visions sliding into the soul of Bradley, and a horrid nightmare of the Slumptown stables for the rawboned steed.

The ample, fur-lined sleigh was before The Cedars piazza, and the horses were flinging their necks impatiently.

"Charley, go hurry your sister and Mr. Horton—what keeps them? My nose is freezing—how provoking."

"I'll polish it for you, Rose."

"Away, sir! Take that for your roughness!—Here they are, at last."

"Now, Sam, give me the leather, and take off their jackets—still—still!—tuck them about my feet—G'lang! and shake out your ringlets," says Mr. Charles Bardleigh; and with a nimble show of hoofs that send the snow shooting behind, they are off.

What wonder, when the stars came out and the night wind lifted up its surly voice, that the blood congealed more and more in the pretty face of Rose Stuvesant. What wonder, too, that Master Bardleigh in his solicitude for her comfort brought a salutary glow to her cheek; or that the warm blood sallied in force to occupy the outposts of his own, challenged by the play of his cousin's eyelashes. Who among us, when we summon the frolicsome days of our youth to give up their dead, do not welcome a resurrection of merry ghosts? Ah! the current of our lives is cold and sluggish now, but something of the old torpedo thrill will answer to the touch of memory yet.

Less ebullient, perhaps, were the feelings which

cloistered in the bosoms of Bradley and Lydia—for it is a delusion of the enamored train, that their sensibility is hidden from the world. Alas! enough of the rapture will escape to betray its presence. Delightful infatuation! 'Twas a divine spark which kindled these unquenchable fires of love. Adam and Eve rejoice alone in their Eden, unconscious of another garden.

> "This visible nature, and this common world,
> Is all too narrow."

The dream of the boy was a poor prelude to this regality of the man, when the heart of the woman assents with passion. *Now*—'tis a kingdom! Concealment, the dragon, which stands between other lives, is stricken down for them by the good angel Choice.

Johnson was right when he classed rapid motion among the keenest relishes of existence; albeit it may be suspected that his conception of a sleigh-ride was not so well defined as his notion of dinners and disputations at the Mitre. What approbation he would have growled could he have sped twenty miles in the nipping air to the mingled music of bells and grating runners. And this, though the blinking "Roman" might not see a vision vouchsafed to many a cooing couple—

> "Flying between the cold moon and the earth,
> Cupid all arm'd"—

A gay time had been concerted, and as they drove from mansion to mansion repeated accessions kept the friskiness—a decorous jollity—at a high mark. Sometimes the approach of a crew of wild fellows was announced afar off by the vigorous blowing of a horn—sometimes a convivial stave was raised, with a tremendous chorus; or a party, oblivious of the hour, and gone in their cups clean into the next day, shouted inharmoniously together,

"Behold how brightly breaks the morning!"

Then, an upset group was passed, scrambling in a snow-drift, or a youthful cavalcade, masquerading as pioneers in grotesque habiliments, brandished the stumps of brooms as they sat or slipped on bare-backed mules, and bandied bacchanal jokes of a punchy flavor.

Mirth beamed from the ladies' eyes and music tripped from their tongues, ere they got to their destination, Woodlawn, the old-fashioned seat of General Cleaver, a hale and venerable hero, who, like Cæsar, gave the world his commentaries, and, like Coriolanus, objected to showing it his scars. The general, however, knew the merits of a well administered commissariat, and his granddaughter, on whom he doted, sprightly Norah McManus, presided at his luxurious board.

There was a dance, of course, and plenty of the general's choicest flip, duly heated with a polished poker kept for the purpose—hearty talk, and raillery without malice—games, and romping. The general had been on the turf, in his day, and bragged to the men of his racers. He deplored, with befitting commendation, the untimely fate of a favorite jockey, who went off triumphant, declining to break his neck short of the winning post. While distributing his fine, old-school compliments among the ladies, he recalled, in a glow of pathetic admiration, the glorious beauties in whose sunshine he had basked—"In my prime, sir—when women were appreciated." There was a supper which the shade of Lucullus need not have disdained, so urging was the terrapin, and so savory the canvas-backs, while the roasted oysters were done to a turn of the singeing of their beards. Woodlawn, in short, was redolent of feasting, and gay with an unstinted measure of fun; and when the rearward of the merry-makers departed, cocks were greeting sleepily the last watch of the night. Out upon your Types, whether civilized or savage, and though they be never so exquisitely painted from a master's palette, and allot us still, O open-handed nature, the generous roughness of our northern clime!

In the homeward drive the lovers conversed in a tone subdued just below the jingle of the sleigh-bells. Rose was sleepy, and Charley Bardleigh had enough to do in the dark to watch the fences and drifts.

"This has been a night to remember, Lydia."

"I have been very happy—and I have been merry, too."

"You put the mirth last?"

"Yes; for I felt above it."

"Darling, I understand you!" said Bradley, gently encircling her waist with his arm.

For some time they spake in soul-talk-pressures—breathings—a common consciousness.

"Bradley! I am proud because I do not belong to myself."

"My noble love, I live only for you!"

"Thank God, for this holy trust in each other!" said Lydia.

"It comes from heaven," said Bradley.

"It gushes from heaven. The very stars reflect our joy, Bradley!"

"Then let them shine, there is enough in my heart for all the constellations."

There was a pause.

"It may be, our happiness is too precious to last," reflected Lydia, pensively.

"My dear, do not cloud the future with doubts."

"I will not. It is ingratitude; and yet—"

"I beseech you, blast not our roses—Not another gloomy word," and Bradley placed his hand tenderly upon her mouth.

Putting it aside, she said, in accents of pleasure, "May I not speak, then, dear?"

"Yes, and make my ears your slaves; but not to torture them."

Judge Bardleigh, while perceiving the attachment of Bradley and his daughter, had been content to perceive it in silence—he felt sure there could be no Jessica at The Cedars. At dinner next day, a quiet family repast, he proposed to his visitor an hour or two of skating on the fish-pond. The ladies determined to go along. While they were preparing, the judge took Bradley, who had requested an interview, aside to his "den," as he styled a room specially appropriated to himself, which contained a jumble of furniture and lumber. The pretext, was a search for straps.

"Sit down, sir," said the judge, who was looking grave.

Bradley started and flushed, but managed to phrase intelligibly, if not aptly, his petition.

"I am satisfied of the earnestness of your feelings, and that they are returned," said the judge.

"I assure you, sir, 'earnestness' is a weak word to describe them."

The judge smiled, and continued.

"So be it. I would not have you say,

'—— comes in her father,
And, like the tyrannous breathing of the north,
Shakes all our buds from growing.'

But there are prudential considerations; so let us be explicit. I do not stipulate, in this matter, for wealth, but a plain sufficiency—for a man's breath is in his nostrils. I suspect you will have it, but I am not sure. I tell you frankly, that I am not so rich as I seem; for I have lived generously. While I am writing a letter, take this sheet, and put down a short statement of your expectations—and leave margin enough for the lady."

Bradley was confounded. A moment's reflection, however, showed him the justness of the demand. It was prompted by no sordid solicitude, but by the affectionate anxiety of a parent. He finished the memorandum while the judge was yet employed, and sat watching him with a new and strange interest. The stream of this man's blood, he thought, would mingle with his own. He saw a tiny hand upon the sceptre given him by that one beloved woman, and he welcomed the rival to the throne.

"It contents mè," said the judge, after an examination of the paper. "Let us return to the ladies."

CHAPTER XXIII.

I do well remember there was a ghost in the narrative, my lord.
                                                    OLD PLAY.

THEY were talking of ghosts. It was twilight, and the flickering fire made appropriate shadows on the wall—uncoerced, it observes no other compact—illustrative of the topic.

"And do you really believe in them, uncle—now, tell us?" asked Rose.

"Well, seeing is believing, I suppose," said the judge.

"So you've seen a ghost, sir?" said Rose, in a dainty little flutter.

"I saw an apparition—whist!"

"How absurd. We are impatient to hear all about it."

"Because you ladies won't keep secrets, you will have us to blab. No, no."

"Now, no more nonsense, uncle."

"It was the ghost of a government contractor."

"What's that?" asked Rose, innocently.

"A fellow who snakes lots of money out of the treasury (after bribing congressmen or a chief clerk) for pretending to do something; and always has an unsettled claim, Miss Stupid," struck in Charley Bardleigh.

"There was no smell of brimstone," said the judge.

"Pshaw! what a proser you are, uncle Bardleigh."

"It was at the junction of the A—— railroad, where I stopped overnight that I might take an early morning train. The tavern stands quite alone, and a more dismal, dissocial hostlery was never dubbed an inn."

"Delicious!" said Rose. "Was there any owls?"

"The night was too gusty for me to hear them, if there was. A spectral cat came down the chimney about two o'clock in the morning, when the gale was piping its loudest. The door would not latch, for the settling of the frame; and I had to stop several broken panes with my less voluminous garments. There was a suspicious shed just under the window, which made me a little anxious, and I secured the sash as well as I could with my pocket-knife."

"Wasn't that the place where the drover was murdered?" asked Charley, glancing at Rose.

"I don't know; it looked like a candidate for a murder—to drop the sense of the Latin primitive."

"Had you not a light all this time?" asked Rose.

"I had—a tallow dip; which burned dim.—I forgot to mention the branch of an old tree, which made mysterious noises on the outside wall, except when it seemed to groan—"

"Like a person in distress?" asked Rose.

"Very like.—I had got under the blankets, and was

speculating on the felicity afforded by fire-arms in such a situation, and wishing for even my grandfather's hanger, which he took from one of Burgoyne's men, when I heard a crash and voices in altercation. I got out of bed, and, shading the candle with my hat, passed into the entry. The draft was too strong for the feeble light, and out it went."

"What an exciting situation. Did it not send a shiver over you, uncle?"

"Yes, my dear; as I was in thin apparel. Just as my light went out, a ghastly figure, with another taper, turned an angle of the passage. It came toward me, paused, and spoke—"

"Aloud?"

"Yes, aloud; though in a cavernous voice."

"What did it say?"

"'Judge Bardleigh—as I'm a sinner!' and it trembled, visibly."

"How odd!—but that wasn't all?"

"The voice I recognized; I should never have known the appearance. It was—and here the confidence comes in—who, years before, after squandering his fortune, had slipped his bail and fled the country to escape the consequence of a forgery he had committed. He was thought to have died abroad. Worn out in body; timid in movement; care-stricken in aspect; he stood before me a suppliant for silence. He had travelled, in a restless and profitless career, through many lands, and here, at last, near the graves of his ancestors, he was hiding, yet afraid to linger, and almost penniless. I spared him what aid I could, and we parted."

"And there was no ghost, after all."

"Only the ghost of the man's former self. Arabs on the plain, my Pekuah! are more dreadful than all the Pharaohs in the pyramid."

"If you want my opinion, uncle Bardleigh, the story is not in the least interesting."

"Judge! you're a great scholard, and knows fluxions as I've heern say, but I reckon a raël sperit would top-sawyer you."

They all started at the utterance of this unexpected impeachment.

"O! it's you, Uncle Steve—How did you come?"

"Wal, judge," explained the oracular Trencher, "I stopped to tell you I found that pointer pup you lost, out in the woods, pesky bad with the 'stemper, and I was showed to the door, but, your folks being a argyin like, you didn't hear me knock, so I opened the door, walked in and sot down, thinkin' I'd wait a spell till you got through."

"If the pup's as much obliged to you as I am, Uncle Steve, he's a grateful dog. I'll send for him to-morrow."

"There was high doins down our way last night. They unhung nearly all the gates, and carried some of them clean off. Old marm Fougeroy found Brady's tied to her cow this morning, and that's more'n two miles off. Brady had just got it as I come along, and was a drivin' spikes over the hinges. He was 'tarnal mad—says they stole the latch, and if he can find out who it was he'll have them up before the grand jury."

"Good people, I hope your hands are innocent of this

grave offence—My folks, you see, were on a frolic last night, Uncle Steve," said the judge.

"Went nary gate but our own, which was a righteous one," answered Charley.

"I guess it was some of them rapscallions from Bullfrog. They don't stop at nothing ornery. Last winter they bored a hole clean through the weather-boarding at Gabriel Wamblebees, and drawed off all the apple-jack in his barrel. Wal, I guess I must be a goin'. Its desp'rate cold to-night."

"I'll see you out, Uncle Steve," said the judge, mirthfully, in view of the parting intimation.

That winter's week at The Cedars, alas! was too soon spent, and Bradley bade the family good-bye. He left, not as a lover trembling with uncertainty, but with store of hope, and just enough melancholy to make it piquant. The judge mounted his horse to look at his cattle, some of the favorite Devons he was feeding into prodigies of tallow, and rode with his guest a few fields length.

"Show your grit, my boy—and God bless you!" was his benediction.

18*

CHAPTER XXIV.

*This is a notable couple—and have met
But for some secret knavery.*—OLD PLAY.

THE Great Republic has produced engineers whose works in magnitude and magnificence have not been anywhere surpassed in modern times; and it is in no spirit of unfairness toward other Americans, of perhaps equal merit, that the names and achievements of Serrell, Ellet, Latrobe, and Meigs, are cited to establish the assertion.

Bradley Horton was proud to be a fellow-laborer of these. There was certainly no fame to be got out of the Tecumseh bridge, his initial undertaking. The *Tecumseh Tomahawk*, indeed, while it was yet only a plan, promised that it should prove "a stately structure, unostentatiously graceful, and far more useful than Cleopatra's Needle," and that it would "rise like an exhalation;" but so wide is the world, even the plunges of the *Tomahawk* scarcely left a shiver on the surface of human affairs.

Tecumseh was delightfully situated among breezy hills, and was a lovely place to be lazy in on a long summer's day; for, billiards left behind, you might smoke on some cool lawn with cultivated men, or eat raspberries and ice-cream in a honey-suckled piazza with charming women in white, who could gallant fans with the love-inspiring brunettes of Castile. A crowd was never known in the place except during court week, and at the agricultural fair. The nearest approach to it was upon the arrival of the evening train, when a group of worthy burghers might be found assembled at each of the two hotels, awaiting the news and commenting upon current affairs. Nobody had been hanged at Tecumseh in a score of years, and included among its notable inhabitants was the tallest man in the county. But its press was the glory of the town. This consisted of two weekly newspapers, the *Tomahawk* and the *Torch*, the first of which was Republican and the last Democratic, and they were edited respectively by Mr. Joab Slunk and Doctor Scammony.

Joab Slunk was a semi-educated writer and roaring politician, in a state of perpetual incandescence, who strove to be venomous, and usually succeeded in being vulgar. Yet he had once or twice achieved the expensive dignity of libel. He was a square, hollow-chested man, who walked with a shuffling stoop, characteristic of his moral conduct. There was something insalubrious in his whole aspect, especially in his complexion, which was the color of inferior putty. Yet no god of all who ruled the middle air from high Olympus, when the quaking sphere answered his nod, could have surpassed in self-esteem the cadaverous editor of the *Tomahawk*.

It was opposite the office of the *Tomahawk* that Bradley one day met Bartimeus Scroggs and Mordecai Dabster, who walked with him to the bridge.

"Ah! 'tis a bridge of size, I see," said Dabster, nudging Scroggs at the idiotic emphasis, who gravely asked him what he wanted.

"I've just bought the mosquito meadows, and I mean to have them drained to promote the health of the town," remarked Scroggs.

"It is a most benevolent project, and will justly entitle you to be considered a public benefactor," replied Bradley.

"Why, yes, I expect to add some reputation of that kind to the undeserved stock I have already acquired."

"And it is a stock in trade you always have a market for," remarked Dabster.

"I will not deny that I have sometimes found money in it, my friends, but I desire only the recompense in my own bosom, and the approbation of the spirit world," said Scroggs.

"The draining you propose is the more meritorious that it will be a costly labor," observed Bradley.

"O, I only mean to pay my share of the expense. We will employ—I will make it worth your while to consider this confidential—a little innocent artifice to excite the public spirit of the place."

"Spotted fever with black tongue—twig, my ace of spades?" added Dabster.

Bradley confessed himself unable to comprehend the explanation.

"We shall take the liberty," continued Scroggs, "to

demonstrate the extreme unhealthiness of the meadows by examples of an epidemic. We have several cases of bilious-remittent, and an African just recovering of small-pox. The latter is horribly speckled, and was procured with some trouble by Dabster, who is about to operate more largely in our vineyard of philanthropic politics. These will be attacked at the same time, and with great violence. We have also a subject in molasses, who was drowned and is much swollen, for a post-mortem. The unfortunate deceased was one of your laborers, just arrived when taken with a congestive chill, and Doctor Scammony will examine the body. Slunk and Scammony are both with us, and will sound an alarm, terrify the people, and secure an appropriation for our project from the town commissioners. They *had* the disease at Sparta, only twelve miles off, you know, a few weeks since. Fraud, my dear sir, is pious when it promotes the welfare of our fellow-creatures; and as to them sickly meadows, they are running down fast to cattails, and the croak of the very frogs is agueish."

Bartimeus Scroggs failed aforetime to get the nomination for Congress which he sought; and thus it was. After many ballottings in the convention he lacked but two votes of a majority over his two competitors. One of these retired and carried his support to the other, Orator Puffin. Three of his voters, however, held off. To catch these patriots, Scroggs cast baited hooks. The night of final trial arrived, and might have brought triumph to Bartimeus but for an unforeseen occurrence. There was a famous medium in town, who pretended to heal the halt, withered, and infirm. This medium was originally influenced by the spirit of the celebrated Fordyce, and took to the line of fevers. In course of time (speaking humanly, and not in the language of the "spheres") Fordyce introduced him to a college of departed surgeons, willing to give their skill sublunary airings on demand. Their manipulations through the medium required an assistant in the flesh, and Scroggs volunteered to act the part. On the night which was to establish or disappoint his personal aspirations, assured that the clinical business would be speedily over, he smiled benignly from a platform the fattest of his smiles upon the assembled crutchees, some of whom he expected to be his constituents. Now, the healing medium, made merry with choice spirits of the earth, failed to appear at the appointed hour. As time lapsed, the assistant grew fidgetty and the patients mutinous. Messengers were in vain. So were assuasive explanations; the cripples had come to be healed, and found no benefit in the words of Bartimeus. One, with a wooden leg, considered them "gammon." The time for the meeting of the convention was already past, there was but one way of exit, and Scroggs charged upon the cripples. Desperate, they formed to repel him. The most determined courage was useless against such an array. Then the cripples charged to the last crutch, and beat him back. Unavailingly he pleaded the importance of his engagement. The man with the wooden leg, who had been constituted leader, was an unnaturalized citizen, and scorned the appeal. While Scroggs was thus imprisoned, Puffin insidiously circulated a report that he had thrown up the contest. The three withholders became alarmed. In another half hour they were open to conviction; and fifteen minutes afterward, in the conscientious discharge of their duty, they voted for the Orator.

And Bartimeus Scroggs did not go to Congress— to its detriment. But the public anguish at his defeat was assuaged by the selection of Puffin, who was altogether as radical, and who could emit a great deal of facile and ferocious rhetoric at short notice. He was a fine accountant, and could tell blindfolded how many eggs any department nest contained, and, with prophetic discernment, what they would hatch, whether old blunderbusses, or the mounting of a cavalry regiment; and he probably smelt their interiors. Not that Puffin was corrupt. On the contrary he was incorruptible. All his constituents were incorruptible. Also his clients—when they paid. His legislative career was brilliant; at least, the newspaper correspondents telegraphed and wrote as much, and he told them so. Ah! very pleasant are our recollections of Puffin flitting from camp to camp to inspirit the dejected soldiers with his furious eloquence. Perhaps it was this peripatetic patriotism which induced some to describe him as a frothy demagogue. But these were his envious enemies. Could they have made speeches equal to Puffin's, they would have made them at the cannon's mouth.

CHAPTER XXV.

*The evening darkness gathers round
By virtue's holiest powers attended.*—WORDSWORTH.

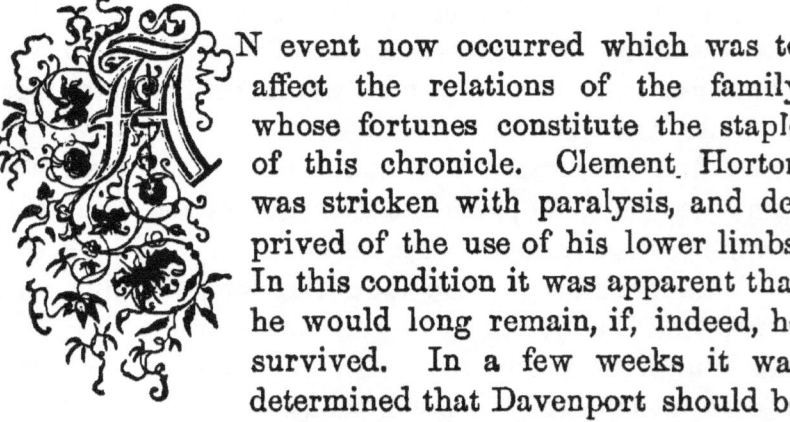

AN event now occurred which was to affect the relations of the family whose fortunes constitute the staple of this chronicle. Clement Horton was stricken with paralysis, and deprived of the use of his lower limbs. In this condition it was apparent that he would long remain, if, indeed, he survived. In a few weeks it was determined that Davenport should be entrusted to accomplish the gradual settlement of the city business, which was become narrowed of late, and that Bradley should take charge of affairs at Brentlands. The year's falling leaves, the sudden death of a young bridegroom, or the fruit of hope ashes on the lips of the fever-stricken, do not moralize you better of the vanity of earthly things than the evolation from the world of a great business house. Poor Davenport had a melancholy time of it dissecting his own nerves.

As a nebula is resolved by a telescope into lights in the firmament, so do the holy affections of woman, which thitherto showed only in the milder guise of grace and gentleness, appear at the summons of suffering. No wounds are too ghastly, no effluvium is too noisome, no vigils are too exacting, no offices are too humble. Full of supernal love, she bares a chaste breast in holy bounty! To such a ministress the foul breath of the hospital is more salubrious than are odors of the conservatory to the soulless votary of fashion. From such, sweet influences of speech and smile are shed, and a fragrance is diffused throughout human lives, and seed, perchance, sown to blossom in eternity. It is thus woman sympathizes with the languishing stranger by ten thousand pallets. How various is her sway! She conquers by beautiful simplicity on the threshing-floor of Boaz, and by slaughter in Shushan the palace; the poet of Olney sings at her bidding, and the triumvir of Philippi softens at her wiles; and many a shattered soldier has been summoned by the Great Commander from a blessed vision of alleviation here, to make her a fame in heaven. But this is a digression.

Emily was now become the light of Clement Horton's little orbit. The nursing daughter was queenly with patience. There was no vulgar bustle in her alacrity—her voice, like Cordelia's,

>—— was ever soft,
>Gentle and low—an excellent thing in woman.

Her smile was ever sweetest when she was truest to her task. Her manner dignified the meanest occupation; it was the motion of music without the sound. And you did not feel it extravagant to think that here was some of the same devotion by which in the Roman dungeon Nature triumphed in the reverse of her decree.

Good Father Tryon often brought his cheerful consolations. In truth, they were quaint parcels; a scrap of news with a moral, a flash of gallantry, a rare thought from Baxter, a reminiscence of adventure, a familiar but unblunted similitude from the "prince of dreamers," or something tougher fashioned on the anvil of a puritan divine, who was intolerant of the shapings of strange theological hammermen. At these visits not a few projects fraught with good for others were conceived; for Christian virtue purgeth sickness of its selfishness. Davenport sometimes chanced to encounter the worthy missionary, whom he regarded with jealous aversion as an intruder in the house of Horton, and he came at last flatly to designate him a jesuit.

CHAPTER XXVI.

To be a husbandman is but a retreat from the city; to be a philosopher, from the world; or rather, a retreat from the world as it is man's, into the world as it is God's. But since nature denies to most men the capacity or appetite, and fortune allows but to a very few the opportunities or possibility of applying themselves wholly to philosophy, the best mixture of human affairs that we can make are the employments of a country life.—COWLEY.

AT Brentlands Bradley donned a suit of homespun, and entered with alacrity upon his newly devolved duties. He rose before day, and when its work was ended made up his accounts by candlelight, read, smoked his cob pipe, and went to bed at nine. There was husking of corn, and putting in of wheat—between one and two hundred acres of each—and the gathering of an abundant crop of potatoes; besides the hauling, feeding, repairing, and numerous other labors incident to the conduct of a large landed property. He placed the operations, great and small, upon the basis of system. He rated his laborers, by a vigilant inspection, at their just value, and discharged the idle and worthless. No implement was allowed to be left in the field when the occasion for it was past. If a team was wanted, no horse lacked a shoe nor wagon-wheel required a tightening of its tire. The cattle were properly groomed, and the stables kept clean, light, and comfortable. Broken fences were restored, and drains cleared of obstruction. Receptacles were made for the fertilizing ooze of stall and stock-yard. He read the best agricultural books, and strove to keep fully up with his work, setting his crops seasonably. Thus forward, he began the year on a level with his undertaking, and resolved that no grass should grow in his middles. The old farmers among his neighbors, who plodded in the routine of their grandfathers, soon ceased to laugh, though they continued to criticise, reluctantly admitted him to be a man with a purpose, and, when their prophecies of crop failures to his discomfiture were falsified, accounted for the results by attributing them to happy accidents.

The labors, various and shifting as the aspects of the seasons, rarely irksome, were often exhilarating in the fresh air and beneath the free sky. The bronzed industry of the fields which is familiar with the elements, when short of "drudgery," imparts a sense of lightness and freedom; though the overworked rustic may be as lumpish as the clod he turns. Orchard, garden, nursery, plantation, meadow, and tillage, exacting timely thought and skill, crowned the year with delights. Fresh from the spray might be plucked at their periods,

"The blushing apricot, and woolly peach,"

a luscious fruitage between the sprightly cherry and the pear of mild and tender flesh. Nor was the ear unsatisfied where the mocking-bird trilled its changeful notes, the partridge, frighted by the trespasser's foot, rose from its grassy nest with sudden whirring, or the pheasant drummed in the wood.

George Dolman and Max Heyhurst came down, to encourage Bradley and have some shooting. Doctor Pledget was to have accompanied them, but, at the last moment, he consulted his barometer, predicted snow, and staid at home. Heyhurst was an artist, and painted the game which he shot. They were genial fellows, electric with good feeling, who honored the hearty welcome which was given them.

The doctor missed of it when he foretold the weather in white, and after a couple of days of rain and half a gale of wind, a clear-shining sun gladdened the landscape. The nice and appreciating eye of Max Heyhurst was delighted by the rural picture. The sky was in color a hazy silver at the horizon, which gradually deepened to a soft blue overhead. The sunrises were fine, but in the more advanced morning the charms of the prospect culminated. Brentlands was high ground, and the surrounding country for miles lay in gentle slopes below it—a mosaic of green wheat fields, and brown squares with their long files of maize shocks in symmetrical array, the succession being picturesquely broken by belts of nearly naked timber. Looking toward the east, the shadows of distant cattle showed on the slanting umber-tinted pastures, as they grazed. A mill-pond, near to, responded to every breeze with sparkling fluctuations. Half hid in clumps of evergreens, or standing boldly out on eminences, the mansions and farm-houses gave a human interest to the scenery; here and there a column of smoke from their chimnies rising vertical and sluggish. A faint mist hung over the course of the remote river, and settled in a purple film upon its further highlands. At sunset, above the cold and crimsoned west, the evening star, brighter than the goddess risen from her yeast of waves, swam up the heaven to meet the Night; oldest of all—not voiceless now as when she knew

"—— the secrets of the worlds unmade."

Bradley and Dolman stood chatting, while Max sketched a cornfield scene in November. There were the nearest huskers pegging away among the rustling stalks—that almost rustled on the sheet—and tossing the liberated ears into the convenient heap of maize. Further on, a group paused at their labor to watch the chase of a rabbit, which a frisking dog had started from its lair. Slow oxen drew cribward the loaded carts. A flock of birds flitted low for forage from a background of brambles.

A red-whiskered man, in a slouched hat and dirty drab overcoat, drove up in a sulky, and contemplated the party with considerable interest.

"Surveyin'?"

"Yes, sir—the landscape."

"What mought that be?"

"Field and wood."

The red-whiskered man scratched his head in unrelieved perplexity.

"Taking the bearins' like, I s'pose; though I never

seen it done this way before. Must be a new how of cipherin' it out.—Mr. Horton, I summons you to appear at Squire Flicker's office, at Jericho, next Saturday afternoon."

Having delivered himself of the latter clause with official promptitude, the constable imparted briefly the particulars of the suit, dispensed a general valediction, and drove away.

It was a suit for an old debt, which was unknown to Bradley. At the appointed time the friends made their appearance at the tribunal of the squire. The temple of justice was a shoemaker's shop, furnished with a few waxy chairs, a hot stove, and an offensive atmosphere, scented with new boots and the village's muggy muslin in impartial proportions. The male adults of Jericho, who occupied the counter, drawled neighborhood gossip to each other, and spat tobacco juice. Behind the counter, Squire Flicker consulted the "Magistrate's Guide," and delivered weighty judgments in the law—usually for the plaintiffs.

Several cases preceded Snap *versus* Horton on the docket, and Max Heyhurst availed himself of the delay to sketch the court-room and its inmates. This proceeding at length attracted the notice of the squire, as possibly an intentional slight upon the dignity of the magistratic character.

"What's that man a doing of?" he asked the constable.

"Makin' pictures. Got you there, Squire—natural as life."

"What! *me*—in open court? This must be stopped.

Young man! who pays you for taking other people's portraits?"

The question, put with stilted severity, brought Max's pencil to a stand-still, and directed the curious eyes of the audience upon him; but it nowise disconcerted him.

"I've had, sir, a prodigality of money from the illustrated journals. They rely upon my pictures to save their dull pages from deserved damnation."

"Be cautious, young man!" interrupted the squire, "or I shall be obliged to put the statue against profane swearing in force."

"May it please the court, I was only replying to its question—"

"Proceed," said the squire, with dignity, waving his hand.

"Latterly, then, I have been taking heads for a phrenological publication—was at Bedloe's Island last week and got Boggs, the pirate. I am also, at present, on a comic almanac."

This was too much. The squire might almost doubt his hearing. He, the duly commissioned representative of Justice, while holding the sovereign scales, to be drawn for a comic almanac, and prejudiced in his place before assembled Jericho!

"Look here, mister! I've no doubt I might hold you for a constructive libel, and I advise you, in my infra-judicial capacity, to put them things up in that portmantel."

Perhaps it was lucky for the delineator that, just then, an excited individual burst into the court-room with the announcement that, "Pete Whitecar was going to run Black Duke agin the stranger's chestnut for ten dollars and the whiskey, right away!" There was a general scattering of the audience to see the sport. The squire was curious, but the man did not prevail at once over the magistrate. "If it's a horse-race," he remarked, detaining the reluctant constable, who had laid a bet, "it's clearly against the law; but if it's only a trial of speed, I'll go and look at it." And the conscientious Flicker adjourned the court and the case.

Max Heyhurst had, in his time, made a happy emendation of Shakespeare, and half a tragedy on Sejanus; had expanded a Greek fable into a pastoral of considerable dimensions, and written impassioned lyrics for the magazines, which, though the firiest stanzas would be sometimes omitted in a pressure of matter, were pronounced by the newspaper critics uncommonly fine specimens of the Sapphic style.

"And you read Spenser, Horton?" he said, as he disengaged a London octavo which was sandwiched between the "Farmer's Cyclopedia" and "Youatt on the Horse."

"Yes."

"No poem in the language contains so much gorgeous imagery as the 'Faerie Queene.' There is in it exquisite delicacy of characterization, tenderness, vivacity, learning, imposing and ever-shifting movement. It is the apotheosis of Virtue by Genius. How the poet hives into his own sweet measure the fable of antiquity, as in the Descent of Night into Hell—how triumphant is his fancy in the enchanted Castle of Busyrane, the House of Pride, and the Temple of Venus!"

"Is it not too long?" asked Bradley.

"Only, as Shakespeare is in his entirety, for the dull and lazy—school exercises and spouting clubs. Thank Heaven! there are some things in the world—Paradise Lost, Cymbeline, and the Faerie Queene—that the *Morning Advertiser* cannot make a synopsis of. Two centuries and a half ago people read books."

"Do you think the 'Faerie Queene' was ever popular reading, like the dramatic poetry of that time?"

"Why, a just discrimination is seldom exercised by cotemporáries. 'Tis probable Marlowe had, in the sixteenth century, a higher rate than Chapman or Ford—that Heywood was more popular than John Fletcher. But of the 'Faerie Queene.' It was written in an age through which the marvels of discovery were being filtered—marvels of enchantment, peril, and fabulous magnificence. Though there remained beneath the surface of society a taint of the old savagery, the staple of chivalric poetry was woven into the common talk of ladies and cavaliers. A new world had been found. There was a grand uncertainty to be attempted by adventure, which allured alike the heroic, the avaricious, and the prodigal. They who listened eagerly to Raleigh's stories of wondrous wiles, and golden cities embosomed in Amazonian forests, and guarded by warlike women, might well hail a higher and purer romance in the encounters for distressed virtue of the

Redcrosse Knight and Prince Arthur with dragons, giants, and enchanters."

"I wish the author of the 'Fall of Rome' would reproduce for us 'the city and the gods' of the reign of 'Gloriana.'"

"A thoughtful face, delicate in its lines, and but little shorter than Sir Walter's; mild, full eyes, and an amiable mouth—O for photographs of that grand Elizabethan choir who drank of the true fountains of Parnassus!" pondered Heyhurst.

"Well, time composes all things. Perhaps there was one, in his day, to regard the poet, where a thousand fawned upon Leicester, and *he* survives as the ambitious villain of a romance," said Bradley.

"Yes.

> 'Pour out for the Poet!
> The Wine of the Immortals
> Forbids him to die!'

Edmund Spenser is more interesting to me in the society of Sidney at Penshurst,

> 'Beneath the broad beech, and the chesnut shade;'

or pacing with Raleigh the banks of Mulla, and discussing the moral virtues, than Robert Dudley aspiring to a throne.—Dryden—Pope—Swift—Churchill."

"Why, with charlatanry and corruption abounding, does not the modern muse produce satire?"

"Because," replied Max, "it takes qualities to make a satirical poet which are rarely found combined—a keen sense of the ludicrous, much self-esteem and capacity of resentment, quickness to perceive frailties of character (which may be quickened by disappointment), thorough mastery of words, the requisite inspiration, and a liver complaint."

"Nay, after all, I think the world has mended," said Bradley.

"Thousands of sewing women coining their souls to save their bodies from starvation—O! Daughters of Zion! they might be Marys and Joannas at the sepulchre of your Lord—while partisan plunderers and shoddy seigniors swarm and swell from their native ooze, like the filthy frogs of old Egypt—and mended?"

"Take England," continued Bradley. "Bacon would not have fingered bribes in Walpole's time, corrupt as it was, and Walpole would not now be tolerated a single day. Read Macaulay. Behold his statesmen, courtiers, and soldiers,

'Calm, thinking villains, whom no faith could fix.'

What a church it was when men were made prelates by kings' mistresses! Where the religion of a nation is surface-faith, be sure the devil digests its politics."

CHAPTER XXVII.

Here feel we not the penalty of Adam,
The seasons' difference; as, the icy fang,
And churlish chiding of the winter's wind,
Which when it bites, and blows upon my body,
Even till I shrink with cold, I smile, and say,
This is no flattery——
As You Like It.

ONE day remained to the visitors, and they determined to enjoy it. There were river coves celebrated for the resort of ducks, that came to feed in the sedge, and host and guests resolved themselves into a fowling party. A light wagon was at the door long before day, and they were rattled off over the frozen road, careless of the cold which tingled in their advancing faces. Arrived at the river, they found a boat, in which they ferried across it. There was then a walk of some miles along the shore to the shooting ground. Bradley laved his face with whiskey, and poured it upon his chest, knowing its freshening efficacy when thus employed. Max took the comfort internally. Dolman carried a supply of cold tea, which Heyhurst insisted was a bequest of choice catnip from his grandmother.

They kept on at a steady pace, losing the dogs in the darkness, and then recovering them—slipping into a ditch, or stumbling at a log, and reached the first of the feeding-grounds about daybreak. Laying perdu behind a screen of brush, they awaited in the eager air the approach of the birds, which were yet beyond shot. At length the ducks came circling shoreward, urging the water before them gracefully in dimples. The almost simultaneous reports of a half dozen barrels invade the quiet, and are prolonged in echoes. The dogs plunge to their work and bring the game, which they deposit with a shake of spray. The birds, at last, are become cautious—will not be toled—and the sportsmen try another cove.

Having dined at a farm-house, with less sumptuousness than appetite, on pickled pork, sauer kraut, and pumpkin pie, they reposed under the lee of a settle before the fire, and while Bradley got consolation from his pipe and the fumes of shredded cavendish, the daintier artist soothed himself with an Havana. Dolman found on the top of the tall clock case a tattered volume of the Spectator, and took a stately turn in Queen Anne's London with worthy Sir Roger. The dogs slept on the hearth, or dodged the sputtering sparks of a fresh hickory log.

"We don't do this every day, Max," said Bradley.

"For which let us be thankful. Who invented fermented cabbage, George Dolman?"

"Hang it, don't bother!—the 'Flying Dutchman,' I suppose."

"No, George Dolman, it was not that marine Hollander. No man given to bellowing nautical commands through a speaking-trumpet could have invented fermented cabbage. 'Twas a rural patriarch, methinks, with aspirations 'for the welfare of his species. He would have made a nobby radical."

"Nice stuff to fossilise a man. I've actually been reading the same page twice without consciousness," said Dolman.

"Do you claim that for an uncommon experience? I find the reading of some pages once sufficient to establish the phenomenon," said Max.

"A truce to quibbling, and let's tramp."

"Agreed:

> 'My boat is on the shore,
> And my bark is on the sea;
> But, before I go, Tom Moore,
> Here's a double health to thee!'"

They added several to the count of birds in their game bags by shooting over a long reach of shore. It was after nightfall when they came to the boat, and pitch-dark with a passing snow squall, from which the flakes fell big and spiteful.

"They come down like quarter-dollars and stick closer—George Dolman! scrape the slush off that seat if you are a compassionate man."

They turned the boat's bow outward, and, bending to the oars, sent her steadily on her blind course. After some minutes of rowing, Bradley's heavy boot, slipping at the stroke, displaced a plug in the bottom of the boat, and the water came gurgling in. They groped for the plug unsuccessfully, and not until the boat was a third filled did they succeed in stopping the leak with a wad of handkerchiefs. Luckily, when they were about to divest themselves of their heavier garments as an act of precaution, the sky lightened, and they saw the shore before them some thirty yards distant. Bradley, who knew the water to be shallow, jumped overboard. Dolman, perceiving him wade, followed, in a plunge to the waist.

"Come on, Max! its only three feet, and a sandy bottom," shouted Bradley.

"Deuce take the soundings! I am subject to cramp. Find the painter and pull me in, and I'll share the salvage."

"The chain's padlocked ashore—Good-bye."

"Here's Dolman's teapot: I invoke the heathen, as he reveres his lares, to return!"

"George, let's try to pull the old tub in."

"Reason triumphant at last over madness and folly. It always is—in novels. No Shallott business to-night!"

There was a shanty at the landing, with a rude fireplace and plenty of drift-wood, but matches and fowling-pieces were alike wet, so they walked to the nearest house, about a mile distant, to the unmusical flapping of their soaked and stiffening garments. Nor was their trouble ended here, for the family, a laborer's, was absent, and the only vestige of fire was a solitary coal which they disentombed in much sifting from the ashes. It was a promise of flame, but an illusory one. They blew it again and again, around the hearth, to the tantalizing verge of ignition, but when they ceased to puff, the dull glow retreated toward the core in a very coquettish manner. Thus foiled, they trudged another mile to the farm-house where the wagon awaited them, shed their last shiver at the blaze of the kitchen fire, and, fortified by a good supper, drove to Brentlands.

CHAPTER XXVIII.

In the morning he rose with new hope, in the evening applauded his own diligence, and in the night slept sound after his fatigue. He met a thousand amusements which beguiled his labour, and diversified his thoughts. He discerned the various instincts of animals and properties of plants, and found the place replete with wonders.—RASSELAS.

THE large cultivator never hybernates. The first two months of the year are his period of preparation for the vernal activity. As the true farmer leads his work, and aims not so much at extent of cultivation as quality, being ambitious of a progressive increase of the products of his land, he gets in timely readiness the implements and appliances of a thorough tillage. He knows that to deserve a large crop from his field, he must generously manure it—plough, harrow, and roll it well. In no pursuit is system more important than in agriculture. The dullest tiller perceives and perverts this truth when he obstinately refuses to depart from the traditions and practice of his ancestors, scoffing at the lights of science as mere will o' the wisps.

The January and February work at Brentlands was

various, and its supervision imparted to Bradley the zest of a novel employment, which exacted healthy exertion of mind and body. Early on the nipping winter mornings he would repair to the hillside woods with his gang of choppers. A sufficient space was soon scooped out of the snow, and a brisk fire built to warm his unexercised blood—that of his sturdy axemen getting its caloric from the swinging of their tools. How cheerily rang the strokes across the frozen landscape, while the chips flew from the widening notch, or the iron wedge was driven slow along the resisting fibres! It was lighter work with the windfallen limbs, which had laid long a seasoning. Some of these were gone far toward mould, to feed those children of the wood, the ferns and mosses. There was hidden treasure in the decay; the fragrance of the arbutus, the scarlet of the pimpernel, and other "fairest flowers," worthy to have sweetened the "sad grave" of Fidele. Perhaps such a sapless log, half buried in the soil, would be the mansion of a tortoise, or the dormitory of a luckless family of snakes. Then the slow oxen, their chests frosted with their breath, drew the logs to the wagon road, in awkward turnings to clear the stumps, while the drivers shouted, and a convocation of critical crows screamed tantalizing allusions from the distant tree-tops, and mocking echoes of the imperative "haw—haw!"

There was field-work in the open spells of winter—ploughing in the drier, loamy soil, and drain-making in a piece of stiff clay, preparatory to its being broken up. Bradley sunk his drains below the reach of plant roots and the sub-soil level, knowing that with a good tilth and favoring heavens his future wheat and clover would not lack food. And there was work when storms beat through the dark days, in shed and shop—fashioning and boring fence-posts, making gates, mending and oiling harness, putting implements in order, and baling hay. The meat-house and garden frames demanded a share of attention. An important part of the superintendence at this season was that directed to the care of the stock—the apportionment of the messes, whether dry or succulent, the cleaning, bedding, and exercising of the cattle. The effects of diet were to be watched, and ailments doctored. Idle currycombs wedged aside, masses of stamped, fermenting dung in the stallways, and waste from rack and mess-box, were held to be undesirable at Brentlands.

March came like a bland guest bound to a banquet. On the twelfth of the month the red spurs of the rose were unfolding to leaves, and Bradley turned the first spadeful in his garden. A few bright, warm days followed, like a mellow slice of later May, and were sandwiched between frosty edges. An ample border facing the south was prepared, and appropriate seed put in; and pulse and radishes were planted. As Bradley placed the hardy legumes, he recollected how a crew of bold British voyagers, wrecked in their little seventeenth century ship on the strand of Baffins Bay, were rescued by the green sprouts of a handful of peas, which they had sown in that unfruitful soil, from slow suffering and death by scurvy. He took upon himself a proxy-ship of gratitude for Neptune, and covered them nightly in their bed with forkings of straw. It was pleasant, ruminating labor to cut the dead wood from the garden fruit trees, and trim the useless canes from the berry bushes—to dig in an apt compost at their roots, or to spread the strawberry spaces with tan. The delved earth gave its tribute of incense, for company there was the westering sun, and a stray bee furnished the music.

It is a breezeless morning, and they are sowing cloverseed. The wheat is a little winter-killed, and it is intended, after sowing the grass-seed, to run a light harrow upon and roll it, to promote tillering. Bradley and a farmer-neighbor are together in the field, and a curious fox, squat, is a safe space off observing them. The farmer picks up an arrowhead.

"This saved pretty considerable farm-work and tradin' round in the old times," he said.

"It tells as full a history, where there was little to be told, as the Pyramids, or the buried coins of Greece," remarked Bradley.

"It belonged to the natives. They was strange critters. Didn't do much tailorin', and wasn't liable to dyspepsy, I reckon. Somehow, when I get to thinking, I like to moralize on such subjects; they make common things look like vanities."

"Yonder sits one of the natives."

"Rot the pesky fox! I've lost two turkies this spring by them varmints. There's natural simplicity with lamb's wool in its teeth! If I had a gun I should stipelate for some of that innocence."

To ensure a future supply of the best fence-posts, a plantation of the yellow locust was made. Two acres were appropriated to it. The saplings, two years old from the seed, were taken from the nursery drills and placed twelve feet apart each way. These were in fifteen years more to become timber. Birds would sing and nest in their branches, and their tressed blossoms sweeten succeeding Mays. Lovers might haunt them, and tender whispers undersigh the breeze. Satiated passion, or meek penitence might be familiar with their dim evening paths. In their noontide shade Truth might bless some votary with a happier inspiration than that which sanctified the grove at old Dodona.

Tom Hance was the herdsman. He was loosely put together, and long drawn out. It might have been a disordered liver, but Tom Hance was a dismal man. In the very relish of his eating, an undertaker could have borrowed funereal graces from his face—transformed into elegy, he would have served a generation of decedents. Tom, under much provocation, displayed little weaknesses of temper that required rebuke, such as persuading perverse cattle with pitchforks. Otherwise he was not a bad-natured fellow. Yet he had but a single associate and friend, a mule; and a more vicious mule, perhaps, never moved hoof in a Mexican pack-train. It was the practice of this diabolical quadruped to make for every one else who entered the field, and, taking his chance, plant himself for the assault, which was accomplished in one movement, beyond the evolutions of military manuals, by dipping the head and sending up the hind heels with unexpected celerity. A belief prevailed among the hands that the creature was possessed. If they laid their clothes within his reach he would tear them, and they never ventured near him without a supply of stones.

Some of the cattle were breachy, and when alone might not be restrained by the stoutest worm-fence. As the corn land surrounded the pasture, it was necessary to overlook them all the time. Wherever Tom was, and however, standing, walking, or recumbent, Badger was close by. If Tom, with his back against a fence-stake, smoked his pipe and watched the fleecy fragments of scud in the blue sky, Badger might be seen a few yards distant, still and grave, regarding him with an almost human interest. Of all our domestic animals, the mule loves best to tumble and roll, and Badger was clumsily sportive in this habit; but he would break off instantly if Tom moved, and follow him. The brute would stoop his muzzle over the man and fondle his face or outstretched hand. He would accompany Tom to meals, leaping fences in the way, and meekly—as if conscious of the trespass, and craving sufferance—wait for him at the kitchen door. Indeed, a marked amelioration became apparent in the animal's entire character. He would probably have kicked an unsuspecting person still, but rather in a spirit of demonstrative familiarity than of wanton malice. Having thus mollified his companion, Tom took a fever, and left the farm. The forsaken brute fell into a melancholy—then into a moroseness—and finally relapsed into a misanthropic ferocity. But Tom Hance made very clear that there was some goodness even in Badger.

This chapter is not an essay on agriculture. Yet if

it were it need not be jejune. No doubt that noble science will sometime be made entertaining reading for lazing July weather, on the lawn beneath the sycamores. Perhaps there is a modern muse for the analysis of soils and the qualities of pasturage. Alas! our American Mæcenas is always busy in contriving to be President. Cowper has sung the cucumber in its eventful history from the stable-heap to the table. Like as not, the next Theocritus will be the inventor of a steam plough. Modern amateur farmers may stride monthly over more space of knowledge than stretches from the Mantuan to old Jethro Tull; though hypothesis outstrip demonstration in the magazines and manuals. Better this than the dulness which disparages methods it cannot disprove. Better Liteprintz, dibbling, in a flush of complacency—better Ravensduck wondering, in a sailor's husky accents, at the refusal of his pistillate strawberries, as he reads his lesson from the "Country Gentleman," than Farmer Crustover, whose tool-shed, where the chickens roost, is a museum of original models, who cherishes fond memories of the sickle, disbelieves in "garden sarse," goes to meeting on a blind-bridled, rat-tailed mare, perpetuates gaunt and ugly swine, ploughs three inches deep, and despises "book-farming." We, for our parts, are simply visitors at Brentlands, this April morning; not at all disposed to sit at the feet of the husbandman who tills it; and who, we hope, will be so judicious—we venture to believe it after that excellent claret—as to keep his chemistry for his crops.

Yonder peach orchard in blossom woos us, as it does the orioles.

It is a smoky day with a south-east wind, and the golden young leaves of the maples sadden for a brighter sun. Bradley is devoting an hour or two, stolen from the farm, to his borders. The floral department is narrow—some roses and other shrubbery to prune and tie, some old-fashioned herbaceous perennials, and a few vines to train. Here elegance and taste are overruled by utility. Nor is there time to know the charms that make attractive the pursuit of a new seedling. These good things are for rich and dignified leisure. They are its privileges—among the minor blessings it can bestow. Sun and shower in the Brentlands garden promote humbler uses—are not woven into gay blooms, but the homespun of beans, onions, and lettuce, and sage for the Michaelmas goose. There are some choice melon seed in these hills, under the glazed boxes, said to be the true Armenian cantaleup. If Pomona is propitious, the cool green flesh of the fruit will melt gratefully in the mouth in August, when Sirius forsakes the night. Set near different plants of the same genus the fruit would hybridize. There is little rest for the soil, and little chance for the weeds. The watering-pot is sometimes needed even in this showery month, now on the verge of May. The strawberries, especially, are great drinkers. The cistern is a sunken cask, near where that cat, wakened awhile ago from its nap on a heap of litter by the note of a bird, is rubbing its nose along the stem of a shrub.

Whoever voyaging home from a sojourn in the tropics has beheld the cornfields in June, which line either of those goodly bays, the Chesapeake or Delaware, without rare enjoyment, ought not to undertake a sentimental journey. Against the monotonous grey of the sea, still the background of sense, their verdure is deepened—after the barren turbulence of ocean, appears the calmly vigorous life of earth. A human interest too, belongs to them, which the sea never originates. Man has no fee in it, more than in the caprices of an untamed tiger—it is a treacherous enemy, whom he can only foil by circumspection. Though a less ardent, the traveller here discerns a more liberal nature than that of the clime which he has left, where languid breezes shake the orange and banana, or tornadoes shatter them. More liberal, because, still graceful in its bounty, its types are those by which *men* strengthen in muscle and in mind.

Yes; contemplating from this knoll the outspread uplands, which fastidious May regards just now with a vixenly frown, we conclude, in the spirit of Captain John Smith's description of Virginia, "Heaven and earth never agreed better to frame a place for man's habitation." There is a deal of work afoot; ploughs going all around, and the wagons of laggard farmers laden with drenched and dried manure from the sloping barnyards. The Brentlands men are striking out their last corn field. This is the final plough work upon it; the tillage will hereafter be prosecuted with hoes and cultivators, the latter to be constantly run until the crop is laid by. The field is fifty acres in extent, and in it the crows find room to forage. Probably but a small replanting will be necessary, for the frosts of winter have purged the upturned furrow slices of the cut-worm. There will be no weeds—why should there be in any arable land, when cultivation will keep them down?

But the neighborhood industry is not all devoted to corn-planting. It is Mr. Potteril in the buggy, followed by his man, Simon Horseradish, with a wagon load of veal for the landing, who is at the gate before us. The load, indeed, consists of two calves hardly in a condition for epicures, but, with Horseradish, who is something plumper, the lank old horses seem to think it is sufficient. Mr. Potteril is of New Paradise. So his great grandfather named the estate which he inherits. It was fat land once, and it has fed several generations of easy-going Potterils. There is poorer gnawing now upon its emaciated vitals. The buried Potterils—the family motto is admonitory, "In the midst of life we are in death"—were mostly fond of field sports, and left the farming to their overseers. The present representative is a more quiet man, whose hobby is "perpetual motion." He has been twenty years perfecting a mechanism which is to astonish the world, and which contains at present about a barrel-full of small wheels. He gets them cast to order, and the calves help to pay for them. Horseradish, who is Mr. Potteril's factotum, entertains a great respect for the "invention," and tells exultingly how it has puzzled the lawyers.

When a prize was promised the discoverer of a bane for the peach-tree borers, Mr. Potteril determined to compete for it. It would probably have gone hard with the worms could he have gone on compounding, for he was daily adding to a collection of the most fetid materials in nature. But just before the crisis of projection, Mrs. Potteril, in a fit of nausea and impatience, cast the preparations to the dogs, and sternly protested against any further essays.

There is plenty of land at New Paradise, chiefly old fields out of heart. Their principal product is a straggling growth of sassafras, though there is no lack of sheep-sorrel. A curious antiquarian may yet find traces of the division fences. The log stables lean so, of late, the rats have grown wary. As to the barns— the Potterils were not a barn-building family. The present Mr. Potteril can make a great deal of a decrepit horse. He prefers decrepit horses, and can get them cheap. He has a theory, that when the lower teeth of the equine quadruped are ground away in natural use, drawing a few of the longest of the upper teeth will equalize the situation. Fortunately, there is not much heavy hauling at New Paradise. The belief of Mr. Potteril is that lime sours land, and that guano burns it; so he reserves his stock manure for his wheat, and makes it go a great way. The other crops draw most of their sustenance from the atmosphere, and the air of New Paradise has long been famous. The Potteril wheat stacks are neither numerous nor corpulent, an absence of conditions favorable to speedy threshing. There is a single dark looking heap, which at conjecturing distance is the fodder of pulse or buckwheat, but which Horseradish will tell you is hay, and he is an authentic witness, having tedded it in the lot after three storms. Such as it is, it infects the Potteril cattle with a chronic discontent at their winter provender of corn stalks and oat straw. Bran mashes are accounted medicine at New Paradise. There are some sheep, which gather their tallow off the old swards. The cows pasture much in the woods, where they regale the flies and mosquitos, and their milk acquires a fine huckleberry flavor. The young Horseradishes loiter on their track of summer afternoons, guided by sound of bell, and drive them home in the twilight at a gallop.

Simon Horseradish, as has been observed, sees to things generally, and pays much attention to the changes of the moon, each of which is favorable to certain labors. He was once so rash as to make a fence in the wrong quarter of that luminary, and it was blown down by the first strong wind. There was a tract of ship timber, quite valuable, but Mr. Potteril stood for his price, until a change of wind when there was burning brush, and Simon was away to consult the almanac, set it afire and destroyed it. However, there will be a growth of pine to substitute it, for the next of the family. Simon often recreates himself at the village, where he discusses with his cronies the Potteril prospects, and brags of the past. Especially has he much to narrate of Colonel Tom Potteril, and his racers, and the stakes they took in their day, till Dick Hoskins, the jockey, broke his neck; when Colonel Tom gratefully buried him beneath a marble slab, upon which was inscribed his equestrian virtues, the whole tagged with some latin verses by the parson, who also planted a tree at the glebe to commemorate him—you may see it any day towering on Hawk's-nest Hill. Toward midnight, on these occasions, Simon will suffer no one to question the prodigious feats he relates of "Harrycane," as he insists on calling Colonel Tom's favorite horse. The bones of Hurricane, nicely scraped, are preserved in a glass case at New Paradise.

Mr. Potteril talks of declaring himself a candidate for Congress. He is staunch in his politics, which are not of the movement school. He decries all innovation, which he imputes to "the infidel spirit of the age," and is ready with illustrative instances from the history of the great French Revolution. Danton is his favorite horror. Simon Horseradish aspires to be constable, and is about to ride the canvass. Meanwhile, the grass will nod approvingly through the long, bright, breezy days to rusty ploughs stuck in unfinished furrows, and the young Horseradishes will gather blackberries, and poison themselves with sumach in the corn middles at New Paradise.

The only son and heir of the house of Potteril, Slogoe—Mrs. Potteril was a Slogoe, of the elder branch, and a niece of Governor Slogoe, of St. Huberts—went into the army, and is expected some time to make a great strategic movement.

But while we are gossiping, the dinner-horn sounds, the dogs howl, and a boy rides in from the village with yesterday's mail. The busy life of Brentlands will grow busier henceforth until the harvest.—The farmer, indeed, should bear a grateful heart. Disappointment rarely brings to him the suffering it allots to other men.

His bread, at least remains. The ground on which he stands passes not from under him, if there be no gripe of debt upon it. Another year, the Hand may be less sparing—another year, a choral strain of thanks to the Supreme Beneficence, who "ministereth seed to the sower," may rise from all the land for the bounty of His harvest.

"Borne on Thy breath, the lap of spring
 Was heaped with many a blooming flower;
And smiling summer joyed to bring
 The sunshine and the gentle shower;
And autumn's rich luxuriance now,
 The ripening seed, the bursting shell,
The golden sheaf and laden bough,
 The fullness of thy bounty tell.

And here shall rise our song to Thee,
 Where lengthened vale and pastures lie,
And streams go singing wild and free,
 Beneath a blue and smiling sky:
Where ne'er was rear'd a mortal throne,
 Where crowned oppressors never trod,
Here at the throne of Heaven alone,
 Shall man in reverence bow to God!"

CHAPTER XXIX.

She listened with a flitting blush;
 With downcast eyes, and modest grace;
And she forgave me, that I gazed
 Too fondly on her face!
GENEVIEVE.

THE most emphatic language of Love is without words. It is spoken from the eye, and is lambent eloquence in the repose of the mouth. By it reproach is transmuted to pathos. It came forth from Eden, a remainder of its first felicity. It has arbitrary symbols, insignificant to the general eye—familiar things sanctified by a touch—the faded petals of a rose, a withered sprig of lavender, the strawberry stains on that handkerchief, laid by in a drawer, years—ah! she knows how many years ago. Bradley Horton and Lydia Bardleigh are silently communing in the shade of the willows, beside a creek which, after winding through meadows at The Cedars, crosses the country road under a small stone bridge.

The road is above them, but it is a quiet by-road little travelled, and they are so low and so close to the side of the bridge that they are out of sight. Nobody has passed in a half hour but a frocked farmer's boy riding bare-back a plough horse on some errand to the village store. She is seated on the bole of a willow which runs a comfortable distance parallel with the ground before it makes its upright growth. He reclines, resting upon his arm, and gazes in her face. The water glides by them with a soothing murmur into the deep pool it has worn at the bridge, the lair perhaps of a gorged pike, for the insects dart undisturbed on its surface, fretting it into puny ripples. The fine red rootlets of the willows reach everywhere from the water-washed bank into the stream, and fluctuate with its flow like ten thousand living feelers. The hospitable trees have harbored ruder guests of late, if a broken tobacco pipe and a veteran jack-of-clubs are testimony. These betoken the Sunday recreation of the quarrymen. Strange rural sound, there rises, by spells, the shrill music of a fife. Yonder is a clump of trees on a knoll, with gray rocks bulging among them, from which the breeze seems to bear the notes. Perhaps an idle youngster stretched on the mould at his practice.

"That grove, Bradley, would be a nice place for a pic-nic."

"Excellent—or to sonnetize in after Petrarch. 'The air nimbly and sweetly doth recommend itself.' And a fine draught there is under this bridge. What a comfort to be a fish such hot weather."

"What sort of fish—a gudgeon?"

"Old Sylvanus never listened to a more patriotic pipe," and Bradley whistled in accompaniment, "Yankee Doodle."

"I wonder, Bradley, you don't like the woods. To walk in them is one of my choice pleasures."

"Well, the ladies are privileged to be romantic."

"Pshaw! it's not sentimentalism, but sensibility."

"Then you are not afraid of poison vines, ticks, and snakes—Did you ever tread on a snake?"

"Do you question my humanity?"

"I've seen a young lady of the finest sentiments jump clean out of her raptures by such a misstep."

"That was a great while ago, I suppose, when women read less philosophy than they do now, and more fiction?"

"O artifice, thy name is woman! It *was* a long while since. There now, it won't pout?"

"As if I care, Sir Tease. I'm only surprised that, with your marvellous perception, you should condescend to look at a lady jump at all."

"Sure, one may gaze at a perturbation of Venus."

There was some minutes of silence, during which Bradley musingly watched the plunge of the pebbles which he threw into the stream.

"Lydia, could you be a recluse?"

"No: religious meditation, I believe, would not satisfy me. It is meant to sanctify religious work, and when unaccompanied by performance, it weakens the character, and lays the heart open to temptation. Faith must be sustained by charity; and charity—the charity of the Apostle to the Corinthians—requires the world for its full exercise—it is the Christian's part and privilege to be *in* the world without being *of* it."

Another pause.

"What progress does the young housekeeper, our Annie, make, love?"

"O, she will need a full year yet of schooling. I cannot leave her with father before she is capable—I owe him that, even at your expense, dear heart!"

"Heigho! I wish I could shorten the year. Why can't housekeepers be made, as French is taught now-a-days, in twenty lessons?"

"I suppose they can—and will be equal to the French?"

"Well, I dare not fret in the presence of such charming patience."

"So may it continue to charm you, I shall pray."

"I think if I could cling to it it would bear me into Heaven!"

She only replied by tenderly taking his hand.

Bradley, looking towards the knoll, exclaimed, "There goes the music."

"It's young Blount," said Lydia.

"The quaker's son?"

"Yes."

"Preparing for the army, I suppose. Well, a soldier's heart has beat beneath the drab before now. Nay; Mars and brave George Fox—who was quite as imperious in his way as the helmeted son of Jove—have had wrestling bouts for a whole family; as that of Barclay. The god got a colonel for Gustavus Adolphus, and a field-marshal for the czar—the quaker took the famous apologist, and won back the colonel."

"Would it not be an odd world all quakers?"

"A queerish. Suppose Philadelphia should be overwhelmed, as was Pompeii, and after the same period of burial be exhumed, a quaker street being first exposed, what would the philosophers say?"

"What would they?" asked Lydia, laughing.

"To begin, that here was a people who had no fine arts, no musical instruments, architectural ornamentation, pictures, nor statuary. With little fancy, it would be argued, and with poverty of imagination, they were probably without poetry. Clearly, they were not warlike, for there is no example of the rudest weapon; and they were doubtless ignorant of gunpowder. They were great travellers, for their libraries consisted chiefly of journeys and journals. Their costume, emphatic as toga or turban, constituted an era in the history of clothes. No evidence of a drama is to be found in their printed books. Their cooking utensils are too numerous and complete to sanction a supposition that they were used by ascetics. They seem to have put their trust in real estate, and to have laid up their treasure in title-deeds and mortgages—the parchment being all made out of a famous pair of leather breeches."

"What an aggregate!"

"You dispute, then, my dead-reckoning?"

"I believe Quakerism to have been one of God's best gifts to the Anglo-Saxon race, as it was an irrepressible declaration for civil and religious liberty when sorely needed—an unfaltering protest against violence, licentiousness, and the tyranny of dead forms. And they surely are established in the Gospel of our blessed Lord in their testimony against

War. When the incarnate and complete Goodness was repulsed by the villagers, and his disciples asked him if they should invoke fire from heaven, as did Elias, upon them, the conclusive reply was, 'Ye know not what spirit ye are of': and they went to another village. How, then, with this example in view, can a Christian justify the accomplishment of partial good by violence?" said Lydia.

"It is allowable, they tell us, to an aggregation of Christians—a State. They are willing to be damned as a prince, if they can only be saved as an archbishop."

"How many precious ministers of Jesus Christ do err in this matter!" said Lydia.

"My ancestors were of the faith a century and a half ago, when there was more meat in the shell of Quakerism, and I respect the traditions. We need, here and now, the protesting spirit of these ancients. Our national lust of gold is ripe in a harvest of mercenary priests, overreaching tradesmen, corrupt judges, and legislatures which are bought. Arrogance, injustice, and dissension are begot in the land. Be very sure, our stripes will not come from a scourge of small cords. So much for the preaching strain, to which you have brought me, you dear little sermonizer!' said Bradley.

There had been a shower, and there was a rainbow in the sky. It was late in the afternoon, and they sat in the portico contemplating the beautiful birth "of vapor and the sun." If you can ever feel the pulses of Nature throb from her strong and bountiful heart, it is in the country after a summer shower. Freshness is in every nerve—the earth is attuned to her primal vigor—she is young again, and a bride—she rejoices, and the splendor in the sky is a fit symbol for her psalm! What Uncle Steve Trencher's thoughts were, as he came toward the house dangling some woodcock, can not be told. He said, indeed, after a sententiously civil greeting, that it had been "a myste afternoon—that's solemn." Uncle Steve was as damp as the meadows where he had trudged for his game, the soil of which the rain had not wholly washed from his cowskin boots. He carried "Proclermation" reversed, its merciless muzzle in advance of him. The dogs recognized and came up to him, eliciting from him pithy scraps of kennel wisdom.

"Fine birds, Uncle Steve—very fine birds."

"Yes, Judge; they've got the right kind of bills."

"Any news your way, Uncle Steve?"

"Wal, none to speak on. Josh Rambo, the storekeeper, has got his daughter Keziah a pianer; and Gabriel Wamblebee is lying at the pint of death, with gastretus the doctors say, though some folks do call it too much apple-jack—but I never knowed that in moderation to hurt any man, and it stands to reason the doctors knows best. Marm Fougcroy told me they give him a ball of quicksilver, and said, if it went through him lively he might get well, but if it didn't void there was no hope."

"He's advanced in years?"

"Nigh on to seventy, I reckon, which looks as if he'd pisoned himself very gradual. One thing I've noticed, most of these pesky people who turn up their eyes at their fellow-creatures for taking a little sperits when ailin' or overdone like, is always a groaning over their dyspepsy or liver complaint. They're unthankful critters that don't know the vally of their blessings.—I calc'late we'll have a sickly fall in these parts, for I see the crows on the graveyard wall every time I pass, and my old woman is troubled with a dreadful ringing in her ears."

"Are these signs, Uncle Steve?"

"So people said when I was a boy, and they was a heap more observing than folks now-a-days.—I've come, Judge, in part, to get your advice, which I always set by."

"Thank you—I hope you don't overvalue it."

"My old woman's brother, who lived in the city, has died and left her a legacy of four hundred dollars; and we've got to go and see about it. I never was there, and don't like the idee of riding in the cars—but life is uncertain, and we must take it, I spose, as it comes. The old woman means to get a pair of new spectacles, and some notions, and we don't know rightly what to do with the rest of the money. I won't hear to the Slumptown bank. If the choice laid between that and a hollow gum, I'd vote for the tree."

"Couldn't you buy three or four acres of your neighbor, to add to your lot?"

"Crimp would want double its vally, and I'd sooner give to the bank than him. He has killed, off and on, six of my chickens, and shot at the pigs, but missed. He don't keep no sort of fences."

"I can place the money on interest, and get you a good mortgage to secure it."

"I'm a thousand times obleeged; that would just suit."

"You can have the interest twice a year or yearly, as you please.—When you go to the city look out for the rascals, for its a naughty place. Keep tight hold of your money, or they will bring you down as sure as 'Proclermation' will a woodcock."

"Aint there constables?"

"Yes; but they don't always catch the rogues."

"I've heern tell, too, it's a passin' place for fires; but I shant stay more'n one night."

Happy glimpses of a promised land were these visits of Bradley to The Cedars. The landscape laughed in tune with the gaiety of his heart, and the birds warbled on a perfect chord. If such a succession of domestic joys should be his! There would be no temptation then to wander. Cintra and Naples would woo in vain. We will dream, in blankets made of Northern fleece, of Mediterraneans laving shores,

"Where the sun with a golden mouth can blow
Blue bubbles of grapes down a vineyard row."

The Northern home where cultivated goodness reigns, with cattle-dotted fields, and groves, whose only orange tint is autumn's gift, outspread around it—though its windows often frame a low and sullen sky, and its dooryard trees are leafless in the winter blast, shall be our Eden still!

He watched the household employments—*her* hands crowned them with grace. Perhaps he was a spooled and stupid fellow, but if so, he was too irrational to know it, and it made little difference. Something of Amphion's touch, which marshalled the Theban stones, was in this country house music. Pray, how much better employed were the pastoral youth with their oaten pipes than he? For the time, he was the good-natured man. Even Annie's pet crow, a bird with a propensity to larceny, failed to vex him when it concealed the candle ends under the collar of his coat, and abstracted his loose property before his eyes. He was fascinated in the companionship of a delicate and kindly nature. And it is suitableness for companionship in a woman, which most charms a sensible man; to produce which, cultivation of heart, and some cultivation, at least, of intellect, are necessary. It is the wretched small-talk of wives of unimproved minds which populates the tavern and the club. Such women may be notable for their housekeeping thrift—able to save a threepence in a pudding, and to higgle the butcher out of the odd ounce of steak. While economy is a minor virtue, and tidiness is an essential to which the goddesses are not superior, your very managing woman is usually an unpleasant female. She may be ranked, with an ample interval, next above her sour-tempered and prickly sister whose perpetual and petty malice makes her the meanest of earthly annoyances. And it is not that false cultivation which begets wishes for political equality with man which is desirable in the milder sex. All such is simply unprofitable road-making into dream-land. There are foolish human females who would rid themselves of all gentle affections and situations to gratify a self-conceit which spurns at the divine will in the creation. Except to dolts and demagogues, Miranda herself howling she-politics upon the rostrum would be as disgusting as Caliban. When conjoined with the Christian virtues, it is home-culture which fits a woman to be her husband's helpmeet, and the almoner of angels to him.

CHAPTER XXX.

The porch of this temple is exceeding glorious, and the gate of it is called Beautiful.—RICHARD BAXTER.

THE cabin had but one window, which was without glass, and was closed by a sliding shutter. There were crevices enough in the walls, however, to admit a feeble light, and in pleasant weather the door could be left open. Such was the habitation given in charity to Dinah, an old negress, who now lay upon her death-bed—a sack of straw on the floor, with a coarse sheet and some scanty covering. Lydia Bardleigh, seated on a stool beside the bed, was reading from a Methodist hymn-book.

"Thank the good Master! I can read my title clear, Miss."

After a little while she added,

"I must soon leave you, Honey; but all your kindness to the old woman has gone to heaven, and when the Lord's angels bring you, you will find it there."

"My poor old friend, let me bathe your back again with the liniment," said Lydia.

"Taint hardly worth while, Honey; the stage is nearly here!"

"I like to do it, Aunt Dinah."

The lovely woman bared the emaciated shoulders and side of the old negress.

"The jelly and chicken you fetched the old woman looks mighty nice, and too quality like, but it 'pears I isn't got an appetite equal to them—my ambition's most clar gone. But I think, my dear missis, if I had a sweet potatoe, I could eat it."

"When I go home, Aunt Dinah, I will send it at once."

"Many thanks, missis! The Lord is very good to me."

At this time the neighboring clergyman entered the hovel. He was a youngish man, very nice in his attire and precise in his manners. He saluted Lydia with marked courtesy, and after a few rather idle observations on passing events, turned to the sick bed, and prayed with a cold but correct emphasis.

"I can't make nothing out of that gospel, missis," said the old woman when the young man had retired; "'pears to me it wasn't preached to the poor. It buzzed in my ears, and didn't go with the life to my heart. But I hear the angels singing now!"

After a short pause she cried in ecstacy,

"Hallelujah! Glory to God!"

Lydia perceived that she was departing.

"My dear young missis, are you feared of death?"

"No, Aunt Dinah."

"Then you, and me, and Jesus, is enough!"

A few minutes afterwards she fell into a doze, from which she awaked exclaiming,

"I shall see my baby once more!"

Directly she cried exultingly, "I AM A KING'S DAUGHTER!" and her spirit ascended from her.

CHAPTER XXXI.

Oh, Men, with Sisters dear!
Oh, Men, with Mothers and Wives!
It is not linen you're wearing out,
But human creatures' lives!
                      THOMAS HOOD.

IT was another year. The cherry blossoms were drifting into the chamber window of Jane Warner at Lokesbur school, and the birds were quietly busy in elm and willow at their annual architecture. A drowsy hum of recitation came from the class-rooms—a hive-like monotone, varied by the tinkle of a teacher's bell. The occupant of the chamber was hastening in preparation for a journey. She had just been summoned by a pressing message to the sick bed of her mother, and while she packed her apparel with womanly neatness still, sobbed her apprehension. Then, aloud, she prayed God to avert a fatal issue—If it please thee, O merciful Father, for poor Frank's sake!

Jane reached home in time to receive her mother's blessing, and close her eyes; and that was all. The funeral was plain and inexpensive, but the grief was real. The bereaved children beside the open grave moved to tenderness every bosom. Frank was not there. He lay at home sick and sorrowful, thinking of the past. The hands that had smoothed his pillow were beneath the clay; the tongue which had cheered his despondency was hushed forever here—but there is God's heaven of angels, O suffering little brother, and that and thy mother are with thee still!

The week after the funeral was one of family rest and affectionate intercourse, subdued in tone, and sanctified by the common affliction. There were no enmities to be forgotten, or wrongs to alienate; and the injunction of the departed parent, "Love one another!" was, in all its solemn significance, the household law. The solicitude felt for Frank was constantly manifested in words and acts of kindness that lightened somewhat the heaviness of his heart. The time seemed chastened, and life went on purged of its tumult and vexations. Then the days were passed, and the cares of the world pressed forward for recognition. To earn money was a necessity stronger than the contemplative dominion of grief. The family must part. An aunt, it was ascertained, would take Frank, on his sister's promise to support him. The small sum to be got by the sale of the furniture it was agreed should be devoted to his wants. A bitterness of sorrow measured the love in the daughter's heart as she folded each familiar garment of her mother's wardrobe. The day of sale came; and then the household separated—"Only for three or four short years, sis," said one of the boys, "when we shall be together again, well-off and happy; and Frank shall have a cab sometimes for an airing."

Jane returned altered to her desk at Lokesbur school. The buoyancy of spirits and alacrity which she had possessed and displayed were no longer hers; a fatalistic lack of personal interest in the future, which took from the present its purpose and energy, had succeeded to them. The two maiden sisters who presided over the select establishment of Lokesbur—at the sere and yellow of womanhood, the latter a bilious gamboge—were unimpeachably respectable and imposingly righteous. They had an orthodoxy of their own, these worthy ladies, knew what was correct socially, and solemnly believed the outside world to be a disagreeable and discontented assemblage of red republicans and shoemakers. They knelt on well-dusted devotional hassocks at church, and read the responses with unhesitating precision out of Oxford prayer-books, extra gilt. Unquestionably the Misses Trimley knew what was proper and pious. They, therefore, regarded the melancholy into which Jane Warner was fallen, after the first fortnight, with severe disapprobation.

Her sadness demanded gentle attentions—some commiserating nature to relax it—and the Misses Trimley were too strict to be sympathetic. Without omitting the duties of her situation, she performed them in a spiritless and mechanical manner. This, with the good sisters, was downright murmuring against Providence. They added to her burden looks and expressions decorously reproachful. How eagerly, when completed tasks allowed, did she seek her solitary chamber! Nor yet solitary, for it was the scene of invisible solace to this woman with her heart-scald—of a life higher than the wonted, as the better world of shadows outreaches the world of substance. How impatient in her ill-informed impulses was she to mingle with it!

The time at last came when such obduracy could be no longer countenanced by the ladies of Lokesbur. One evening, after prayers, they summoned to their presence the delinquent teacher. With some pertinent reflections on the wickedness of a complaining deportment, in a select establishment, they announced to her their purpose to dispense with her services. The salary due to her was paid the following day, and she departed.

She took quiet and humble lodgings in the city, where she could prepare her food and live at small expense. This done, she went to Frank. Old prejudices, clung to with the obstinacy of ignorance and age, had indisposed her aunt to cordial relations with her. There was also in Miss Cluskey some leaven of that envious antipathy with which uninformed persons, though otherwise worthy, are apt to regard their better instructed family connections. Jane's visits to her aunt, therefore, had been rare.

As her niece's situation became apparent to the spinster, the spirit of selfishness waxed strong within her. To the prospect of losing the stipend she had received on account of Frank, was added a probable appeal for aid by his unemployed sister. And Jane had wilfully abandoned her place; for she preferred no complaint against the Misses Trimley. The spinster would not refer this silence to a generosity which she could not understand. Indeed, had she known of her niece's unhappiness, she would have esteemed it as nothing but perversity, or the vapors of a woman. While her indignation mounted, she hit upon an explanation of Jane's conduct—incipient insanity. Miss Cluskey was of a saving temper, and kept no cats.

Having made this diagnosis of her niece's case, it was perhaps illogical in Miss Cluskey to censure her as an offender. But pure reason is not the forte of an incensed woman, with whom, when argument fails, there is always a refuge in crimination.

"Well, miss, I suppose your fortune's made, since you have contrived to part with your situation."

"What do you mean, aunt?"

"Just this; that people can't live without money or occupation, and as you don't seem to care for the last, you should have enough of the first, either in hand or prospect."

"You are unkind to say that I don't want employment—I was never idle through indolence."

"It's as bad if people don't try to please, and put on airs. Beggars can't be princesses, and boarding-school teachers mustn't think themselves full-blown ladies."

"If you mean, aunt," replied Jane, nettled by this tirade of reproach, "that I have aimed at habits and indulgences which my means will not warrant, or deported myself toward any one with affected grandeur, you accuse me falsely: if you only mean that I have known how to respect myself, you are right."

"Hoity-toity! so I lie. You think yourself a pretty

diamond, I don't doubt. I believe you're a little crazy, but that don't mend the matter. I'm sorry for that sick child."

"You may make yourself easy about Frank, aunt, for the present. I have some money, and I shall try to earn my own expenses by sewing until I get a place. I shall pay you, as heretofore, while I can."

"Well, miss, I hope fair words will continue to butter parsnips. You can come see your brother, of course, when you please; but after what has passed I don't think it's necessary you should see me. Young people nowadays don't respect age—bears wouldn't make 'em. I dare say I'm a deal too common for your society—not to speak of my want of veracity—and I shall keep away from it when you call, if it is my own house, being a meeting-going woman and a peacemaker," and with an odd jumble of assumed meekness and spiteful pretension in her accent and carriage, Miss Cluskey took herself off, satisfied that, whatever else might result, she had shut up every avenue by which her niece could approach her for assistance, on the exhaustion of a slender purse.

When the door had closed behind the flouting spinster, the sick boy broke a momentary silence with a deep sigh of relief.

"I wish aunt had more self-control, sis. It is very wrong and trying, though she's mostly good to me."

"Never mind, Frank; I won't let it trouble me. *You* can't think ill of me, I'm sure."

"If I could, dear sister, I would be a wretch."

"Then let it pass. Always, Frank, treat your aunt

with respect; it is your duty, and will be to your advantage. We are all frail, and must allow for each other."

"It will be hard to hear you talked against, and don't think I can without speaking."

"Be guarded, my dear! To know you were unhappy, would make me so."

"I sometimes get discontented, sis; then I think mother—I think I see her smiling upon me, and I cry, and grow very calm."

Jane sat by her brother, holding his hand, while earnest, patient eyes looked into her own, where constrained cheerfulness contended with starting tears.

"I have brought you a new book of tales, Frank."

"Thank you, sis; thank you very much."

"And something you will like better—a parcel of figs."

"No, I like the book better; it lasts longer," replied the lad, laughingly. "But I don't care for all books of tales alike. I would rather follow the fortunes of the poor, and find them at last comfortable and happy, than read of the most splendid victories of kings and soldiers—even the adventures of Bruce and Wallace. As a good missionary who came here once, Father Tryon, said of his acquaintance—when they get rich I generally give them up. That was the reason, I suppose, he wore such a shabby coat."

"The robe of Christ, my dear, is ever new. You don't let the spiders spin along your bookshelf, Frank."

"No, indeed. It's a nice little library—isn't it? Those three books at the left are the first real books I ever owned, except a testament—of course I don't count nursery stories. 'The Glory of America,' father gave me when I had pleurisy—was getting well of it, I mean. I liked Mad Anthony Wayne, but thought I would rather be Decatur or Lawrence, and live on the ocean."

"You would rather be, I guess, a nautilus on a summer sea."

"What's that chap know of life?—There's my 'Pilgrim's Progress,' pages of which I know by heart. And that is 'Robinson Crusoe,' which set me drawing and peopling islands, and building cities, and inventing governments. Heigho! old as I am, I draw them in my head sometimes now. I was making a navy for one the other day, in a sort of reverie, and listening the while to 'Pop goes the weasel' from an organ in the street, when a monkey stole in at the window and poked his red cap in my face," and a twinkle of merriment played about the youngster's mouth.

Considering the temper of her aunt, Jane deemed infrequent visiting of her brother best for his comfort. She left at regular periods the sum agreed upon for his board, assiduously sought employment for herself, and pinched on bread and butter and tea, with an occasional morsel from the butcher. She sought employment, and only sometimes got it—coarse shirt-making; the wages of which helped to supply her scanty allowance for food and shelter. But she had not been trained to the use of the needle, and was a slow sewer. There was a dearth of rough seamstress work, and a competitive strife for it. Once or twice, when she attempted finer garments, she was rudely rebuked for botching them, and refused compensation. Spring passed away, and summer came, with a mockery for her of leaves and sunshine.

As time wore on, the stitching vigils for bread, and the fearful uncertainty which harassed her spirits, showed more and more ghastly in her face and wasted body. Her attempts at cheerfulness when with Frank were unsuccessful, and the visits—made shorter now—brought to the boy anxiety and grief. Strange thoughts began to possess her, and inklings of new and dread temptations. She had lost her way of life, and the longer she wandered the more she must go astray. Human happiness, after all, was in nowise, as she had thought it to be, dependent upon human will. Individual misery was an inevitable evil. There was a grave for all—and a sleep. Yet she still believed in the goodness of the Almighty, with a fervorless conviction, as in the essence of an inaccessible Being. She could not curse God, but she could die! She could die out of the seething and selfish crowd for the pittance which would not furnish her a meal.

On her return from a clothing store with a parcel of work, the fruit of several solicitations, Jane Warner one gusty evening in June stopped beneath an awning for shelter from the rain. The vehemence of the storm had subsided to fitful showers from some broken rearward clouds, that were slowly following the mass of lightning-riven blackness which overhung the east, and which was still resonant with rapid peals of receding thunder. The gas-lights flickered on the plashy crossings, along which damp and detained wayfarers picked their homeward course, or avoided, with surly expressions of resentment, the spattering onset of a cab. As she stood before a shop window and contemplated the procession of umbrella-bearing passers-by, she was suddenly conscious that an earnest gaze, partly shrouded by the slouch of the hat, was directed at her. Turning her head to meet the look, she observed that while it was steady it was not disrespectful, and concluding that the person from whom it came had some motive for delay besides impertinence, she averted her face and turned to another train of thought. Presently, reminded by the striking clocks of the lapse of time, she hurried onward in the rain.

In her speed, she slipped at a smooth grating in the pavement and fell heavily upon her outstretched hand, dropping the parcel which she carried. Directly she was lifted and supported by a ready arm. The spot was rather dark, but she recognized by his dress the person who had shared with her the shelter of the awning.

"Are you hurt, Miss Warner—for I believe I am right in thus addressing you?"

"A little stunned, sir, and my arm seems sprained."

"I see you don't know me."

"Mr. Bloker—excuse me, I did not.

"Can you stand without aid?"

"Very well, thank you."

Bloker picked up the bundle and his umbrella. Spreading the latter above Jane, he said,

"Lean on me, Miss Warner, and permit me to conduct you safely home."

"By no means, sir; I am but little hurt."

"You are shaken by the fall, and lame in that arm; I should be lost to all civility to leave you. I have known your family too long and well to think of it, and it is my duty to attend you, both as a gentleman, and, whatever you may mistakenly consider me, a friend."

Finding by the positive tone of her companion that remonstrance would be decorously unheeded, Jane forbore to urge it.

"I did not know of your being in the city—Is your wrist painful?"

"More than at first."

"Let me bind it with my handkerchief—I will not hurt you."

Mastering by promptitude her indecision, Bloker soon converted the handkerchief into a rude bandage, and applied it.

"You will need a doctor, perhaps. There may be a fracture; when you are at home we can examine."

At the entrance of the street where her lodging was situated, she protested against his accompanying her further. He courteously said that she might be doing herself injustice, but that he was bound to respect her desire. He insisted, however, that he should be allowed to send on the following day to inquire concerning her; and wishing her a deferential Good-night, he left her.

When she was alone in her room the pain of the

hurt increased. Casting down her eyes she beheld the handkerchief. Recollections of its owner came to vex her spirit, and, in a fit of indignation, she tore it from the limb. She poured water from her pitcher on the red and swollen part, and, relieved by the douche, was swathing it with wet muslin, when the thought arose in her mind—I cannot work!

That thought was a terror. But a few small coins remained for her subsistence. The pawnbroker was before her—beyond that she dare not look. She had been compelled to omit the last payment for her brother. Sorrowfully she persuaded herself that it was only an obligation postponed; and thus much she meant to explain to her aunt, when she could announce that she had obtained fresh employment which promised to continue. Stretched on a rack of solicitude, she went to her bed, and awaited through weary hours the respite of oblivion grudged to nature—she did not weep—alas! she did not pray.

CHAPTER XXXII.

Imogen.—I have heard I am a strumpet, and mine ear,
 Therein false struck, can take no greater wound
 Nor tent to bottom that.—CYMBELINE.

AWAKENED late the following morning by the cries of the hawkers, Jane Warner arose and prepared a scanty breakfast. Scarcely had she finished it, when a slovenly girl, the child of a fellow-lodger, ushered Bloker to her chamber.

"My dear Miss Warner, I could not deny myself the happiness, being on business in the neighborhood, of calling on you."

"Take a seat, sir," said Jane, with constrained civility, while the blood burned in her cheek.

"I hope you are better of the injury?" he asked, with an air of concern.

"Decidedly."

"Truly glad—I thought you much hurt."

"O, no."

"Did the handkerchief help you?"

"I took it off."

"Permit me," he said blandly, advancing his chair

and reaching to her hand. "You must know, I am part of a doctor—had charge of a ship's medicine chest when I was a supercargo, and set a sailor's leg once, on a pinch; or, rather," he continued gaily, "to be precise, on the forward hatch. It mended finely—with castor oil."

His gaze shifted as he spoke from her wrist to her eyes, while she regarded him with forced composure.

"Yet inflamed. If I might advise, keep it wet with a solution of sugar of lead.—A hand for a sculptor, by the goddess of beauty!" and he emphasized the compliment with a gentle pressure and an amatory look.

"Enough, sir!" and she was withdrawing her hand, when Bloker exclaimed,

"I must feel the flutter of that breast—it outdoes nature!" and with his disengaged arm he clasped her waist with compulsory ardor.

With surprise and sudden anger she started from his embrace and fled to the window. There she turned, her bosom heaving and disdain in her kindled eye, and cried, "Leave my room!"

"Hear reason, my dear Miss—"

"Go! or I'll call help!"

Scowling vindictively upon the incensed woman, Bloker departed.

A week passed; during which Jane was unable to use her needle. She thought to return the tailor's work, but still hoped to complete a part of it by stitching till the midnight chimes. Dime by dime, her purse was emptying. At length, she took back the unfinished work. With misgiving she approached the counter of the great slop-shop, and presented her excuses. A foreman snatched from her the patterns, with an oath, and bid her begone. A score of women were standing by—sewers like herself. Some echoed the man's depreciations, others laughed, and two or three seemed to sympathize with her.

On the morning of his repulse by Jane, Bloker visited Miss Cluskey. He was known to that gentle spinster, she having previously appealed to him with some success, of her own motion, in behalf of Frank. Therefore, when the merchant pulled the porcelain bell-knob at her portal, after reconnoitring from the area, she slapped the small servant with the lid of a saucepan for keeping her "always in a mess when gentlemen called," cast off her apron, tidied her cap, and admitted him, with a serene aspect which showed superiority to every carnal instigation.

"Why, Mr. Bloker, I declare! Walk in, sir—who would have thought it? As I was saying to our Susan—that's my help, sir, that I took a bound-girl from the poor-house and send to Sunday-school regular —Susan! I dreamed last night of a thunderstorm, which is a sign that something agreeable will happen."

"I could wish my mission more pleasant than it is, Miss Cluskey."

The spinster lapsed instantly to a state of suitable melancholy, and gave a feeble sigh.

"Yet it is benevolent."

"I am very sure it is," responded Miss Cluskey,

brightening. Benevolence, to Miss Cluskey, was symptomatic of bank notes.

"Captain Warner was long my respected friend, and I owe something to his memory."

"The rich have blessed privileges," observed the spinster, with anticipatory promptitude.

"Duties may be so called, madame."

"That poor child, Frank, is completely forsaken by his sister. Ah! sir, pride must have a fall."

"It is of his sister that I have come to talk—I believe her mind is diseased."

"I can't help it, sir, nor her either. She's been going on ridiculous since her mother's death, as if she felt more than everybody else in the world who has losses. As Miss Trimley told her, it's a sinful repining. Then she must lose her situation by her conduct! I couldn't overlook it if I was the robin red-breast that covered the babes in the wood."

"Last night I found her hurt on the street, where she had fallen, and attended her home. I proposed to get a physician, but she would not allow me, and I reluctantly left her in a great deal of pain. This morning I called to learn her condition and offer my services, when she exclaimed violently against me for insulting her, threw a tumbler, and threatened me with an outcry. I saw, with sorrow, her state, and came straight to perform this painful duty."

"Well, sir, I really can't say what's to be done. She has quit coming here. *I* have no money to spend. I suppose she ought to be taken care of by somebody."

"I believe, Miss Cluskey, your means are limited—'

"You may well say that, sir."

"And insufficient to bear the charge of properly caring for your niece. Perhaps the money can be elsewhere supplied. But it would still be necessary for you, her nearest adult relative, to appear in her behalf."

"Regarding her state of mind?"

"Yes. I may be imposing on myself a heavy obligation, but her father served me well, and I will venture it. I will pay the expense of skilful nursing—I think it will soon cure her. There is a pleasant and secluded asylum, of which I know something, though it costs high."

"I hardly see how far I can testify—Do you think, sir, a few weeks would restore her?"

"So I hope. You will not be rigorously questioned. You must state what you know of the particulars of her melancholy to a physician—there's the celebrated Doctor Conium, a pleasant-tongued gentleman, I can introduce to you—who will make a personal examination of the patient and give a certificate."

"They treat the patients kind, I suppose."

"Their treatment is altogether mild and considerate, madame. They have the best-tempered nurses, music, books, games, conversation, and shady, spacious grounds for exercise and recreation."

"I am sure I am willing to do all I can for the poor thing."

"I am thinking how we shall contrive an opportunity for the doctor, without duly exciting her. I have it!—send for her here. Doctor Conium can call, as if by chance, or for an assumed purpose, and converse with her. An attendant can be in an adjoining room, and a coach in readiness. If the doctor should give a certificate, it will be easy for you to persuade her to take a drive. It will save tumult."

"I shouldn't like to take such a step, sir, if I didn't think it for her good. If it will only cure her of that dreadful downness! She isn't really fit for anything now. Yes, there's no doubt her mind's affected."

"She may need suitable clothing, and here is thirty dollars to supply it. She will be in the society of ladies. Prompt action on our part may save her from suicide."

Doctor Conium called at the Cluskey abode by appointment, and Jane was inveigled into engaging in a few minutes conversation with him. He was on his way to dinner after his professional rounds, and was to hold a college clinique at three; therefore he came briskly around the corner to his awaiting carriage and Bloker.

"It's hardly pronounced insanity," he said, "though the girl may be a little shaken at top. Tried the Shakesperian test, and found her gambol some from the matter of our talk—it might, indeed, have been natural confusion—Moody, eh? Would like to look further into the case, but I am overwhelmed, literally obstructed with labor. Her aunt's story, coupled with her wildness toward you—strange freak of expostulation! I hope there was no method in it—must satisfy me. Take her to Norey's? I don't know much about the place; I nearly always send to the regular institutions; I suppose it's all right. I'll give you the paper;" and Conium wrote it on the carriage cushion, pocketed his fee, and drove away. In another hour the doctor was reëstablishing his energies with Madeira, and Jane Warner was in Norey's Retreat.

Norey was a Scotchman, with a stony calmness of bearing, features that might have been molten, so immovable were they in repose, and a methodic graciousness which started in the recipient of it a doubt of its sincerity. He had been educated to his business in an English asylum conducted in accordance with the old mad-house system, and where a commitment was sometimes as effectual as the Bourbon *lettre* to restrain an obnoxious and constrain an unwilling person. With such a training, he held in little favor the milder modern hospital administration, although he affected to acquiesce in it, and, compelled by the prevalence of popular assent, in some respects adopted it. Though the ancient privacy and profits no longer prevailed, separation from society for the friendless or the solitary was still possible; there was still gold to be paid to a discreet jailer, unrecognized, but tolerated by the law; so a large stone country mansion, remote from the high-road, was purchased and painted by Norey, dark cells and shower-baths introduced, the rooms furnished with double doors, the windows stoutly wired, a lofty wall of light-colored, cheerful bricks built around the grounds, and all together constituted the "Retreat." For, said Norey in his adroitly suggestive circular "Insanity often, perhaps most frequently, exhibits itself in an aversion to the nearest relatives and kindest friends; and this should-dictate temporary seclusion."

Norey was not originally a physician. He began his career as an under-keeper—became a keeper—an apothecary's assistant—apothecary—attended a course or two of lectures at Edinburg, and from superintendent rose to be proprietor of an asylum. His first officer at the Retreat was a gaunt, sinewy Englishman, blind in one eye, who was close, sombre, and watchful with the hard grey eye which remained, and who professed the faith of a Covenanter. Indeed, his religion—such as it was to him—was the only topic upon which he was not habitually reserved, inasmuch, it seemed, that there was unusual acerbity and discomfort in it. He was not, in his silent grimness, a pleasant man for a nerve-shaken patient to behold. The matron was fat and florid, passably polite, and of a positive fibre—just the kind of woman, in short, to be reckoned upon as unconscious of irregularities in the management.

Perhaps it was to adapt Jane to her new situation, perhaps it was by a suggestion of the humane Bloker, that she was aroused every half hour the first three nights to receive medicine, administered with uniform suavity, and was not permitted to sleep during the day. Her protests were disregarded, and her indignation at its height answered in dumb show. Two stout women were summoned, who led her along a hall to a windowless, gas-lighted bath-room arranged for showering, the walls of which were garnished with a collection of stout straps.

24*

CHAPTER XXXIII.

Nay, you shall see mine orchard; where, in an arbor, we will eat a last year's pippin of my own graffing, with a dish of carraways, and so forth.—HENRY IV.

HENRY DAVENPORT was as much lost to accustomed uses as a displaced brick or a dispossessed abbot upon the dissolution of the house of Horton. As the gradual settlement of the business invested him with more and more leisure, time went wearily with him. He grew dyspeptic, took an interest in the adulteration of food, and was observed to look truculent when he passed the corner grocery. In extreme fits of indigestion he publicly proclaimed his purpose to join a fire company, or talked wildly of a whaling voyage for the recovery of his health. He procured a carpenter's chest of tools, and undertook the construction of a labor-saving washing machine after an original model —crowning his yard fences in the resting spaces of graver toil and cogitation with intricate paling, cunningly devised for the exclusion of vagrant cats Finally he bought a farm.

It was a small property of forty acres, situated in the

Belair neighborhood, and near to Farmer Gregg's. Upon receiving the deed, the old clerk obtained a bull-dog of game reputation and despatched him to his rural purchase. Next, he transmitted for the stocking of his new domain a coop of hens, which he took on the averment that they were prime double-yolked layers of the true capon breed; and a pair of veteran cab horses, that had not smelt a fresh furrow since their colthood. He got also, a lot of seeds from an insolvent herb doctor, which, though they were somewhat old and musty, were had a bargain. As for agricultural implements, except those immediately necessary, he resolved to pick them up as they offered at country vendues. At the time of harvest, with a just sense of his importance as a proprietor of the soil, accompanied by his mother, he went down and entered on possession.

Thither Emily Horton repaired, shortly after the investiture, to pass a few days beneath the roof of her father's friend. She was soon at home with his excellent housekeeper. Mrs. Davenport was a gracious, motherly body, who rejoiced in occasions to comfort her ailing fellow-creatures with the proper physic. She wore spruce caps with inlayings of black ribbon at the borders, and was dexterous with her knitting-needles. She was not friendly to innovation, and, among other singularities, insisted on counting winter to the twelfth of March inclusive; "The good old style," she observed, "which her mother kept before her; and which was altered by the Pope of Rome, and she would like to know what business *he* had to meddle with it." Good Mrs. Davenport—who had already contracted a friendly alliance with Aunt Becky Gregg through a commendation of her butter—had grievances, and rehearsed them, ranging in the scale from the pump down to the pismires, and declared it as her well-matured opinion that the country would be endurable if it were paved and cleared of wasps. Her son, on the contrary, was constantly contriving new possibilities of enjoyment. He set a weir in the river and visited it daily for fish, bringing sometimes two or three perch with appropriate exultation. He weeded, mulched, and trained in the garden, pursuing the plant bugs with unrelenting animosity. He learned to talk glibly of fallow and ley; took studies in the anatomy of the plough; and began to experiment on patches with rival fertilizers. He affected cattle medicine, and kept the cab-horses up to their provender with drenches. By patient observation of Farmer Gregg, he mastered the mysteries of harness. Not that this exuberance of knowledge was acquired suddenly; it came to fructify like seasonable showers.

Bridget McFadden served the Davenports in the capacity of woman of all work. She was a decent body with warm sympathies, who strove in her humble but honest way to cultivate good gifts and live in hope. She had worked for Miss Cluskey in the felon and fever stages of Susan's kitchen career, and at general house-cleanings; and as it was her judicious practise to improve such connections, she called occasionally for gossip and the rare chance of a dole of fragments. Thus she became a favorite and semi-confidant of Frank, for whom she acquired a fondness, which she showed by considerately regarding his little requests for attendance, cheering him with her good-humor, and amusing him with her quaint Irish fancies. On her last visit at the spinster's she found the lad very low in spirits and tormented with apprehension by the prolonged absence of his sister. So much did Frank's dejection interest Bridget, that she made inquiry at the lodgings lately occupied by Jane. She could only learn of her sudden departure; when her clothing, being all that belonged to her on the premises—that were hired furnished—had been sent for, and the rent paid to the month's end. The one additional scrap of information which she procured was from an acquaintance near by, whose son, a fish hawker, had seen the young woman out airing in a carriage, on the day of her disappearance. This was just enough intelligence to whet, without in the least satisfying Bridget's curiosity; and there was no help, for if the hawker could tell more he was at the time on his business rounds in the suburbs. Still she deemed what she had heard sufficient to alarm Miss Cluskey, and incite her to an instant search for her niece. Her surprise was great when her disclosure was received by that lady with unconcern, and her zeal rewarded with a rebuff; all further communication with Frank being denied her.

The more the disappearance with its circumstances of haste and mystery was revolved in the McFadden cerebrum, the more inexplicable it seemed; for Bridget's ingenuous bosom harbored no sinister suspicion concerning the conduct of the missing girl. In her perplexity she made the subject a theme of discourse, and as she colored it with the hues of her imagination to a gloomy and even horrible extent, she at length withdrew her mistress from a diligent quest of a recipe for the colic, with which complaint the stable boy had been afflicted the day before, and persuaded that matron to give ear to her narrative; which, in turn, was imparted to Emily, who was at once interested by it.

The event was discussed in a family conference, and Emily easily induced the old clerk to aid her in an attempt to explain it. They went for this purpose together to the city and waited on Miss Cluskey, who received them with stinted civility. Emily could not induce her to engage in a public inquiry. "No, miss; it is in vain to urge it; I'm not such a fool. If you could prove to me this wonder is not another of the girl's strange fancies, there might be some room for hysterics; though then it would be as well perhaps if they were kept in the family—not that I mean reflections. To make a judy of myself in print, blindfolded, is what I don't mean to do—I'm obliged to you, all the same." The spinster permitted Emily to have an interview with Frank.

"Hoping, miss, you won't put anything into the child's head to frighten him, for he's trouble enough now."

The sick boy's face beamed with a welcome fit for a good angel; for though he had seldom seen Emily, he had heard his lost sister speak of her with all the warmth of esteem. His solicitude for his sister found speedy utterance. Emily could not remove, but strove to allay it by ingenious suggestions. But, hopeful as they were, they produced little effect. She assured him no endeavor should be spared to discover Jane. Her whereabout, indeed, since she had left her lodging had been reported; and although the clue might result in nothing at present, all would surely be clear in time. It was not impossible that, allured by some unusual advantage, she had left hurriedly; and that her letters had miscarried. Feeble consolations, scarcely less like December in the young invalid's heart than its own forebodings.

As Emily sat by the settee holding Frank's white and wasted hand while they conversed, a thought arose in her mind.

"Frank! wouldn't you like to be in the country at this pleasant season?"

"Ah, Miss Emily, a poor cripple like me must be content. I can *think* of the country, you know; see brooks in the cool woods, sunshine on the birds' backs, and almost hear the rustle of leaves."

"Can you hear the birds and eat the fresh fruit in your dreams?"

"Yes; and behold flowers of gorgeous colors too, that sometimes mingle with each other while I look; and the other night I awaked trying to wipe the stain of mulberries off my mouth. Ha, ha! the berries dissolved with the dream."

"I see you are a pet of queen Mab. Seriously, Frank, if you choose, with your aunt's consent you shall go for a few weeks to a quiet farm-house. A friend of mine is a good-natured gentleman, and I know he will take you to please me."

"It would be delicious, Miss Emily!"

"We will see, then. I think you will be allowed to go, but I must persuade your aunt."

Upon hearing Emily's proposition, which Davenport seconded with enthusiasm, Miss Cluskey assumed to hesitate, but it was plain that, for so self-willed a lady, her objections would yield to gentle assaults. She was to be relieved of all expense of the boy's maintenance during his absence, and that charge she asserted, with some appearance of truth despite the neighborhood whispers of considerable savings shrewdly invested, was a burden disproportioned to her ability. The attendance upon her nephew she declared to be at once a duty and a pleasure, and, in justice to her, so long as the weekly stipend was paid it had so appeared; but the demand of late upon her purse had altered her demeanor, and kindliness was being daily throttled in the stronger grasp of avarice. Miss Cluskey probably had not wronged posterity in remaining single. It was arranged that Frank should be called for the first bright morning of the ensuing week.

Henry Davenport, having set down Emily at Doctor Mellen's, proceeded to prosecute according to direction a search for the hawker of fish. That itinerant of traffic had just left the parental abode, and was supposed by a coatless and bare-footed cadet of the house, to be producible in an adjacent street. Under the stimulus of a dime, which he deposited in his mouth by an exact fling, the urchin led off briskly, and presently announced, "our Zack jist ahead, a giving of it woice;" which the stentorian cry of, "Yer-ers your fresh pogees! *only* three cents a pound," abundantly confirmed.

"My friend!" commenced the old clerk, "can I say a few words to you?"

"You oughter know best, sir."

"I see you are a wag, and none the worse for that—I'm something of a wag, myself."

"I say, none of that gammon, uncle. You can't have them fish no less than three cents if you take the lot—nary red. Figsey!" to an associate, "sound your melodeon a bit, drive up the cart and stop at the corner."

"I don't want to buy, but to question you about a matter which interests me."

"Figsey! you needn't exert yourself uncommon while I transact some private business with this gent, but keep an eye to the purceeds, and don't take none but bankable money—Now, sir!"

"You remember Miss Jane Warner."

"The sewing girl what lived near us? Yes. Well?"

"You saw her about the time of her disappearance, I think, in company with others."

"I say, uncle, what's the reward?"

"The reward!"

"Any information concerning the party will be liberally re-money-rated, you know, as they puts in the newspapers when they advertise for people supposed to be drownded or they want to nab—Is it stiff?"

25

"O! there's nothing of the kind, my friend. There is nothing to come of finding the girl in the shape of profit to any one; and there is not a suspicion against her. She has a few friends who are anxious; that's all. The search is purely humane."

"That squares it—so I seen her."

"Where, and with whom?"

"A taking an airing on the river road in a kerridge, with a man and a woman."

"What was your impression of her companions?"

"That's what the lawyers call an opinion aint it, when they requests the party to pint?"

"Something of the sort—what you thought, now," explained Davenport suasively, slipping a half-dollar into the hawker's hand.

"Well, then," proceeded the latter, in an oracular tone, "I considered the turn-out tip-top, and the lady and gent as was with her prime for fortygraphs, and remarkable nobby and fire-proof."

Whether the last attributed quality figured an appearance of secrecy, or was a flowery manner of expressing pecuniary responsibility, Davenport could not determine; and it seemed, indeed, the only feature of the account which admitted of speculation.

Pillowed in Davenport's dearborn, the brickyards left behind, and the real country before and around him, Frank was a happier mortal than the Egyptian queen when she floated down the Cydnus. The orchards; the grouped cattle, standing or recumbent beneath some wide-spreading tree; the yellow wheat stacks; the restless corn, fretting with its blades at every breeze; crows winging their way from field to wood; the scarlet tomatoes in the gardens; were brave sights—the very dust was parcel of a new nature, as it rolled lazily beside the wagon in the sunshine. And when, after cheerful welcomes and ministrations by Mrs. Davenport and Emily, dinner came, the vegetables were tasteful beyond example, and for the lamb—age could not have made it mutton, while the juicy peaches blushed from the table at their praises. Soon the boy became a centre of interest to the Davenport household, and a favorite also of Farmer Gregg, who persisted in regarding his state as one of the deplorable results of a city training.

CHAPTER XXXIV.

I vow he is a lovely man—and such bravery of speech!
OLD PLAY.

WHILE Emily remained at Davenport's, Bloker availed himself of a general invitation which he had received from the hospitable old clerk and drove over behind his trotting team, one horse of which was milk white with a spacious chest, and the other a chestnut bay, in new, silver-mounted harness. His arrival flustered Mrs. Davenport, who was employed in the preparation of a valuable salve, quite out of her self-possession. Henry was open and hearty, and looked after the horses; keeping a prudent distance however, upon the stable boy's pointing out, "a cloud in the near 'un's face, which was a nugly sign." Frank, reclined in an easy chair in the hall, breathed the cool breeze which came from the western landscape, and luxuriated among the pictured pages—wondering voluptuary!—of a volume of the Penny Magazine. Jacob Bloker accosted the lad in a sympathetic tone which indicated yearnings under his fawn-colored waistcoat. The venerable matron discovered at once the tender locality. "My word for it," she subsequently said, "my word for it, Emily, that man possesses a noble nature!"

After tea Bloker presented his arm to Emily and begged the honor of her company for a twilight walk. He was in smooth spirits, comprehensively benevolent, and of mild conversation. A cat, startled by their approach and stopped by a wicket, plunged into a sunken cask half-full of water, which served as a provision for the garden, and for the propagation of mosquitos. Bloker's sensibility was aroused, and discarding his coat he hurried to puss's rescue.

"Suffering, Miss Horton," he said, "in every shape distresses me. Whenever I see a dog ill treated I think of that fine line of the poet,

'Even as it fawned he struck the poor dumb tyke.'

I started a petition lately to prevent the cruel tying of calves in the market carts."

"We would be glad, sir, to have your help in a search for a missing lady: Jane Warner has disappeared and cannot be heard of."

"It is singular—How long has she been gone?"

"Since the middle of June."

"And there are no traces of her, you say?"

"None."

"Why, then, it looks serious. There was no despair in the case, you think?"

"We cannot tell. I believe, however, that she possessed enough moral vigor to resist it. The people where she lodged say that, though melancholy, she was right in her mind to the time of her departure. That is all we can learn, except that she was quite poor, and was last seen in a carriage with two companions."

"The little information you have got will at least sanction the supposition of an unsettled mind; and the shades of insanity, the doctors say, are often so nice as to elude common observation. But what was she doing alone in a city lodging?"

"It appears her lowness of spirits after her mother's death displeased the school-teachers who employed her, and she lost her place. I did not know of her condition, or I would have gone to her."

"That, again, points to a disturbed intellect; made worse, perhaps, by the trials of unaccustomed poverty. I wish I could think otherwise. She may have wandered to some remote spot, and be still alive. If so, she will have been cared for, and can be found. There is another and a sadder conclusion. She has an aunt, I believe, in the city—what does she propose?"

"Nothing."

"Nothing!"

"She pretends to think that Jane has gone away in some caprice, and refuses to search for her."

"You astonish me. She cannot prevent our searching: such cases are the common property of the humane, among whom Miss Warner hitherto has not been inclined to number me. But I bear no resentment—to forgive such enmities is as much the interest of the philosopher, as the duty of the Christian; and I, at least, wish the equanimity of the one, if I cannot claim the added happiness of the other. If the lady had been prosperous I would have kept aloof from her affairs; but now I am anxious to show that I have been misunderstood. It is possible though, that her aunt's conjecture is right—I don't think so, still it is possible; in which case a public inquiry would tend to frustrate its purpose; for the young lady might seek a more secluded place of concealment. I think the search had best be private, and I will undertake to employ a detective upon it."

"I did not hope for so much zeal when I asked your aid. Accept my poor thanks, and be sure of the richer gratitude of her brother."

"I wish I could promote his comfort. When you think I can, command my purse;" and he felicitated himself that an obstacle to his desires was timeously and securely removed. Norey's had not come to his relief a day too soon.

As they sat together that summer evening in the porch and chatted, while the moonlight crept stealthily upon them, Bloker felt that he occupied a higher plane in the regard of Emily Horton. They chatted of flowers, affections, pleasant people, and the comet; and it was as refreshing as would have been a zephyr tempered by the pole, that measured recitation by Jacob Bloker of some nervous lines of old Chapman:

"—— Innocence, the sacred amulet
'Gainst all the poisons of infirmity,
Of all misfortune, injury, and death:
That makes a man in tune still in himself;

Free from the hell to be his own accuser;
Ever in quiet, endless joy enjoying,
No strife nor no sedition in his powers."

It was surely Marcus Antoninus set to music among lilies beneath the fawn-colored waistcoat.

CHAPTER XXXV.

Behold I see the haven nigh at hand,
To which I meane my wearie course to bend;
Vere the maine shete, and beare up with the land,
The which afore is fayrly to be kend,
And seemeth safe from storms that may offend:
There this fayre Virgin wearie of her way
Must landed bee, now at her iourneyes end—
FAERIE QUEENE.

THERE are experiences in life which put an enduring impress upon the individual, and yet cannot afterward be adequately described in detail. The traces that remain are but separated memories emitted from the depths of our consciousness; as bubbles sluggishly rise to the surface of a lake when the storm is over. A stroke of affliction was suddenly laid upon Bradley. Seemingly in the full vigor of health when Spring came with bloom and brightness, Lydia Bardleigh was now dying of a cancer in the neck. She had been told all—the knife would not avail; and she had calmly replied, "Even so, come, Lord Jesus."

Bradley was often at The Cedars now, a worn, subdued man, waiting to part with his betrothed in the ante-chamber of Death. A sepulchral tranquillity seemed to rest upon the old mansion and its surroundings—a sepulchral tranquillity open to the garish day, and dressed in a poor pomp of sunshine. The hospitable fires were quenched. Carriage wheels still grated on the approach, but the challenge of welcome was hushed; there was no gay sally and answering laughter under the sheltering elms, nor gambols to make cheerful the shadows of the hemlocks. The flutter of midnight merriment had risen to these hoary rafters; but now the lights were out.

Our illusions overmaster us, and men tread among latent shapes of mortality as if their feet were eternal on flint. So the eye sees not in the beautiful flowers of the aconite a lurking poison which can paralyse the heart. Perception itself is hoodwinked by hope, and bidden to contemplate the possibilities of Providence—and prayer without resignation invokes a miracle to stay dissolving nature. Hence the bedside trust of friends in a final effort of skill, some potent remedy to rally the sinking powers—ammonia, phosphorus, be it what it may—even while the sick man's features sharpen into the last fleeting fashion of the mortal mask. But where the fate rankles in the corrupting flesh—where the ulcer day by day spreads corrosive, searching toward the sources of vitality, and naught can stop it, even the mercy of deception is denied. Then fails the heart which loves. Yet solicitude, like a shadow, attends on certainty—it is David still stretched fasting upon the earth for the sick child after the prophecy of Nathan. This sense of dependence is established for the subordination of the creature. For relief from his heaviness, Bradley tried to read, but there was no spell in eloquence and fancy now. He sought consolation in remembrances of the past—the past with her, which he had thought consecrated forever to happiness; but it was no longer joyous—it answered him with hollow echoes, as do solitary midnight streets the tread of the wayfarer. Better there had never been a dawn, since there was to be no day. Philosophy presented motionless lips—your only stoic without a heart—like the Sphinx in stone, where dwelt neither complaint nor comfort. He knew not the love of "the First begotten of the dead, and the Prince of the kings of the earth." He sought in the world of Shakespeare, who of uninspired men he reverenced most, instances of heroic resignation to calamity, that he might lesson himself withal. There the troubled resolution of Brutus was able to bear the death of Portia,

"With meditating that she must die once."

But the buds of young love never yet unfolded beneath the Roman's cold and lowering sky. What, he urged, were the tears which the scarcely lingering Lear—for sorrow dignifies like wine, and hesitates at no comparison—what were the tears that that "great decay" shed over the dead Cordelia, to this slow distress; to the pangs when are riven affianced hearts. Even the wisdom and pathos of the greatest of poets were thus measured by Bradley with a glance of the mind. A sickening horror sat upon him, and he shuddered in spirit as at an apocalypse of terror issuing from the bosom of an Indian summer noon.

No portion of his suffering escaped the vigilant tenderness of Lydia. As a woman—in spirit a wife, she accepted it as a testimony of his affection, and from the amplitude of her love could have returned a keener pain for every pain of his. But she beheld in it also a dangerous growth of discontent tending toward a defiant reprehension of the Supreme Wisdom. One morning, a fair September morning, warm and still, and fragrant with the sun-pressed odor of grapes, she called him to her side.

"Dear heart!" she said, "let us never lose sight of the Divine intention, that we should grow strong by suffering."

"It has been often said."

"And often proved, dear Bradley, to salvation. 'As many as I love, I rebuke and chasten.' To be so chastened is to be cherished by the Spirit, and our sick souls, when they humbly long for the Love and the Power, are watched and ministered to by angels, as our blessed Saviour was comforted from heaven after the temptations of hell in the wilderness."

"I do not find the comfort, Lydia; so let us pass it, and I shall endure as best I can."

"That, Bradley, is a confession of darkness; and 'If the light which is in thee be darkness how great is that darkness.'"

"It is true; there is no day in me."

"Then join me in prayer, dear Bradley, that a ray

of the Divine brightness which proceedeth from Jesus Christ may shine into our hearts."

"I have no power of prayer."

"Our blessed Saviour has invited us to ask; and we can, if we approach Him in a spirit of penitent meekness, forgiving all men, as we desire to be forgiven and favored. As we grow to be poor in heart, we grow to be prayerful. 'Come unto me, all ye that labor, and are heavy laden, and I will give you rest. Take my yoke upon you and learn of me; for I am meek and lowly in heart: and ye shall find rest unto your souls.'"

"If affliction like this be good, why does nature agonize?"

"It is the earthy nature. These ties of time while we live together here, are for a holy purpose in God's economy; but in heaven our affections will probably not be limited. It is a fine thought of Richard Baxter's—'The enjoyment of His kingdom is, as the light of the sun, each have the whole, and the rest never the less.' And the sanctified heart, even here, should rejoice at the prospect of a love rising to the Highest and boundless as the universe. The purified, who are congenial here, will find an unspeakable rapture in that emulation which embraces heaven. That we are soon to be parted," and her voice trembled, "is perhaps because we are assigned for higher purposes hereafter. God, in his infinite and bountiful compassion, grant it!"

"We should accustom ourselves, then, to meditate on the loss of—of—"

"The beloved who are ready to depart, dear Bradley."

"—With composure—nay, exultation. I know it is the Christian's consolation. To me it is only a solemn abstract solace, which sheds no relief. We want them *here*—we need their benign influence more than do the saints above."

"That, Bradley, is a presumptuous reflection! Each earnest wish, I grant, will find an argument, but the strongest argument is weakness when arrayed against the possibilities of life. 'How little should God hear from us if we had what we would have!' Believe that I feel it when I say again that, His purposes are not bounded by the narrow limits of time; beyond them His heavens are full of days. Our Father's providence, which has numbered the very hairs of our heads, is sufficient. Remember, 'That which thou sowest is not quickened except it die: So also is the resurrection of the dead. It is sown in corruption, it is raised in incorruption: It is sown in dishonor, it is raised in glory: it is sown in weakness, it is raised in power.' And that power implies uses; as yet concealed behind the vail, but we know them to be the uses of Beneficence."

Charley Bardleigh came home from college. He was really distressed, but nineteen and a Freshman. He brought studious intentions and several text-books, which were usually shelved together, giving place to a novel or the last magazine. Most of the time he was out-doors, looking after the education of a pair of young dogs, or taking apart, polishing and oiling his guns, in a quiet way. Yet Charley Bardleigh was really distressed; kept from social gatherings, and even declined to pull a trigger on the game which abounded alluringly. Now and then, the judge's wonted hilarity would show itself for a moment, like a spark in tinder, and go out in the sombreness that prevailed. There was a cast of womanly gentleness in his bearing.

The time was come for Bradley to depart. She had fallen into a slumber with her hand clasped on his. The wings seemed folded up within her. He would have gently disengaged her hand without awaking her. Conscious of the attempt, she, smiling, opened her eyes.

So serenely lay The Cedars landscape around him as he rode away, so peaceful was it in a world of clamor and care, that his heart grew passionless and reverential, and he paused to contemplate it. The high ground rose in terraces, planted with fruit trees, from a broad margin of smooth-rolled meadow which stretched along a creek, the further boundary of which was a sloping hill-side heavily wooded. An array of trees that would have gladdened the critical eye of Evelyn flanked the mansion, among which some noble weeping willows, their tresses tinged with yellow, were conspicuous. All was repose; only a few sheep were to be seen nibbling in the nearer pasture. The afternoon sun cast the shadows of the orchard forward on the upland, and each growth seemed bending to reach its unreal counterpart in silent eagerness.

CHAPTER XXXVI.

With these drugs will I, this very day, compound the true orvietan, that noble medicine which is so seldom found genuine and effective within these realms of Europe.—KENILWORTH.

FARMER GREGG had, as he styled it, "an attack of the bilious." Driving in his ox-cart to a schooner which was receiving grain and moored a quarter of a cable's length from the shore, by a freak or fright of the cattle he was shot into the river. Farmer Gregg had been taking calomel, and was lifted out of his involuntary bath an alarmed man, for he cherished a belief in the damaging result of cold upon the use of that remedy. His case, however, might not be hopeless, and the fame of Mrs. Davenport's curative skill had reached him. Accordingly he put on his "bettermost" suit, including a well-preserved bell-crown hat of great antiquity, mounted his sleek mare Dolly, and fared forth to consult the oracle of healing. Thither let us accompany him, and keep the worthy matron's pharmacopœia at a salutary distance.

The old clerk is leaning on a fence and considering his melons in a rapture of admiration. Farmer Gregg's,

"How d' do, neighbor?" as he ambles up on the grass, startles him as would a congreve rocket, and after looking foolish a moment he coughs with dignity and returns the address somewhat as if it were an accusation.

"Reether a fine lot, neighbor—I've seen 'em grow bigger though, in the shade of tater vines."

"*I* never saw larger in the city markets."

"Haint? Well, that beats! Why, I've tuk 'em there nearly twice the size. But I'll own that was an uncommon season. Sut's good on the young vines to keep off the bugs.—I feel dreadful strange, internal."

"Sick at the stomach?"

"No; I reether think—its—in—my—bones."

"Appears to me you need something searching—I dare say mother can tell."

"Why, that's jist what I'm after. Beckey, she tried to persuade me not, but to take some hot barm tea instead; but I reckon there aint much grip in that. Your mother, neighbor, is getting among folks an awful reputation for doctorin'."

Frank accosted the farmer cheerfully, as the latter deposited his diseased bones in a melancholy manner on an end of the settee.

"Tired, Uncle Gregg?"

"No, little one; I don't feel bright like—I haint worked off enough bile, I expect."

This was a subterfuge; the ailing agriculturist had determined to unbosom himself only to his medical adviser. Mrs. Davenport shortly came in from her clear-starching. She produced an adequate remedy from the receipt of a celebrated German woman, whose two immediate male ancestors were physicians of great repute, the elder having been the seventh son of a seventh son, and imprisoned in a castle as a wizard. The farmer received it with gratitude, and the respect due to a medicine so assured, without caring to inquire whether it was counteractive or preventive. As he rose to leave, he suddenly bethought himself of a purpose, and plunging his hand into the pocket of his coat drew forth a cucumber which was oddly curled upon itself.

"It's a cur'osity for you, Frank. I've watched it grow a purpose—it's as perfect as a twist in a pig's tail. Sich are the wonders of nature!—And that puts me in mind of something curious I found the other day, and meant to show Miss Emily."

"She is in the city now, but we expect her here the last of the week—Mr. Horton insists she shall come for her health," remarked Davenport.

"Wife thinks it may turn out kind of supernatural, but I say it was the wind."

"What was it, neighbor Gregg?" inquired the old lady.

"O! I haint told. Well, I took my corn to a new mill to get ground—for to my mind, neighbor, Job Smelt is a raising this year a leetle too much pork. It was a good stretch further, but I wagoned quite a jag. Coming back, in the road by the hospital for crazy folks, I seen what I took to be a letter, and 'lighted and picked it up. Then I seen it was only a letter cover; but I read the hand-write, and it was Miss Emily's name in full. So I kept it, and here it is."

"That's almost as strange as a circumstance which happened to aunt Betsy Harper's daughter, only instead of thinking it supernatural, she called it romantic; and so it turned out. Let me see—was it the great strawberry year, or not—*that* was in thirty-five, warn't it, neighbor? No matter. Aunt Betsy—"

And here the old lady's reminiscence was interrupted by an exclamation of surprise from Frank, to whom in turn Davenport had handed the envelope:

"It is Jane's writing—I know it well!"

CHAPTER XXXVII.

You have a nimble wit: I think 'twas made of Atalanta's heels. Will you sit down with me? and we two will rail against our mistress the world, and all our misery.—JAQUES.

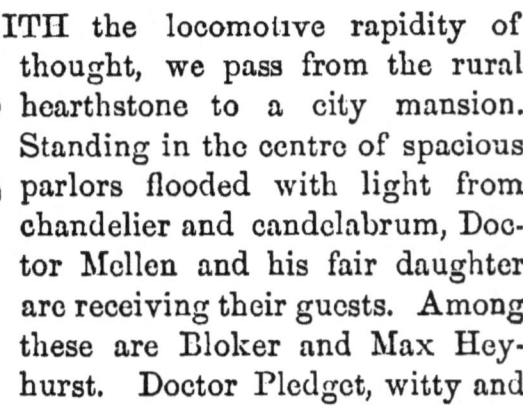

WITH the locomotive rapidity of thought, we pass from the rural hearthstone to a city mansion. Standing in the centre of spacious parlors flooded with light from chandelier and candelabrum, Doctor Mellen and his fair daughter are receiving their guests. Among these are Bloker and Max Heyhurst. Doctor Pledget, witty and debonair, would perhaps be present but for the shadow of a dead dog which separates him from his scientific brother.

It was a butcher's terrier suspected of being mad, which Mellen had bought to vindicate his theory of the harmlessness of *rabies*. His servants, who, in consideration of high wages, had put up with a great deal in the way of snakes, fled in dismay; but the doctor in spite of the exodus persevered with unruffled temper toward the conversion or confutation of Pledget. It was at the very height of a hot dispute for and against the existence of hydrophobia, between the two gentlemen, that the terrier, which had been fastened with unphilosophic carelessness to a rope, escaped from its tether and burst into the apartment where the controversy was proceeding. Doctor Pledget grasped a poker and skirmished with the intruder, while Doctor Mellen called loudly upon him to desist. But, at length pressed into an angle of the room where further retreat was impossible, in sheer desperation with one blow he fairly finished the dog and the experiment together; and at the same unlucky moment the friendship of the disputants terminated.

The philosophical occupations of Doctor Mellen kept him much apart from his family. He made minute and wonderful experiments on the hairs of various animals, dividing and sub-dividing them, and pressing them to the utmost verge of microscopic scrutiny. When he had digested his labors and discoveries in this important department of natural science into a fat quarto, and printed it, he turned his attention to hides. He dissected them—he macerated them—he tested them with acids. On a supply of biscuits and hard boiled eggs in his laboratory he would convert the integument of a crocodile, as hard as the heart of Pharaoh, into a pultaceous analysis. Even the skin of the armadillo defied in vain his researches. Outside of his peculiar province he was an urbane and unassuming man; but in it he thundered his tenets in the journals of learned societies and ponderous pamphlets. These were answered by other Mellens, in other parts of the world, with dogmatical speculations on the other side; which the doctor, in turn, derided in sinewy English as very vagaries of fancy. He had been scathed by the explosion of retorts, and rescued in a state of suspended animation from unwholesome gases; but he was in harness still, patiently investigating, and as good as ever for his part in the clash of controversy.

The ladies rustle and trail their graceful finery in the promenade. The talk is humorous; a little censorious, perhaps, if the frequent breaks of answering laughter which sometimes seem derisory are its index. It rises and falls with the performance and cessation of the opera airs. By-and-by, when night and morning are at meeting, there will be a supper creditable to gastronomic art; nothing lean and tough disguised in condiments, you may believe, but veritable oysters, quails, *pate de foi gras,* ices, and fruit. When the blithe milkmaids are out in the grey morning with their pails, these gentle bosoms will be fluctuating, to the time of sounds more or less melodious, toward the half way of their rest.

"So you think, Miss Emily Horton, the German was right who said, 'American women resemble tulips, in whom only the head delights?'" asked Caroline.

"No; but not altogether wrong. You must allow, too, for the point of the simile."

"And you, Mr. Heyhurst—as an artist?"

"A beer-guzzling libeller, on my conviction as an artist and a man."

"Talking of heads—Heyhurst! I wish you would borrow those Peruvian skulls you spoke of; I want their angles for a paper in confutation of Occiput's March-hare theory. The traveller's offence is, I suspect, that he declares that our ladies are running down in a regular muscular atrophy," said Doctor Mellen.

"It may be safely averred that, of American women not obliged to labor not two in ten take the bodily exercise which nature requires," persisted Emily.

"I don't know, Miss Horton: Nature is an indulgent parent," observed Max.

"She seems to be; but disobeyed, presses a little here and a little there, and punishes in generations. A woman in the cultivation of her powers, physical as well as moral, should consider that she is, like the old Greek, planting for posterity.—Do we walk?"

"No; but glide, like goddesses," responded Max, gravely.

"Fantastic compliments apart, Mr. Heyhurst, you know how many of our countrywomen languish into pale, expressionless beings, with chests that court consumption. The influence of the father—who should be in all vital matters the household's head, accountable to *his* Head in heaven—is too little felt in the education of his daughters; and in a Christian this neglect is a delinquency. To take a more restricted view, there is too much work which may be called by a general title time-waste, done by young women who are just well enough off to live without labor, and who pass their spiritless lives, when employed, chiefly in knitting cotton thread for glove-money. This trifling business, when not pursued for a livelihood, while it stimulates vanity, ensures a neglect of the cultivation of the heart, the head, and the body. The home industry, that tasteful tidiness so necessary to the comfort of a civilized family, is slighted, because the young ladies have orders for thread collars from the shops. The confusion of the house is never mended, nor is it possible to shut all the dirt out of sight, and spiders spin blissfully on the very looking-glasses. Besides, this idle occupation is a wrong to the poor who *must* work for bread, and the virtuous and incapable destitute—the children of our common Father—who have a claim upon the hand-charity of their sisters that are blessed with leisure."

"Tilt your needles against every other woman's—'tis your vocation, coz! Work moral uglinesses into their absurd embroidery, and exigences into their edging. I am of Rosalind's uncle's mind touching the evils to be laid to the charge of women: 'There were none principal: they were all like one another, as half-pence are; every one fault seeming monstrous, till his fellow-fault came to match it.' Nay, never talk to me; I am all tears!"

"'Well, this is the forest of Arden'—in that vein at least."

"Will you recommend punching the dummy, Emily, to our suffering sex?—You never saw a lady punch the dummy, Mr. Bloker?"

"Never had that felicity."

"I was born a dummy, if any dear creature wants exercise," said Max.

"It belongs to a calisthenics of our own. The dummy is a canvas case stuffed with straw, and suspended from a beam in a clear space. The operators are Emily and I, who stand opposite to each other, and use our arms with a purpose upon the swinging sack."

"A pilfering from the prize ring, and a movable of Mr. Benjamin Caunt's!" exclaimed Heyhurst.

"Do you know it is actually thought vulgar in many neighborhoods for ladies to walk by the mile? And I have seen American women, pretending to cultivation and rich in luxurious surroundings, who considered it gross and unrefined to confess a good appetite," said Emily.

"What do the delicate darlings feed on—macaroons moistened in maraschino?" asked Caroline.

"When I write a romance I shall make the heroine eat apple-dumplings, even if I am compelled in the end to use poison and finish her with an Italianized strawberry," said Max.

"To change the subject—Mr. Heyhurst, have you seen Crome Green's famous picture?" asked Doctor Mellen.

"Yes; my eyes have partaken of the general gladness."

"What is it?" inquired Bloker.

"Ah! there you pose me. *He* calls it, 'The Coming Man.' I suppose it is."

"Coming from where?" asked Bloker.

"And for what?" added Caroline.

"The Man of the Future, seen through the Mist of the Present."

"It can hardly be a fog worth speaking of which permits him to be seen," said Bloker.

"He is not distinctly visible, which, if it hurts the prophecy, helps the imaginative spectator to suppose a grand conception. For my part, it looked so like one of my late landlords, who did me the honor to die my creditor, that I half suspected his ghost inspired the design."

"And you didn't feel reproved?" asked Caroline.

"In the very mild effects of the ideal I saw no reproach; of course it would have been superfluous politeness in me to reproach myself. If the picture is at all typical of the time to come, we may expect the abolition of duns."

"I object to the anatomy of the figure," remarked Doctor Mellon.

"I object to the mist," said Max: Who can paint a mist?"

"He who aspires to, had better try his 'prentice hand' at a dew drop on a rose leaf. Mist, itself, is a painter to the man of fancy," said Emily.

"It is; not understanding by the term your dirty English fog. The true creative mist is not city-begotten, neither does it canopy the level landscape, but it dwells in the pure air of the mountains."

"Then you have seen some of its finest works," said Emily.

"I have; in a Californian winter. Sometimes, at night, I would steal apart from the glare and noises of the camp, and, climbing an overhanging hill, listen to the surging of the troubled water that rolled beneath, a solitary sound deepening the silence, and gaze upon the shifting imagery of mist, that rose and sunk along the mountain sides. Rose and sunk in shapes fair and fantastic—alternating—contrasting—mingling; the graceful curves of classic sculpture; domes richly robust; the fretted spire, lifting itself in air; arch; temple; tower; cataracts, converted in their fall to stony immobility, art-created forms of past and present; nature's wildest aspects; grey, all grey and ghastly, in the vapor-filtered moonlight."

"To turn from the palette to the lyre—they say that Funeman's last volume has taken," said Emily.

"So! Is Funeman among the poets?" inquired Max, in a tone of solicitude.

"It is the muse's livery, I believe," replied Emily, as she handed Heyhurst a book from the table beside her, as gaudy as a Dutch tulip.

"Um—a portrait. Funeman risible—Thalia couching at his mouth. Hear this—'The Catfish Crier's Complaint.'"

"Sorry to object, but don't read it!" exclaimed Doctor Mellen, alarmed by a preparatory gurgle in Max's throat.

"I will not; I wouldn't distress anybody. Benevolence was my foster-brother."

"To ascend from Funeman to the gods—When shall we have a song that will leap to the national heart, and make it throb applause in the spirit of a higher than a bloodletting heroism. A martyred missionary is far more deserving of song than was Sir John Moore. In this matter, poets lackey to the brutal adulation of the mob, and the partiality of Laura Matilda for a uniform. It is not the immortal in them which sings." said Emily.

"Is not Campbell's 'Mariners of England' potent to excite the circulation?" asked Max.

"Yes, as a bottle of brandy is, unhealthily. Every drunken Englishman is a sea-king, and fights Trafalgar over again. Campbell was a true poet, and wrote better than that. The Farewell to Kemble, though the theme was not high, is much better poetry."

"Campbell is certainly compact, polished, and a poet.—So you are a non-resistant, Miss Horton?" said Max.

"The more christianized a man becomes, the nearer he approaches the posture of non-resistance. Non-resistance is the spirit of the gospel of our Lord. All men recognize this when they are revolted at preacher-fighters. Everybody feels that a bellicose bishop is not a servant of Jesus Christ. Yet why should a layman not be as perfect as a bishop, according to his measure of light? Now, all divine light is in its nature the same, whether it be in a blacksmith or a bishop. We are commanded, in the Gospel, to be perfect, even as our Father in heaven is perfect. What, then, are the perfections of War? Cupidity, revenge, bad-faith, outrages upon the person, spoliation of industry, ravage of nature, desecration of sanctities, destruction of life, maimings, political corruption, private malice, fraud in business, impurity of thought, forgetfulness of God, pauperism, intemperance, and arrogance."

"I believe that one man may rightfully slay another in strict self-defence when driven to the last wall, or for the protection of the virtue of a woman," said Heyhurst.

"I read the 'Corsair' when I was a supercargo, and I thought it very good," observed Bloker.

"What did Byron want with that 'young earthquake' in his Alpine thunder-storm by night; and what is a 'young earthquake,' since one full grown only lives a few seconds? But I'm no poet," said Doctor Mellen.

"It is a patch on the face of beauty. The poet who could make the hues of an Italian sunset instil the deep-dyed Brenta with

'The odorous purple of a new-born rose;'

who could show us the tide-tossed hand of Selim menacing the shrieking sea-birds; was rich enough in imagery to disdain even fresh-littered convulsions of nature," said Heyhurst.

"As there are shallows in the sea, so the greatest poet will sometimes shoal upon a rigorous criticism," said Emily.

"Indisputable: and a lax criticism too. With what avidity Shakespeare in his noble flights swoops some poor quibble. Laertes, after the pathetic and picturesque description by the queen of the drowning of Ophelia, forbids his tears because his sister has, too much water—Juliet, just after the vehement soliloquy in which she adjures the night, misled by the nurse's ambiguous reference to Tybalt and thinking Romeo slain, plays fantastic variations on the letter I," said Heyhurst.

"A little poetry in long intervals, like mushrooms once or twice a year, is well enough; but what, after all, does it for us?" asked Bloker.

"Does it for us!" replied Heyhurst; "it makes progress in society possible, by inspiring us with an ambition to reach in life the ideal excellence which it presents. The spirit of poetry enters into patriotism—it is the source of exalted actions and characters. Benevolence is full of the afflatus. In poetry the common is forgotten—by the highest poetry the sensual is depressed. It ennobles the pursuits and objects of every-day life, by investing them with the attractions of fancy and the refinement of taste. It heightens pleasure, and diminishes pain. It connects the ages, and makes the heroism of the past tributary to that of yesterday. Florence Nightingale is a nobler object of rational Christian contemplation than

'Divine Scamander purpled yet with blood.'

It is the expression of the natural piety of the human heart from the dawn of history. It is Magnanimity and Devotion—love of man, and praise to God. The Christian Poet is a new man who lays his ear close to the heart of nature, and hears in its rhythm the voice of the Almighty. And the pagan conqueror who ravened an empire from Darius, respected the house of Pindar."

"Some of our best prose has been written by our best poets," said Emily.

"It has. Milton's controversies and Dryden's prefaces are models of English, and Cowper is never more graceful and tender than in his Letters."

"Speaking of letters—" said Doctor Mellen, addressing Max, "I received one the other day from Professor Berzelius Retort, in which he undertakes to controvert my theory of metallic bases. I am getting up a reply, which I shall publish. Some afternoon, when you have leisure and inclination, I will allow you to read both."

A dozen talking and laughing groups have been formed and dissolved, and Bloker and Emily Horton are together in the conservatory. At the further end a lady with the folds of her fragile dress caught in a lemon tree is being extricated by her gallant. These pass out, and the former are left alone.

"And you hear nothing of Jane Warner?"

"Not a syllable. I have prosecuted a diligent search in all probable quarters hereabout, including the insane asylums, public and private. To the latter I have been in person;" and Bloker enumerated them.

"Then we are baffled still—What do you propose?"

"To search on. My heart is in the inquiry—may I not say sympathetically and hopefully with another's?" Bloker looked his meaning at Emily, and found her regarding him with a countenance which showed no displeasure.

"I wish, my dear Miss Horton, you could understand my entire willingness to walk the world at your command with benefactions!"

"O, of course, I *can't* understand it," replied Emily, pleasantly and in some confusion.

"You are not above learning to, I hope—say you are not averse to learn!"

"Sure, good instructions are alms-deeds—They are coming here from the supper-room; let us walk."

CHAPTER XXXVIII.

I sometimes wonder at the incredulity of good people when they hear of unusual outrages for gain; for if they would but consult their own experience they would perceive gold to be the most persuasive of orators.

UPON the return of Emily to Davenport's she was shown the envelope which was found by Farmer Gregg, and made acquainted with its history. Of course it occasioned much speculation. The superscription had been confidently identified by Frank as the writing of his sister. He was a sharp observer, accustomed to her penmanship, and not accustomed to that of other people. This, in Farmer Gregg's view, was not conclusive as to the correctness of the lad's opinion; for, he observed, he had "known droviers recollect a beast's make a year with only seeing it once, and dealing all the time, when its owner couldn't have picked it out of a lot." Concerning the intended destination of the letter, however, there could be no question; the address was plain enough.

While the perplexity was being discussed, Bradley and George Dolman drove up. Dolman was a lawyer, and the matter was at once submitted to him as a person trained to scrutinize. The particulars of the inquiry Bloker had directed were told, and the worthy Gregg assumed his wisest look, satisfied that in the flood of light expected all objections to his cherished hypothesis of the wind must disappear.

"If we grant the writing to be identified as this lady's, whence came it where it was found? Now, there is no blemish nor inaccuracy in the superscription itself to account for its rejection by the writer: that is the first and a slight consideration. Was the envelope discarded by the writer, that she (supposing the sex) might add an afterthought to the letter? I think not; for, notice how cleanly it has been cut; yet the postage stamp is still upon it—is it likely a person, with a knife at hand, so careful in the one respect, would have been careless in the other? The envelope has not gone through the post-office, for it is without mark. But see, here is something which has escaped your attention, or to which you have attached no importance—some apothecary's characters in pencil. It seems to be a hasty calculation—f℥vi=℥ii ss=m 57=484½.

"The numerals don't quite multiply to the result. Perhaps the double *s* makes it—what does it stand for?" said Bradley.

"I don't know—an abbreviation, I suppose—solution of scorpions, may be—and it don't matter for the reasoning. This pencilling was not the person's who wrote the address; nor was it done before the address was written, for a part of it is under the cut. Again, it is probable it was not done remote from the spot where the envelope was found, for that is fresh and clean, and as the country has been wet of late it could not have been blown far unsoiled. Nor, for the same reason, can it have been long exposed to the weather."

The complacency in the visage of Farmer Gregg abated to a dead calm.

"Apothecaries are not numerous in the country," continued Dolman, "and, doubtless, drugs are compounded at the asylum near which this envelope was found. There was no evidence of the missing girl's insanity, you tell me, up to the time of her disappearance. All that follows, then, is supposition, based on her melancholy. Her relatives are poor, and unable to pay the charges of a private asylum?"

"Yes," said Emily.

"She had no prospective interest in property?"

"No."

"And there is no reason to suppose that she has been spirited away for a sinister purpose by an acquaintance?—I believe you spoke of her appearance as being sprightly and pleasing."

"Not that I know. And I feel very sure that she will not be found at this place, for I recollect Mr. Bloker mentioned Norey's as one of the asylums he had visited in person, fruitlessly."

"How long since?"

"Within a fortnight."

"That fact furnishes a presumption against my inference. Still, she may have been confined there since his visit; removed, we will say, from some other place—assuming that she *is* restrained."

"You seem to think it's not certain she's shut up somewhere, sir," remarked Mrs. Davenport, a little disappointed.

"The evidence of it is circumstantial, and not at all conclusive."

"Well do I remember, when a girl, being at cousin Debby Shute's in harvest, and Paul Gurney, who had been chained mad in the county-house eighteen years, breaking out. He got into the woods, and they didn't capture him for nearly a week. They said he had an axe, and we women folks was dreadful scared, and even the men went to bed with their scythes. It was the year of Mungo Brown's prophecy of the end of the world. One of the Boyles drowned herself in a well the day he set, which was the sixteenth of August, and a terrible thunder-storm," said the old lady. She was about to proceed with her reminiscences, when, turning her head, she perceived Frank's distress, and paused to comfort him aside.

"Can Miss Warner have been in possession of a secret which would criminate some one?" speculated Dolman.

"Are people smuggled into mad-houses for that reason—is such an atrocity possible?" asked the old clerk, with vehemence.

"Possible, sir! Yes; and of not unfrequent occurrence. It is only a rarer shape of the advantage which the gold of vice gets over honest, unfriended poverty.

Some have been kept so imprisoned with the means of which they had been previously defrauded."

"Why is it not made impossible?" urged Davenport.

"It will be when our legislators are chiefly virtuous men, and vigilant—not this alone, but a score of equal evils. But there is no bribe in this sort of legislation," replied Dolman.

"It were best to consult with Mr. Bloker," said Emily.

"I confess I never had any liking for Bloker," said Bradley; "to my thinking, the man has ambiguous ways. Once, at least, he was not this lady's friend, and I do not entirely credit his sudden conversion."

"That was long ago," replied Emily; "and I have reason to believe the letter which irritated him was unnecessarily caustic. But upon this inquiry I know he has entered zealously, and prosecuted it with not a little expenditure of money. And what ground have you for intimating that he is unprincipled?"

"In part, your own distrust of him heretofore, which seems to have departed.

"So there was a letter—about what?" asked Dolman.

The incident of the rejection of Bloker's gratuity after the death of Captain Warner was recounted, together with circumstances that indicated his anger thereat; and Dolman continued:

"This may, or may not justify us in arraigning Mr. Bloker's integrity; I know too little of the man's principles and temper to determine. But it is a maxim of games to take the trick if you doubt. This gentleman, I think, should be left out in the initial proceedings; in short, until we can see further—if Miss Horton will pardon a seeming want of gallantry in a lawyer's suggestion."

"I agree with you. What is your plan of action?" asked Bradley.

"I propose to associate Heyhurst with us; we will then go together to the asylum, and in a confident manner request an interview with Miss Warner. This certainly will not be granted, but we may learn something by the character of the reply and our own observation. We will then set a watch on the premises—if you consent, Heyhurst and yourself—while Mr. Gregg, Frank, and I go before one of the judges and procure a habeas corpus."

"I approve of the arrangement, for I think a bold push with precaution better than tedious strategy. Will it suit your convenience, Mr. Gregg?"

"There's nothing to hinder that can't be put off—and I'm not sorry it has turned out sort of supernatural, but I won't let on to mother."

"Well, to-morrow, then, we will proceed," said Dolman.

CHAPTER XXXIX.

"It is no affair of ours!" is a common colloquial disclaimer with two very different classes of people—the selfishly bad, and the timidly good. Every wanton injury to the soul, the mind, or the body of a fellow-being, no matter how mean is his estate, is the "affair" of the virtuous, whether they be considered as men, as Christians, or as citizens.

HE morning and George Dolman were recognized together by Max Heyhurst, who was awaked by the entrance of the latter.

"Hallo! What's up?

'What misadventure is so early up,
That calls our person from our morning rest?'"

"Come! off of Shakespeare's stilts and out of bed; for you are to play the knight-errant this day in the rescue of an imprisoned lady."

"Then you must lend me a clean shirt. The laundress don't bring my wash till this afternoon, and I thought meantime to keep in the cage, and give a little tone to the head of Darius the Persian."

"If you don't joke, Max, I'll send for one."

"Joke! You must suppose me lavish of linen—a very Dives. I have been to two evening crushes this week, and have nothing presentable but a paper dicky.

I cannot consent to sally forth for the benefit of distressed beauty in a paper dicky — Don Quixote wouldn't have done it."

They took up Bradley, and drove to Henry Davenport's. At the appearance of Farmer Gregg, armed with a stout, warty stick, and with his unique beaver worn back in a resolute way, Max inquired of Dolman in a whisper, "If that was his idea of the Bayards and the Herberts, or whether his friend was a head-keeper out of employment?" Mrs. Davenport had Frank dressed and brushed, and displayed in her movements a sense of unusual responsibility. Emily was ready to coöperate, but not expectant of success. Soon the four explorers were off, and in due time they arrived at Norcy's.

The summons of the party at the portal was answered by the Covenanter.

"We have called to see Miss Jane Warner," began Dolman, with matter-of-fact deliberation.

The man brought his hard grey eye steadily to bear on the inquirer for nearly a minute, and then responded,

"Well, do you see her?"

If Dolman had been looking into a telescope for a particular star, his tight-tied answerer could not have exhibited less personal feeling.

"O, that won't succeed!—we know she's here," persisted Dolman.

"Give me leave!" said a person broad-set in figure and with a face of inflexible composure, as he advanced and elbowed aside the official. "I have remarked your communication, sir—Have you anything more to impart?"

"That as it may be when I see the lady," replied Dolman, decisively.

"If I am so fortunate as to understand your reply, it is tantamount to a negative. Mr. Angus Norey, therefore, has the honor to wish you a good-morning!" and bowing, he shut the gate.

Upon this repulse, Max and Bradley were posted to watch the house, and the others repaired to the old clerk's for Frank, with whom they proceeded to the city. They found the judge at chambers, and Dolman made application in form for a habeas corpus, which was granted, and made returnable the following day. Mr. Angus Norey then appeared, and declared under oath that he had control of the person of Jane Warner; that she had been regularly committed to his care by her nearest adult relative, after an examination certified by Doctor Conium; and that her present condition was such it would be hazardous to produce her. In these cases the oath is based upon the professional opinion of the private mad-house doctor, and if the professional opinion of a conscientious physician does not usually belong to pure mathematics, it may be supposed to possess a great scope of flexibility. So Norey put in a medical affidavit in attestation of his account.

Next to the clerical, medicine, though men ungratefully grudge its practitioners both their gold and their applause, is the most humane and honorable of the professions. There need be no falsehood in it. It has given philanthropy to suffering, genius to literature, and progress to science. If benefactions ennoble, then are its ministers, from Saint Luke to Jenner, the heroes of history. It has let the light of God's day into the poor man's habitation, and driven pestilence from the mansions of the rich; every ship which sails the ocean carries its benignity; it has hushed the shrieks of the operating-table; it has lengthened human life in cities, and made it worth the lengthening; it has taught that a physical education is necessary for the future parents of the race; it daily sets ten thousand noble examples of disinterested patience in the performance of duty; its offices are often made subservient to the cure of souls, coöperatively with the sacred ministrations of Christ's priesthood; while it strengthens endurance with sympathy, it scatters broadcast the amenities; it turns from its beaten ways to laugh with Rabelais, to listen to the muse of Schiller, and rejoice in the genial pleasantry of Holmes. But, notwithstanding, if an accomplished, dissembling, replete and quintessential villain be required, physic can produce him!

To old Justice Fumbleback, Norey's return to the writ, fortified as it was, would have been satisfactory, and the attempt to liberate Jane Warner defeated. According to the rotation of the court Fumbleback would have heard the case, but he was gouty, and opportunely subjected to a course of colchicum and confinement. Ironbeak represented him, a wakeful magistrate, who was crustier than the old port which he liked, because it was drank by the Templars. Two characteristics of Justice Ironbeak were favorable for the applicants; there was a touch of Timon under his ermine which made him habitually suspicious of artifice, and he was very sensible to the appeals of distressed childhood. The solicitous, imploring look of the young invalid, aroused in him a personal interest in the proceedings. So he took the trail of the obdurate Norey and kept it with a bloodhound's pertinacity, until, after questions and cross-questions, he ventured to conclude that the woman's infirmities of neither mind nor body would be aggravated by her appearance before him, which he imperatively directed.

And on the following day she was produced, when Mr. Angus Norey declared, that he had been instructed to no longer prefer a claim to her custody. It is probable they who stood behind him, Bloker in chief, considered that the hunt was growing too loud; and, doubtless, Doctor Conium desired no conspicuity in the matter. That Norey himself wanted assurance to browbeat the acutest scrutiny, or to face a tumult of indignation, will not be supposed by any one acquainted with the small but pestilent class to which he belonged.

It is useless to enlarge on the extravagant joy of Frank as he rode back to Henry Davenport's with his sister beside him, *free*. Mrs. Davenport, when she heard of the release of Jane, and had welcomed her, not indeed, as she expected to, in a straight-jacket, was in high spirits. The hospitable matron abandoned herself to short-cakes, and even forgot her hoarded wisdom, a frailty of memory the more wonderful, that deaths in the family had failed to produce it. Serene satisfaction sat enthroned in the face of Henry Davenport.

Aunt Becky Gregg was present; having come expressly, fortified by a dream of the skeleton of a murdered peddler discovered directly under her churn in the milk cellar, which well-scoured butter-barrel the ghost had used, to her consternation and disgust, as a drum—having come expressly to triumph with the triumphant supernatural.

CHAPTER XL.

"Well, Moses," cried I, "we shall soon, my boy, have a wedding in the family; what is your opinion of matters and things in general?"
VICAR OF WAKEFIELD.

ENRY DAVENPORT was warm for a suit against the parties concerned in Jane's imprisonment, of whom all now suspected Bloker to be the principal. Dolman discountenanced the design. In the widely conflicting views, he said, of the boundaries of insanity, with the hebetude of conservative Fumblebacks on the bench, Conium's certificate, which he would be compelled to justify, and the legal adroitness which could be purchased with Bloker's gold, there was ample room for their escape. To illustrate the uncertain solution of such questions, he cited the instance of a gentleman who was held to be crazy on the ground that he recited gibberish, fancying the while that he was speaking in unknown tongues, and carried weights about the house; the truth being, that the man was acquiring a pronunciation of the Hebrew proper names of the Bible and exercising his muscles at the same time, in his daily ambulations.

In the quiet of the farm-house, where there was just enough movement to please a convalescent person tired of watching the shadows of the trees as they crept noonward on the sward, the poultry, and the blinking dog beside the porch, Jane Warner recovered her serenity. Now and then, indeed, when she gazed on Frank and thought of his and her own future, a cloud of anxiety would overcome her; but worthy Mrs. Davenport on such occasions, divining the gloomy tenor of her thoughts, cleared her mind with cheerful words or diverting employment, imparting to her cherished mysteries of housekeeping, in the preparation of pickles, preserves, and savory messes. Once, when Jane was unusually dejected, the friendly matron was at the point of exhilarating her by the production of two or three choice prescriptions of the German wizard; but she recoiled in time, and put her benevolence on the footing of a promised legacy.

One of the cab horses having died, Davenport had bought a pair of lusty mules, and released the survivor from the drudgery of the field. Oats, leisure, and promotion seemed to endow the quadruped with new life, and he was sometimes observed to switch his tail in a dissolute manner, as if recollections of an obstreperous colthood were upon him. Crockett was his name, and he knew the country roads as well as the Davenports, or Jane, or Frank, who so often rode behind him. Of his own volition he crossed the bridges at a walk, and kept to the right as the law directed; he would have scorned to bilk a turnpike. The old clerk habitually moistened his hay to keep off the heaves. Poor

Crockett! these were his sunny days. He lived to help fill one of Clanalpin's famous contracts, and to endure a purgatory of rations after the third sub-letting. He never snuffed the battle, but succumbed to seven pounds of provender a day. Rest to his mouldering hoofs!

On a quiet country Sabbath they would go together to the old tree-encircled church. There was a tranquilizing shadiness about the house of worship, but plenty of sunshine among the tombstones in the grassy graveyard—allegorical, perhaps, of the light of heaven after the shadows of earth. Sometimes the birds would flit into the very aisle, and chirp in unison with the worshippers. If ever human face was benign, it was that Presbyterian parson's. Surely his altitudes were spiritual Pisgahs! There was no grand music, and there were few grand words—hardly ever anything that sounded like Greek to the rural auditors. But the grieved heart was comforted, and the seeking spirit satisfied in that old tree-encircled church. 'Tis likely the parson's place is another's now, for he was shaken with labors in his Master's vineyard. His cough was ominous. Death to him, come when he might, would be a messenger of Love. Doubtless, still

> "They chant their artless notes in simple guise;
> They tune their hearts, by far the noblest aim;
> Perhaps Dundee's wild warbling measures rise,
> Or plaintive Martyrs, worthy of the name;
> Or noble Elgin beats the heavenward flame,
> The sweetest far of Scotia's holy lays:
> Compared with these, Italian trills are tame;
> The tickled ears no heartfelt raptures raise;
> Nae unison hae they with our Creator's praise."

A fortnight after the deliverance of Jane, Emily Horton and Bloker met at Doctor Mellen's. She bowed coldly in reply to his salutation, but repelled the bland advance with which he would have followed it. He started, and an angry flush showed in his face.

"May I ask —— " he began.

"No, sir!" she quickly replied, and turned from him. There was no scene. He saw that a vehement tide was against him—that his designs were as a sum rubbed out.

It was evening twilight, pensive hour sacred to old memories, in Caroline Mellen's chamber, and thus ended an earnest conversation.

"You insist, then, on continuing his acquaintance. I cannot subject myself to the unpleasantness of meeting him again," said Emily.

"You need not, that I see," replied Caroline.

"It will be always possible if he and I come here."

"This, then, follows: that I must surrender my free-will and have my acquaintanceships hereafter depend on the license of a censor. I regard the revelation of that sewing girl as the purest vagary of fancy. I believe there was a reason for her being in the asylum, and that you did her no good when you took her out."

"There we differ—but I do not mean to debate the question. I think that the true dignity of our sex, which is purity, hangs as much on the virtue of a sewing girl as upon that of a princess. The women are only separated by the poor trappings of life, and are equal before God. I am sorry that events have brought us to this night."

And so they parted.

CHAPTER XLI.

If we could, from one of the battlements of heaven, espy how many men and women at this time lie fainting and dying for want of bread; how many young men are hewn down by the sword of war; how many poor orphans are now weeping over the graves of their father, by whose life they were enabled to eat; if we could but hear how mariners and passengers are at this present in a storm, and shriek out because their keel dashes against a rock or bulges under them; how many people there are that weep with want, and are mad with oppression, or are desperate by too quick a sense of constant infelicity; in all reason we should be glad to be out of the noise and participation of so many evils. This is a place of sorrows and tears, of so great evils and a constant calamity: let us remove from hence, at least, in affections and preparation of mind.—JEREMY TAYLOR.

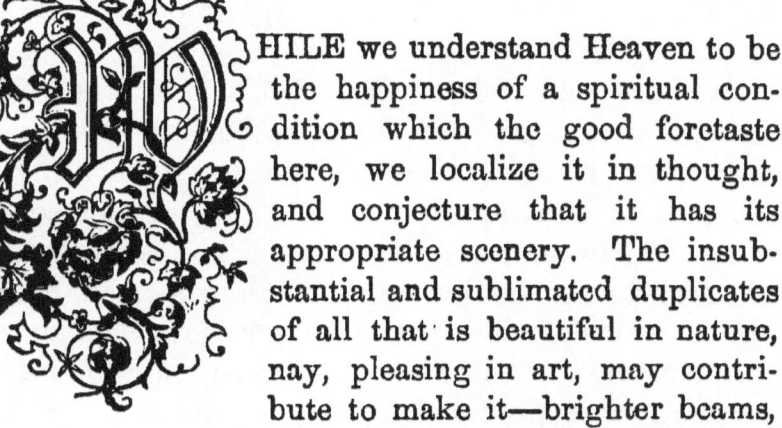

WHILE we understand Heaven to be the happiness of a spiritual condition which the good foretaste here, we localize it in thought, and conjecture that it has its appropriate scenery. The insubstantial and sublimated duplicates of all that is beautiful in nature, nay, pleasing in art, may contribute to make it—brighter beams, rarer flowers, bluer skies, and a celestial architecture. Amid these delightful surroundings the perfected spirits of the just may exist, glorifying God in love and purity.

Once more the violets looked meekly up to catch the smiles of their froward mistress, April, or hung pensive heads beneath her frowns; while the unfilial pyrus flaunted in scarlet, careless of either. At The Cedars, under the trees, which seemed almost sentient with the swell of vernal life, they bore a coffin into the old mansion. Up stairs in Lydia Bardleigh's chamber there was a stark similitude and twilight out of time. The uses and disorder of occupancy no longer characterized the room. The watch which had ticked upon the bureau was put aside; the medicines, trays, and napkins were removed. A Bible had been left, but even it was clasped. Silently they came and went; acknowledging that she was with them still—and yet alone.—Across the threshold with measured steps—where the robins will not come to-day to seek the generous crumbs—then a short, dull, sliding sound, and the slow wheels go on a space, and pause.

Bradley returned to Brentlands a sterner man. Though an exacting employer, as became an accurate and active man of affairs, he was governed by an innate love of justice. This not only restrained him from unfairly imposing labor, but it induced a humane attention to the bodily wants of his workmen, both in health and sickness; sound and various food, clean, spacious and ventilated lodgings, and a well-ordered hospital, were provided by him. He recoiled from thrusting a disabled servant naked upon the world.

Now his rebukes were become keener, and his bearing was grown austere. For himself, regardless of the weather, he wrought on in his laborer's garb. He was in the fields, in the smithy, among the stalls, or at the desk, as heretofore, but a harsh and silent man. His prospect was as dreary as the South Atlantic, where, a dark and desert waste of tormented water, it is scourged by Winter against the scowling cliffs of Patagonia.

At length he resolved to seek in the bustle of a great city diversion and tranquillity; to exchange the uneventful quiet of nature for the pursuit of pleasure, the tumult of controversy, and the charms of intellect, where all the sounds and shows of population prevail. In such a whirl of various occupations, he thought that the recollections of the past which distressed him could be cast off; in the vigor of youth, and stung by disappointment, he knew, at least, he would find allurements, if he failed of happiness. It was his purpose, therefore, at the completion of the ensuing harvest to relinquish the management of Brentlands.

And so the days went by, bringing sun, and shower, and promises of ripeness. Wide reaches of clean brown loam were arrayed with the green and sturdy maize, some five weeks up; the heavy-headed wheat fluctuated in yellow billows; rank oats declared the fertile slopes that nourished them. It was the morning of the twenty-fifth of June, when, by one crushing stroke, all was blasted. Just before the dawn of day, Bradley was awakened by a strong, cold wind which blew upon him through the open blinds of his chamber.

A sharp, rattling crash of thunder pealed upon the stillness of the night, and then, in sudden tempest, came the hail!

Sunrise smiled from a cloudless sky, which, like the smooth ocean pressing upon the wrecks of yesterday, bore no trace of treachery—smiled upon a desolation. The mangled bosom of the green earth, the trampled and shattered grain, the orchards ravished of their fruit and foliage, and the despoiled nurseries, attested the pitiless smiting of the storm. The birds flitted in confusion and bewailed their riven habitations, and theirs was the only voice of mourning. The world measures calamities by their dignity, and has no attention for private griefs; but the population of a war-scourged province or a burned city is an aggregation of single sufferers.

One of Bradley's last acts at Brentlands was to bury a favorite horse of his father's. "Rock," twenty-seven years old at the time of his death, was a tough-constitutioned saddle sorrel. Like some well-preserved men who can look backward to the psalmist's figures, he had acquired the art of living with the minimum wear and tear of life. For some years he had done nothing but graze upon an ample range in summer and stand or lie in his well-littered winter stall, where the rack was never empty; except when his master had made infrequent visits to the place, when he was sometimes bridled for his service. The merchant declared that his record was without a stumble. The fall before, "Rock" had got a wound, an ugly gash eight or ten inches in length, luckily where there was a fair protection of muscles. This it was thought would prove fatal, but upon being stitched it healed, and the old horse was soon again in ballast, his mane and tail prickly with the fresh-gathered sandburs. He passed the winter well, and, though his eye was a little dull, and his ribs could be counted in the sunshine, it seemed that you might notch thirty on his manger and safely call it a prophecy. It was on a dismal October afternoon, when, with a sort of human impulse, he came from the field to die. There was no evidence that he was in pain, nor of any ailment except the years. He died in the night, while the rain pattering on the roof made a soothing monotone in the great hollow of the barn. Next day, when the storm had ceased, Bradley had a pit dug in the orchard—dug deep, to balk the hounds. "Rock" was brought on wheels—that much was due him—and put beneath the clay. The spreading pearmain, which will lie light in summer shadows above him, will be the greener for his grave.

29*

CHAPTER XLII.

> Nor is it well, nor can it come to good,
> That, through profane and infidel contempt
> Of holy writ, she has presum'd t' annul
> And abrogate, as roundly as she may,
> The total ordinance and will of God;
> Advancing fashion to the post of truth,
> And cent'ring all authority in modes
> And customs of her own, till sabbath rites
> Have dwindled into unrespected forms,
> And knees and hassocs are well nigh divorc'd.
> THE TASK.

A PRESIDENT is to be elected. Europe listens to the tumult of a heterodox politics, and even John Bull, paragon of animals, wipes the beer from his sprightly visage, and condescends to bellow contempt.

Bradley Horton was now become a citizen of New York, into which he entered a stranger. He found it a metropolis where life presented many phases, as it was variously devoted to traffic, knowledge, art, ambition, ostentation, and folly. He found some who were occupied with their own devices, and others with the devices and destiny of the world at large, and not a few who were torn of devils. He beheld Commerce fluttering about his altars, and Pleasure garlanding her cup: now he communed with some rare ancient, perhaps an Elizabethan whom Elia loved, at the Astor; and then, in the saloon at midnight, noted how hope deluded folly still from the bottom of a faro-box. He heard the dirty and disreputable Funk intoning on his perch allurements to pinchbeck, and the cadences, suasive and silvery, of the priest in spotless linen. In the same hour he passed from the elegant tranquillity of a breakfast at Delmonico's to the hum and movement of the Exchange at Whitehall—from pacing the cool morning flags of the stately avenue, or the solitary labyrinth of the breezy park, to the wheel-clashing ways where the chimes of Trinity buffet, like strong swimmers of the upper air, the sea of uproar which billows from the town; only less loud than the noisy anarchy of Chaos which smote the ear of the exploring fiend at pause on the brink of hell.

After a period of sight-seeing and idleness, Bradley was engaged to write up the "*Keynote*"—it was so settled with Cochin Neal, the publisher, over antemeridian hock at the Blue Wing. He was expected to produce quantity, sound, and coarse pungency, together with humor in a set of dictionary words, rather than elaboration. These are the characteristics, for the most part, of first-rate American newspaper editorials. With perhaps a score of exceptions, our able editors are high-reaching polemics, superficially "smart," outlaws from syntax, without scholarly exactness and literary elegance, whose matter is spumous, and whose looms produce only gunny when they mean to weave velvet. But this is a young country, and they will probably improve.

The editor of the "*Keynote*" had many opportunities to admire the Radical worthies who vie with each other to promote their country's good. They rented halls, and bought coal oil for illuminations by the barrel—with the assessments of the party. They went about to circumvent the adversary with documents and declamation. Some invested their capital in the canvass, as they would have invested it in corn, hoping for a profitable return in offices and contracts. No alchemy could assimilate these to—neither badge nor shibboleth would identify them with many wise, earnest, and conscientious men who acted with them. For months the "*Keynote*" was prolonged in a strain of appeals and animadversions, like the creak of an ungreased axle. If voters were not converted it was their misfortune, for Bradley never allowed a topic to wither for want of "copy." He was as sweet as Hybla for his friends, and as bitter as Marah for the enemy. Alas! the lost books of Livy are not less accessible than is the "*Keynote*" now. The last number which its editor saw, and which contained his strongest article in behalf of civil liberty, was beneath the spectacles of his laundress, who was laboriously spelling over its contents. It had invested the foul linen of a censorious fellow-citizen who was restrained in Fort Rochambeau, till he should

"—— rebate and blunt his natural edge."

CHAPTER XLIII.

The rogues were very merry on the booty. They said a thousand things that showed the wickedness of their morals.—GIL BLAS.

THE rebellion came—begotten child of Mammon,

"——the least erected spirit that fell
From heaven."

Behind the awful aspects of the war there was a greedier scramble, a baser grovelling for gold than in the less profitable days of peace. Clanalpin was in power, and Expectation Biles was his Chief Armorer. It will be seen that Biles had risen. Tumultuous eras are the opportunities of greatness, and Thomas Carlyle's "French Revolution" may be had of all respectable booksellers. Great, like other men, must have beginnings. Even Clanalpin was not always a councillor of the earth. So Biles had ripened to Chief Armorer; and there was a Camp Biles, and there was a gunboat christened Expectation Biles.

What countless pruning-hooks were beaten into spears to fill the contracts that were lavished by Clanalpin! There was a premium on shoddy. Ancient hangers, that had been last drawn at the command of

Mad Anthony, were hunted from their hiding-places. Prodigious orders were given for castor oil and linen pantaloons. How delightful were those Washington nights in "The Ring," where the smell of villainous gunpowder was unknown, while the ear was soothed by the rustling of treasury notes and the trickling of perennial punch! Placid hours! coffers not coffins received your fruits. That "Ring"!

> "When the treasury failed—and the people storm'd,
>   They bore the brunt—
> And the only cry which their grave lips form'd
>   Was 'blunt'—still 'blunt!'"

Last of all the expressions of that period to be forgotten, was the great horse-fair at Hepzidam. To say that it was never equalled, is feeble description; it never was approached! At Hepzidam the Clanalpin influence was predominant. There were many rogues at Hepzidam, who carried sweat-cloths in their carpet-bags; and the honest part of the people dealt, when times were dull, in counterfeit quarter-dollars. Horse contracts were likewise currency at Hepzidam.

If it had been meant to establish a veterinary hospital, instead of to furnish forth the dragoons and artillery, there could not have been completer success. There were trembling knees and capped hocks; broken wind and botts; tumors and ulcers; spavin, consumption, and staggers; and a dreadful concert of roaring and wheezing. There were horses that balked, and horses that bit. Some were decrepit, others blind; some were wall-eyed, others had lost their tails. The external appearance of most of the animals was of a piece with their sanitary state, nor was either much improved by deficient provender. The vermiparous condition which was apparent might reasonably have been excused, it was so little premature. The atmosphere was surcharged with asafœtida, and drenches of black pepper and whiskey were in constant readiness for sudden gripes. The most distressing part of the spectacle was the fresh arrivals of misery. They came from the four quarters and were accompanied by needy politicians, subordinates of the more fortunate contract-holders—postmasters, village editors, tax-collectors, township constables, decayed good fellows. Mingled with these were prosperous farmers, wide awake to their opportunities and sound on the "anaconda." Mr. Potteril of New Paradise was also present with an ancient gelding, adapted by his favorite process to the short-ration system which prevailed.

Clanalpin had come down by an express train and moved briskly about, the admired of all beholders; inciting with his gold-headed cane a friend's sluggish nag, now and then, to the moderate amount of movement required by the inspection. He was attended by the Chief Armorer. It was a study for high horse art, the Chief Armorer a tiptoe, looking—a cyclopœdia of farriery in his countenance—looking through his spectacles into the mouth of a new arrival! Bradley unexpectedly met Doctor Pledget, who seemed desirous to elude observation, and appeared to be dejected. He was in search of a valuable gray which had been stolen from him. He deeply regretted, he said, the inconsiderateness which had brought him with a hue and cry to Hepzidam. He regarded the journey as the severest stroke of satire to which he had ever been subjected.

Jacob Bloker's star was now above the horizon. Bloker owned ships and steamboats, in whole or in part, some of them mere sieves plugged to float, and the Administration paid him for the use of them the revenue of an Asiatic prince. With this great income he bought farms and factories, and speculated in gold. Jacob Bloker was become an irreproachable patriot, somewhat indifferent, perhaps, to the welfare of the sewing-women whom he employed, in the execution of his contracts, at thirty cents a day, but an irreproachable patriot still, who believed in Fort Rochambeau, pyrotechnics on the Fourth of July, and a censorship for disputant newspapers.

CHAPTER XLIV.

I am now in the nineteenth book of the Iliad, and on the point of displaying such feats of heroism performed by Achilles, as make all other achievements trivial.—COWPER'S LETTERS.

AQUILA GLUMP was meditating in his counting-room in Phœnix-block, Commerce-street. It was a drizzly night, and the clock had just struck nine. The *Evening Popgun* lay outspread upon his knees, and the jar of a passing omnibus as it tinkled from tier to tier of the hollow hardware mingled with his reveries. "It is the very thing!" thought Aquila Glump, nodding his head with sage emphasis as he contemplated the dim outlines of the pots and kettles by which he was surrounded; "a currency of iron is the remedy for the distress and extravagance of the times—with brass for high values. It would prevent speculation; it would keep out luxuries, and punish John Bull and the French; it would foster frugality and patriotism; and it would promote human health by compelling your nice feeders to adopt a more simple and natural diet;"

and he particularized this point in his reflections with a ghastly grin, for Aquila Glump was dyspeptic, and dined sometimes off a Digby herring, which he preceded with a mixture of magnesia and charcoal. "The soldiers wouldn't have it?" he continued interrogatively in his cogitation: "Shoot 'em for mutiny, and make another draft! But there is a precedent—the Spartan soldiers took it; and Broil and Blacking, of the War Office, two of the most remarkable men of this or any other country, can fix it in an opinion or general orders. The statesmen can have their cast iron heads, labelled, to transmit to the latest posterity. As a sharp-sighted patriot, I'll sell the Treasury my stock in trade at ten per cent. less than retail prices, for—" he had nearly thought "cash," but jerked his mind at the inconsistency, and at the same time looking toward the door he perceived beyond it the figure of a man like unto Bartimeus Scroggs.

The figure indeed was Scroggs, but the habiliments were martial; a six-shooter was in his belt, a trenchant sabre hung at his side, and the military shape had been given to his unassuming whiskers. But the day before Scroggs had taken Phœnix-block *en route* for Washington, and was this his brow again, lowering like the front of battle, beneath a corded hat?

"'Tis he!—how came he thence?—what does he here?"

Not with the strides of Tarquin—not with the rush of spear-launching Achilles when through the imperfect armor he transfixed the neck of Hector, nor yet with feline spring, advanced Bartimeus upon Aquila Glump; but with a steady, deliberate, and majestical limp; while thus he spake.

"I had rather see no money in an army contract than be here to-night."

"Mad!—poor man, the spirits have turned his head," muttered Glump, as he retreated behind a desk and furtively seized a ruler.

"But feelings for softer times! Friend Glump! I arrest you for misprision of treason, and I hope, as a reasonable citizen, you will submit without a murmur."

"Stand back, Scroggs, or I'll prostrate you! It's a trick—you are imposed on, I say!"

"I got the warrant at Washington, and it's regular; based on the depositions of two detectives."

"I'm a loyal man, and invest in Government sevens —I read all the war articles in the *Popgun*—my patriotism, sir, is indisputable!"

"I hope so, but I must do my duty. You can write to the Administration from Fort Rochambeau; peradventure it will correct the mistake."

"I'll stay in Phœnix-block and save it the trouble, being free-born and of lawful age—in short, an American citizen."

And now it was that the wranglers grappled each other in fierce contention, till the heightening clamor appalled the rats and was answered by a deep-mouthed bull-dog from the vault. Glump dealt with the ruler rapid and resounding blows upon the corpus of Scroggs, while that Rowland was prevented drawing his lethal weapon for the extirpation of his adversary, who had promptly grasped the scabbard and held it with the hilt jammed into its owner's abdomen. Unable to assume the offensive with his virgin blade, he seized a pattern pot-lid which was luckily at hand, interposed it as a shield between his person and the strokes of his antagonist, and under its cover, dexterously putting his body into the position of an antique military engine, butted with such irresistible impulsion as to carry the enemy clean off his legs. And so the issue of the struggle seemed declared. But the Cloud-compeller, beholding, sent an Olympian to the rescue— business worthy of a god! A package of flat-irons was timeouly jostled from a shelf above upon the sinewy buttock of the victor as he stooped with fell intent. Seized with agony and amazement, he fled amain.

The excitement of that eventful night was fatal to Bartimeus Scroggs. At twenty-seven minutes past twelve he died in a fit. He had just been appointed Commissioner to the Bey of Biscay, and his credentials with the official creases undisturbed were found in the lining of his hat. Myrtles grow at Biscay, and orange trees blossom all the year round. The summer solstice at Biscay is one siesta, and little birds sing ditties to their innocent mates. Yet had the patriot who has left us chosen, even against this Eden he would have voted for the storied grave, where, wrapped in the star-spangled banner of his country, he sleeps in peace.

CHAPTER XLV.

> I would have thee know,
> He does not breathe this air,
> Whose love I cherish, and whose soul I love,
> More than Mounchensey's.
> OLD PLAY.

> Thou art Arthur, of the golden crown!

EVIL likings, as hatreds often do, distil in darkness drop by drop, and harden like stalactites. With music and merriment, amused by fancy, charmed by animal pleasures, and impelled by sensual desire, Bradley Horton glided into a whirl of excesses. There was mad gaiety in brandy, and he sought it—oblivion, and it was welcome. His intellect flashed to the blaze which was consuming it. He could see the sparkling of its reflection in the eyes of his boon companions, and he beheld it with exulting vanity. He became "as a city broken down, and without walls." His daily life was a tide of excitement which swelled into the turbulence of midnight.

Against this continued and unsparing assault, the efforts of nature to maintain her integrity were arrayed in vain. Delirium came, with its attendant horrors, to seize the empire which Reason had abdicated. Indescribable are the mockeries, the infernal insultations, the overpowering dreads, the agonizing suspenses, the loathsome shapes, the countless tortures exquisite beyond human contriving, and the voices of accusation and doom—voices to which cloven tongues of fire would add no terror, that arise from that hell of the cup!

Under God, he owed his life to the devotion of one true heart. Paul Mervine was a Southerner—the Good Samaritan belongs no more to geography than an angel. In this noble friend a woman's tenderness and refinement were united to lofty courage. The well-tempered masculineness was seen to gleam like the limbs of Adam among the flowers of Eve. There was a dignity in his nature which, to common observers, seemed but a large measure of amiability; and a tone which, though it pleased them, was above their comprehension. His prejudices were those of a man who despised duplicity and all meanness. Every moment which he could spare from an exacting business was spent in attending to Bradley. He soothed him with kind words; he suggested, gently considerate, many comforts, and provided them; he bore him in his strong arms. On a sofa, beside the sufferer's bed, sleeping fitfully at best, with the solicitude of a young bride, he watched through many nights. And when amendment came, the gladness of his good heart leaped to his lips in smiles.

Paul Mervine's kindnesses may not be recorded here. Rich jewels are lessened to strange eyes: to such, even goodness of mark is like water locked in diamonds, the flash of which they see above the common light and cannot count its value. It is better to live well in the meanest human heart by its memories of the timely oil and wine, than to be able to weigh the satellites of Jupiter!

Paul Mervine was fond of birds, and kept them; he was the gentlest of gaolers. Gradually he accustomed them to enlargement, and the more docile knew the cage only as the shelter of their choice. When a boy, the martins never left the village boxes but he knew beforehand they were packing up; and, sure, the troubles of moving would have been lightened had the ebon emigrants understood how fully they were shared. Bradley passed many of the calm hours of convalescence with his friend's family, and at these times Paul would steal apart from his occupations to taste the tranquil scene. So they were together one morning, when a person of threatening aspect entered at the open door, trailing a musket.

"Paul! this thing cannot go on longer—it is inexpiable—it must stop here!" exclaimed the intruder.

At one startled look Bradley knew that he had seen the face before. It was Blumenbach of the old counting-house days in the city.

Paul's composure disconcerted his purpose, if purpose he had. He was, it seemed, one of Paul's unavailables; and, in truth, they were a queer lot. Spiritism had desolated his fine intellect, never robust, perhaps, but once attuned to the choicest chords of harmony. He was become an idle, meaningless man, who heard voices in the air and wrestled with spirits in the night—the surges of the pit had passed over him. The wretched stir of the invisible-infernal was to him the mysterious music of the spheres! Incapable of continuous attention to any pursuit, he would yet talk with pleasing intelligence if the theme was foreign to the engrossing subject of his thoughts. Once there, chaos came again. Confidence and suspicion possessed his mind successively, as his impressions varied; and its delicate organization aggravated the torment. Probably his dog was the only creature which he did not distrust, until he conceived some metaphysical absurdity of transmigration that brought the poor animal to disgrace.

Paul Mervine was unmarried, though his presence was as goodly as that of Absalom. Perhaps he was deficient in small-talk; or it was his modesty that—but we know that the heart of woman turns instinctively to unobtrusive worth in men. Witness the consecrated union yesterday of Burnish, the banker—octogenarian Burnish, with that dove of dulcet cooing, the promising child whom you fondled, friend and fellow-militiaman, when your whiskers began to bud! Or, and like enough, Paul had never willed it otherwise. Such was the flow of thought in the mind of Bradley as he sat in the bird-room over a newspaper. At the height of it, his eye fell upon this paragraph.

A FASHIONABLE WEDDING.

On Tuesday, the 22d inst., in the presence of a large and brilliant assemblage, at Saint Simons, by the Rev.

Hildebrand Mildman, assisted by the Rev. Sharon Gawscloome, Jacob Bloker, esquire, to Caroline, daughter of Doctor Peter Mellen.

In a paroxysm of surprise, Bradley dropped the newspaper. There was a sudden chirp. It came from a bright-breasted canary, which, with its head on one side, was gazing in dreamy rapture at a snake in a bottle of spirits, whose golden scales gleamed in the sunlight.

CHAPTER XLVI.

The course of a rapid river is the justest of all emblems to express the variableness of our scene below. Shakespeare says, none ever bathed himself twice in the same stream, and it is equally true, that the world, upon which we close our eyes at night, is never the same with that on which we open them in the morning.—COWPER'S LETTERS.

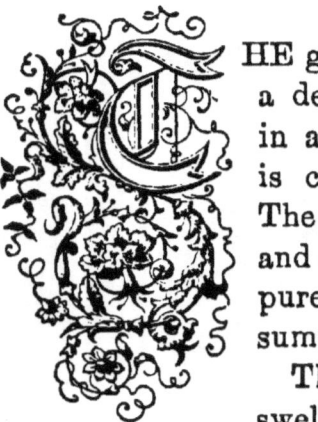

THE grey autumn morning looks upon a death-bed with mourners beside it, in a city chamber. Clement Horton is calmly approaching the Unseen. The tender words have been spoken, and offered the silent prayers, and his pure and peaceful soul passes at the summons.

The noises of the awakened town swell in the streets, but they are no longer heeded by the dull ear of one who loved the stir of busy life. Henceforth, action for him shall have a better voice. There is a repose in his face, as he lays gasping, which tells of more than an enforced submission. The heart is surely in that look! Though it cannot allay their present grief, the bereaved will remember it and rejoice. They will keep his picture with sacred care, but they will carry within them a more cherished image of a departed father and friend. With heaviness for the virtue earth and we are losing, and thanks to God that it was given, we turn sorrowfully away.

"I have news for you, sis!" exclaimed Frank Warner as Jane Davenport entered the sitting-room; "Miss Emily is coming here."

"Yes, Frank; you must keep as cheerful as a cricket."

"It is crying nice news, and my sick mocking-bird begins to sing again!"

The marriage of Henry Davenport and Jane Warner scandalized the decayed virgins. They went about with noses full of snuff and hearts full of malice, and croaked confusion to the match—"Fifty, if he's a day! Seraphina Blessing caught him a pulling out the grey hairs with tweezers—and, my dear, the *bride* is a few years younger than I, a mere chit!" Regardless of the dismal old ravens, Henry Davenport walked with a step as springy as when he tied fancy knots in his cravat and punched Wilson's ribs with McCullough at the counting-house in the city long ago; and looked, indeed, as if he might live to be a contented cotemporary with his grandchildren. Jane changed naturally and gracefully into a matron, and was in all respects, Henry's venerable mother declared, like herself at that period of existence.

That good-hearted veteran persisted in accumulating receipts for posterity, and accomplished fresh cures, that brought her increase of reputation, with an original eye-water made of the last spring snow in a fluid state, and strengthened by undivulged combinations. When there was a severe pressure for salve she sometimes took Frank so far into her confidence as to permit him to watch the boiling; during which she recounted for his instruction the various instances of healing which had resulted from the use of the remedy. But, despite the excellence of her system of teaching, she discovered in him little genius for medicine, and was not encouraged.

When the expectation of the year had past, and the door-yard trees stood bare and gaunt beneath the winter sky, it was still June at the unpretending hearth of Henry Davenport. Thither came good angels with healing in their wings. The faith which lives within us, works without us, and Heaven is radiated from a cheerfully virtuous family wherein is set up an altar to the Lord! The number of Frank's pets was increased by a quail and a squirrel, the gifts of Farmer Gregg, and a parrot from the Spanish Main, which escaped soon after its arrival to the farmer's house and alarmed his good wife in the middle of the night by shrill cries in choice Castilian. Farmer Gregg often brought a pocket-full of nuts for "Bonny," and after feeding him would sit and watch the rapid gyration of the cage with child-like simplicity of interest; or tell the boy legends and experiences. What the princess of Abyssinia failed to find in the land of Egypt, was here—a happy household, thankful for humble pleasures, and superior for the main to the littlenesses and vanities of life.

CHAPTER XLVII.

They were simple bubbles, blown hither and thither according to the child's fancy, yet they caught something of the sky, and something of the human face.

THE Horton experience is approaching an end. It has not been diffusely told. As a veracious history, it has not half the tragic spice which a cultivated taste in fiction demands. There is not a bandit in the book, and neither battle nor murder. Only the illustrious Scroggs comes to sudden death. It is true, one or two of the characters should have perished for their offences, but they did not. It must be considered that most pilgrimages survive the simoom.

Jacob Bloker, probably, has no other twinges than those of gout. That disease of late has thrown out skirmishing pains toward his stomach. This is unpleasant, both as a declaration against good dinners and as investing with doubt the continuance of the tenure by which he has his ships and merchandize, his patriotism, houses and lands. Perhaps he is not certain that he shall thrive so well in another life. Meantime, Caroline Bloker is a queen in Shoddy, dispensing much fine action and brilliant conversation, to the annoyance of rival sovereigns who lack her parts and polish. Whatever else there may be, there is no gout, sure, in her world.

That, at least, is the opinion of Max Heyhurst, whom she has ceased to know. Max has sometimes seen the outside of her carriage at a crossing on opera nights, as it was driven before him. He is preparing for the ministry. He was converted at a prayer-meeting, and has deserted his pictures. His vivacity is subdued, but there is enough of it left, and he will probably never be an austere Christian. He is at Princeton.

Bradley Horton and Paul Mervine are in Brazil, contemplating, perhaps, from Tijuca the beautiful bay, and the city of St. Sebastion beside it flashing in tropical sunlight amid its emerald hills; or wandering in the Serra dos Orgoes, where the cascade gleams forever on the cliff, where nature is most bountiful and gorgeous in flowers, fruit, and foliage, and pictured prospects of sky and sea, and all the sumptuousness of summer.

www.ingramcontent.com/pod-product-compliance
Lightning Source LLC
Chambersburg PA
CBHW031425230426
43668CB00007B/435